Hope Revealed

Hope Revealed

The Message of the Book of Revelation—Then and Now

ROBERT P. VANDE KAPPELLE

WIPF & STOCK · Eugene, Oregon

HOPE REVEALED
The Message of the Book of Revelation—Then and Now

Copyright © 2013 Robert P. Vande Kappelle. All rights reserved. Except for brief quotations in critical publications or reviews, no part of this book may be reproduced in any manner without prior written permission from the publisher. Write: Permissions. Wipf and Stock Publishers, 199 W. 8th Ave., Suite 3, Eugene, OR 97401.

Bible quotations are from the *New Revised Standard Version of the Bible*, copyright © 1989 by the Division of Christian Education of the National Council of the Churches of Christ in the United States of America. Used by permission.

Wipf & Stock
An Imprint of Wipf and Stock Publishers
199 W. 8th Ave., Suite 3
Eugene, OR 97401

www.wipfandstock.com

ISBN 13: 978-1-62564-419-0

Manufactured in the U.S.A.

To Peter and Sara
and their children:
Jacob, Benjamin, Katherine, and Emily.
Surely here is hope revealed.

Children are a blessing
and a gift from the Lord.
Like arrows in the hand of a warrior
are the children of one's youth.
Happy are they whose quivers are full.
—Psalm 127:3–5

Revelation Song
Worthy is the,
Lamb who was slain
Holy, Holy, is He
Sing a new song,
To Him who sits on
Heaven's Mercy Seat
—lyrics by Jamie Lee Riddle

Holy, Holy, Holy
Is the Lord God Almighty
Who was, and is, and is to come.
—Revelation 4:8

Because John offers his Revelation in the language of dreams and nightmares, language that is "multivalent," countless people for thousands of years have been able to see their own conflicts, fears, and hopes reflected in his prophecies. And because he speaks from his convictions about divine justice, many readers have found reassurance in his conviction that there *is* meaning in history—even when he does not say exactly what that meaning is—and that there is hope.
—Elaine Pagels

Contents

Preface / viii
Acknowledgments / xv

Introduction / 1

PART I
Christ's Message to the Church: Addressing Complacency

CHAPTER 1: A Vision of Christ (Revelation 1) / 23
  Essay 1: The Christology of Revelation / 33

CHAPTER 2: A Vision of the Church Imperfect (Revelation 2–3) / 39
  Essay 2: Internal Conflicts in Early Christianity / 52

CHAPTER 3: A Vision of a Rightly Ordered Universe (Revelation 4–5) / 58
  Essay 3: The Centrality of Worship and Doxology in Revelation / 71

PART II
God's Message of Warning: Critiquing the Prevailing Order

CHAPTER 4: First Vision of Judgment: Seven Seals (Revelation 6:1—8:5) / 77
  Essay 4: The Old Testament Background of Revelation / 91

CHAPTER 5: Second Vision of Judgment: Seven Trumpets
    (Revelation 8:6—11:19) / 96
  Essay 5: John's Strategic Use of Interludes in Revelation / 113

PART III
God's Message of Judgment: Destroying the Destroyers of the Earth

CHAPTER 6: A Vision of Evil: Seven Significant Signs
    (Revelation 12–14) / 119
  Essay 6: Permeable Boundaries in Revelation / 145

CHAPTER 7: Third Vision of Judgment: Seven Plagues
    (Revelation 15–16) / 149
  Essay 7: Interpreting Revelation's Violent Imagery / 158

CHAPTER 8: A Vision of the Harlot and Her Demise
    (Revelation 17–18) / 162
  Essay 8: Interpreting Revelation's Symbolism / 173

PART IV
God's Message of Hope: Making All Things New

CHAPTER 9: A Vision of Final Judgment and the Demise of Evil
    (Revelation 19–20) / 179
  Essay 9: Eschatological Approaches to Revelation / 194

CHAPTER 10: A Vision of the Church Perfected (Revelation 21–22) / 199
  Essay 10: Interpreting Revelation's Inclusive Language / 212

Epilogue / 217
Appendix—The Essentials: Key Ideas from Revelation / 223
Bibliography / 225
Subject/Name Index / 227

Preface

What do Armageddon, Antichrist, Apocalypse, Four Horsemen, Seventh Seal, Red Dragon, Lake of Fire, Mark of the Beast, Return of Christ, Imminent Judgment, Global Destruction, Millennium, Eternal Life, and the number 666 have in common? They are all hot topics today, they all appear in the book of Revelation, and they all tend to be distorted or exaggerated by preachers, televangelists, pundits, and the popular media.

The book of Revelation has been a godsend to those who like to predict "doomsday" scenarios. It is the favorite book of those who believe that events in modern history are the fulfillment of biblical prophecy. Every generation of Christians has had in its number those who believed themselves to be living in the last days, some even putting a date on the end of the world—and they have all been wrong. To use an analogy from baseball, every person who has stepped to the plate—taken Revelation literally—and set dates accordingly has struck out; no one has even gotten on base. How could many people be so mistaken?

A helpful way to look at confusing concepts and misunderstood notions is to think in terms of antonyms. For instance, what is the opposite of sin? Most people would answer "salvation," but that response is clearly influenced by theological assumptions. Could the antonym of sin be "justice," or better yet, "compassion"? And what about "faith"? Is the opposite of faith doubt, as commonly affirmed, or might the opposite of faith be "certainty" or "arrogance"? When it comes to theological, spiritual, or existential matters, our imprecise vocabulary can confuse.

The following pairs represent what we typically construe as opposites: type/antitype; poison/antidote; hazardous/safe; vice/virtue; wise/foolish; small/large; blindness/sight; and active/passive. Although clear and precise, they are bland and unappealing. John of Patmos, the author of Revelation, holds a much richer palate, and he uses tints and hues to create a kaleidoscopic world of colors, a typology of harsh and subtle contrasts. His polarities are vivid and imaginative: Calvary/Armageddon; Angelic Choirs/Demonic Locusts; Christ/Antichrist; Bride/Harlot; Sea of Glass/Lake of Fire; Heavenly Throne Room/Bottomless Pit; New Jerusalem/Babylon; True Prophet/False Prophet; Holy Trinity/Unholy Trinity; Loving Lion/Dangerous Dragon; Seven-horned Lamb/Seven-headed Beast; Seven Benedictions/Seven Plagues; Heavenly Horseman/Earthly Horsemen; Sealed Martyrs/Branded Slaves; Silent Sound/ Noisy Sound; Redemption/Destruction; New Creation/Old Creation; Faithful Witnesses/False Witnesses; Praises/Laments; Restorers of the Earth/Destroyers of the Earth; Eternal Life/Second Death. One can think of many other contrasts in Revelation. For John, the latter item in each set generally represents the antithesis of the former, whether a parody, a counterfeit, a caricature, a travesty, or a reversal. These pairs and the remarkable cast of characters in Revelation produce the storyline for one of the most intriguing, most discussed, and most life-changing books ever written. Join me for the adventure of a lifetime—or more accurately, of an eternity—as we explore this remarkable display of spiritual artistry.

REVELATION: BANE OR BLESSING?

Foundational to reading the Bible is a decision about how to view its nature: is it a divine product, a human product, or somehow both? Biblical scholars suggest three broad possibilities regarding the inspiration of the Bible, to which we add a fourth as corollary:

- *verbal inspiration*—the view that every word of the Bible is divinely inspired and therefore inerrant;

- *human response to inspiration*—the view that biblical writers were witnesses to divine revelation; their words and experiences may be human but they serve as vehicles to a higher voice and a deeper reality;

- *inspired imagination*—the view that the Bible is great literature, designed to capture the imagination; though the books of the Bible contain heightened insight, their message is conditioned by historical, sociological, and cultural factors. When the Bible is studied academically, it is the third of these possibilities that scholars generally have in mind.

Corollary:

- *inspired process*—the view that scripture requires ongoing interpretation. This assertion, flowing naturally from the preceding options, recognizes that the sacredness of scripture is validated by its ability to inspire Christians in every age. Scripture, defined and finalized by the canonical process, has an open-ended quality both dynamic and alive, thereby extending the revelatory process to the present. Viewing scripture as "inspired process" safeguards the original revelation while authenticating its enduring meaning.

Viewed in this context, the book of Revelation can be examined as a unique piece of literature—for it was crafted at a specific time, by a specific author, and for a specific audience—but also as the final book in the biblical canon, integral to the Bible in that it represents the culmination of the biblical narrative and brings its message to a fitting close. Contrary to those who regard this book as a biblical oddity or appendage, Revelation can be considered a biblical capstone, for it incorporates the Bible's central topics and concerns even as it brings its message to a close.

The book of Revelation, known also as The Apocalypse of St. John the Divine, barely made it into the New Testament. Every great interpreter had difficulty with it. It was one of a number of apocalypses in circulation during the church's early centuries, and most if not all such writings were regarded with suspicion by church leaders. The reasons for this suspicion are obvious: apocalyptic literature conveyed a note of desperation and finality, its imagery was bizarre, its vocabulary extreme, its tone vindictive, and its God vengeful. The book itself seemed incongruous with the reconciling message of forgiveness found in the Gospels and incompatible with the self-sacrificing love of God exemplified by Jesus. Even after its official acceptance into the canon, many Christians remained hesitant to include Revelation as a part of their Bible. The Protestant reformers often sided with this hesitance. Martin Luther, for example, included the book in his Bible, but denied it functional status because he found its Christology deficient. John Calvin passed over it in silence, writing commentaries on every other New Testament book. Among modern biblical scholars, Rudolf Bultmann, who wrote a famous commentary on John's Gospel, relegated Revelation to the margin of the church's faith and life. To this day, Catholic and Protestant lectionaries include only minimal readings from Revelation, and the Greek Orthodox lectionary omits it altogether. On the other hand, Christian thinkers from Irenaeus to Augustine in the early centuries to Walter Rauschenbush and Paul Minear in modern times have found Revelation to measure up to its canonical role of providing direction and sustenance for the church's life and mission, particularly in extraordinary times.

Having taught courses on Revelation for many years, I have always been impressed by the high level of interest and curiosity that college students have about this book. The teaching experience is rewarding because the class is always full, the level of sincerity is high, and the degree of interaction is intense. When I ask students their motivation for taking the course, their answers reflect both curiosity and apprehension. Many are curious about the book, having heard that it contains coded predictions about the end of the world, with current conflicts in the Middle East perhaps leading up to the great battle of Armageddon, which will end our known world. Some assume that Revelation provides clues to the identity of the figure known as the antichrist, whom they think will soon gain control of the global economy and dominate the whole world. Others are apprehensive, having been repelled by the views of religious groups that seem obsessed by the coming end of the world. Some assume that Revelation is a dangerous book understood only by experts. Many adults are repulsed by the book's intense imagery, feeling that exposure to this literature could add to the high level of violence already present in our society.

We are not alone in these assessments. Major historical figures were also drawn to the Apocalypse for different reasons. For example, the brilliant scientist and mathematician Sir Isaac Newton was absolutely fascinated by Revelation, spending as much time studying the Bible as he did math and science. In a book called *Observations upon the Prophecies of Daniel and the Apocalypse of Saint John*, Newton indicates his desire to decipher the mysteries of Revelation, much as he had been able to decipher the mysteries of the natural world. Having formulated the law of gravity and the laws of motion, he figured he could formulate the laws for interpreting apocalyptic writings. He thought that if his telescope could help people to see into the deep mysteries of space, then Revelation might help people look into the deep mysteries of time and history, accurately predicting specific future events. Using a chronological understanding of particular visions in Revelation, Newton thought that the mysteries of history were unfolding with a kind of mathematical precision. His scheme involved a great deal of guesswork, and his approach to Revelation was not well received. The reason is clear: he was not trained in theology or in biblical interpretation.

Another famous individual who had his own issues with Revelation was the British novelist D. H. Lawrence, author of such novels as *The Rainbow* and *Lady Chatterley's Lover*. Lawrence also had a kind of obsession with Revelation, not because he found it fascinating but because he found it appalling. Near the end of his life he wrote a book called *Apocalypse*, completed just two months before his death. In it he called Revelation unpoetic, ugly, and vindictive. He thought that the book was written by a second-rate mind for people with second-rate minds. He insisted that its violent imagery was the opposite of Jesus' message of love. He thought that Revelation was written by someone who could not wait for the world to end so that he could see cast into the eternal lake of fire all the people he didn't like.

As we begin this study on Revelation, we must recognize the book's extraordinary ability to generate both curiosity and confusion. And we need to set the record straight. The book is not as bizarre and vindictive as many have imagined. And its message need not be viewed as incongruous with the biblical message of love, reconciliation, and forgiveness. While Revelation's method and theological conceptuality are relatively different from the rest of the New Testament, once they are appreciated in their own right, they contribute to make this book not only one of the finest literary works in the Christian canon, but also one of the greatest theological achievements of early Christianity.

DISTINCTIVE FEATURES

My goal in writing this book is to produce a commentary on Revelation that addresses the interests and needs of a general Christian audience, providing guidelines for understanding the message of this ancient work and its application to twenty-first century readers. *Hope Revealed* is not an exegetical commentary, for it does not offer verse-by-verse analysis of the text. Neither is it a textual study, in which a scholar makes a case for a preferred reading. Instead it offers perspective on specific topics that arise as one follows the narrative, always with an eye on the big picture, namely, hope for daily living.

This study divides the book of Revelation into ten units, each discussed as a whole, providing biblical, literary, theological, historical, and textual comments where appropriate. My goal is to proceed from text to understanding and from understanding to application. To that end, each chapter includes the following features:

1. overview of the passage
2. key verse(s) of the passage
3. central theme of the passage
4. learning objections for the passage
5. outline of the passage
6. analysis of the passage
7. an essay related to the passage
8. questions to ponder

Having conducted seminars on Revelation with students during a forty-year teaching career, I have always paid attention to the literary form and the spiritual message of Revelation. While the book contains passages of great beauty and comfort, other passages appear bizarre and bewildering at first sight. But when one approaches the book recognizing that it belongs to a particular literary type (the apocalyptic genre), then one can begin to appreciate the book's intent. While some parts remain enigmatic, attentive readers will be pleased to find how much of the book makes sense.

Acknowledgments

It is fitting that this, the seventh book and closing project of my scholarly career, addresses the book of Revelation, the literary and theological capstone of the Bible, where the number seven represents completion, totality, and finality. In this way my career ends as it began, focusing on biblical studies—my intellectual first love—the linchpin of my teaching and scholarly expertise. The topic of eschatology—the study of the end of history and the return of Christ—has always fascinated me. It also intrigued the first Christians and many others throughout church history. My notion that history is purposeful and moving toward a climactic resolution was fueled by my parents and theological mentors but also by classes, professors, and experiences during my high school and college years. Eschatology occupied much of my free time and led to additional research—generally with conservative scholarship and always centered on the Bible, which I considered the ultimate resource on the topic and God's reliable authority on all matters spiritual, past, present, and future.

My academic exposure to the study of Revelation occurred at Princeton Theological Seminary, where I studied with the late Bruce M. Metzger, one of the renowned biblical scholars of his era. His brilliance as a scholar, wisdom as a teacher, and humility as a mentor encouraged me to appreciate the overall message of John, "the theologian of Patmos."[1] Under his tutelage I was exposed to the writings of G. B. Caird, the eminent New Testament scholar and author of *The Revelation of St. John the Divine*. Caird approaches Revelation as a profoundly Christian book but also as a great work of art, one that can speak as eloquently to our world as it did to John's time. The perspective I gained from these formidable scholars profoundly influenced my approach to biblical theology and helped maintain my academic, theological, and personal interest in Revelation.

---

1. Metzger, *Breaking the Code*, 9.

In addition to the influence of Bruce Metzger and G. B. Caird, I am particularly indebted to the scholarship of Richard Bauckham, M. Eugene Boring, Craig R. Koester, and N. T. Wright on Revelation.[2] I acknowledge with gratitude my reliance upon the insights and methodology of Barbara R. Rossing's "Journey Through Revelation: Apocalyptic Hope for Today," the 2010–2011 Horizons Bible Study published by Presbyterian Women in the Presbyterian Church (U.S.A.).

Over the years I learned much from students in my seminars on Revelation, due in large measure to the participatory format used in those classes. At the end of each term I experienced a renewed love for the subject matter, a new understanding of the message of Revelation, and a greater appreciation for the genius of its author. Writing *Hope Revealed* has renewed my love for scripture, challenged previous conclusions and interpretations, and convinced me that Revelation, properly understood, speaks as profoundly to the present as it did to the past.

I am grateful to Mary Ann Johnson for reading the manuscript and offering editorial advice. My wife Susan provided regular support and perspective, as did my colleague Dan Stinson. I dedicate this book to my children Peter and Sara and their children Jacob, Benjamin, Katherine, and Emily, leaven from the Lord and loves of my life.

---

2. Their works are listed in the bibliography.

Introduction

HUMANS ARE MADE IN the image of God. That is a biblical given, but it is only part of the story. The other part, which each of us must determine for ourselves, is this: in the image of which God? Perhaps we have no more important theological investigation than to discover in whose image we have been made. Our sociology—including our values, priorities, choices, and behavior—is derived from, legitimated by, and reflective of our theology. I propose to discern a vision of God found in the book of Revelation that will enable readers to examine their theological face, exchanging whatever temporal masks they might be wearing in favor of an eternal image, so that when they look into their theological mirror they might see revealed the Bride of Christ, who, like Jesus, reflects God's glory and bears the imprint of God's very being (Heb. 1:3).

THE PROPHETIC TASK

In *The Prophetic Imagination* (1978) Old Testament scholar Walter Brueggemann begins his study by reflecting on the theology of the exodus and on the covenantal tradition associated with the ministry of Moses. In that book Brueggemann makes clear the implications of the God we choose to represent. We can worship and serve Yahweh, the God of Moses, who provides a radical alternative to the dominant surrounding culture, or we can gather around a static god who protects the status quo and legitimates the social agenda. If we choose Yahweh, freedom cannot be far behind. Conversely, if we choose the religion of the Pharaoh, oppression cannot be far behind. If we are made in the image of a God who is free from all regimes, free to hear and answer the cries of victims, and free from goodness as defined by empire or society, then that perspective will bear decisively upon our sociology, because the freedom of God will surface in the marketplace, the boardrooms, the halls of congress, and in personal, corporate, and national priorities as justice and compassion.

As Brueggemann notes, the task of prophetic ministry (of which apocalyptic literature is a part) is "to nurture, nourish, and evoke a consciousness and perception alternative to the consciousness and perception of the dominant culture around us."[1] That nurturing task displays itself in two contrasting ways: (1) by *criticizing* the dominant consciousness, attempting to do what the liberal tendency does, engaging in a rejection and delegitimatizing of the present ordering of things, and (2) by *energizing* persons and communities, attempting to do what the conservative tendency has done, to live in fervent anticipation of the newness that God has promised. To choose between criticizing and energizing is the temptation, respectively, of liberalism and conservatism. Liberals are good at criticism but often lack a word of promise; conservatives invite to alternative visions, past and future, but often lack germane criticism.

Jeremiah's "call" passage (1:10) is instructive in this regard. In that passage Jeremiah is entrusted with a compelling message. Framed in a double metaphor, one rural and agrarian (plucking up and planting) and the other urban and architectural (pulling down and building), the message addresses everyone in society, from the greatest to the least, and every dimension of society. God's first word, entrusted to the prophet, is a negative word, critical of the dominant consciousness. God's world-breaking and world-nullifying activity, which announces death to some worlds, precedes God's final world-creating and world-energizing message. The prophetic promise both destroys and creates worlds. Plucking up and breaking down the false and the wicked must precede planting and building of the true and righteous. As the apostle Paul notes, the old must pass away before the new can emerge with finality (2 Cor. 5:17). The God who "plucks up and pulls down" is the one who "plants and builds."

Christians are called to imagine alternative visions. The key word is "alternative," and believers are called to engage in a struggle with that notion. Quite frankly, most Christians belong to communities of faith that on the whole do not understand that there are any alternatives, or are not prepared to embrace such if they come along. Their prayers, hopes, and dreams are "man-sized" rather than "God-sized." The church will not have power to act or believe until it recovers its tradition of faith and permits that tradition to be the primary way out of enculturation. John of Patmos, author of Revelation, knew this, and so must we. This is not a cry for traditionalism

---

1. Brueggemann, *Prophetic Imagination*, 13.

but rather a judgment that the church has no business more pressing than the reappropriation of its memory in its full power and authenticity.

In the late first century AD, John of Patmos advanced a thorough-going prophetic critique of Roman power, making Revelation the most powerful piece of political resistance literature from the period of the early Roman Empire.[2] It is a mistake, however, to suppose that John opposes Rome because of its persecution of Christians, for the full-scale persecution of the church that John foresees was not yet happening when he wrote. Rather it was because Christians must dissociate themselves from the evils of the Roman system that they were likely to suffer persecution. John sees the nature of Roman power to be such that, if Christians are faithful witnesses to God, then they must suffer the inevitable clash with Rome.

In Revelation the two major symbols for Rome, which represent different aspects of the empire, are "the beast from the sea" (chapter 13) and the harlot of Babylon (chapters 17 and 18). The beast represents Rome's military and political power and Babylon the city of Rome in all her prosperity, gained by economic exploitation. John's critique is political and economic but in both cases also deeply religious. In chapter 13 John recognizes two sides to the imperial cult. On the one hand, the beast blasphemes: it gives itself divine names and claims divinity (13:1, 5). In other words, it absolutizes itself by claiming the religious loyalty due only to the sovereignty of God. But John also recognizes that the imperial cult was not imposed on unwilling subjects. A second beast, elsewhere called the false prophet, promotes the imperial cult through willing subjects, who in many cases provide the initiative and impetus for that adulation. From John's prophetic viewpoint this idolatry was dangerous not only because it deified political and military power, but because it compromised the justice of God. According to 18:24, Rome would be judged not just for the martyrdom of Christians but for the slaughter of all innocent victims: "in you was found the blood of prophets and of saints, and of all who have been slaughtered on earth." John takes the perspective that Christians, in dissociating from Rome's evil, would become victims of Rome in solidarity with the other victims of Rome.

When John counters Roman dominance, expressed through oppression and exploitation, he does so not out of vindictiveness or retribution, but with a vision of justice and compassion. The reality emerging from this climactic book of the Bible is not just a new religious idea or a vision of freedom but a call for the emergence of a new social community, one that matches the character of God as displayed in its risen Lord. This means that John's critique of Roman power is closely tied to his theology: the power

---

2. Bauckham, *Theology of Revelation*, 38.

of resistance to Rome comes from faith in the one true God. For John and those who share his prophetic insight, it is the Christian vision of the incomparable God, exalted above all worldly power, which relativizes Roman power and exposes Rome's pretensions to divinity as a dangerous delusion.

The alternative consciousness imagined by John provides a model for criticizing. We will discover how John criticizes and dismantles the Roman Empire, nullifying its social, political, economic, and religious claims, noting how Rome's politics of oppression is overcome by the practice of justice and compassion. For John, the dominant culture cannot counter God's will; the gods of Rome cannot; the merchants of the regime cannot. The imperial religion and its allies have failed and are doomed to annihilation.

Whenever we encounter judgment language in Revelation, its tone is decisive and bears a note of finality. The reason is clear: evil is a temporal power, and its influence cannot last. Readers easily get caught up in Revelation's images of violence and language of retribution, thus failing to grasp its corrective and illustrative nature: such language is penultimate rather than ultimate, a means to an end rather than representative of God's will or action. Revelation's punitive rhetoric is illustrative of divine discipline, a principle found in Revelation 3:19: "I reprove and discipline those whom I love" and also in Hebrews 12:6-7, 9-11: "for the Lord disciplines those whom he loves, and chastises every child whom he accepts. Endure trials for the sake of discipline . . . Moreover, we had human parents to discipline us, and we respected them. Should we not be even more willing to be subject to the Father of spirits and live? For they disciplined us for a short time as seemed best to them, but he disciplines us for our good, in order that we may share his holiness. Now, discipline always seems painful rather than pleasant at the time, but later it yields the peaceful fruit of righteousness to those who have been trained by it."

Examples of this disciplinary principle are found in Genesis, where "curse" (3:14-19) precedes protection (3:21), judgment (6:7) precedes blessing (9:1), and confusion (11:7) precedes covenant (17:2); in Judges, where punishment precedes deliverance (the fourfold pattern: Disbelief, Punishment, Repentance, and Deliverance is established in 2:11—3:6 and repeated seven times throughout the book); in the prophets, where "bad news" precedes "good news" (contrast Isaiah 1:4 and 21 with 1:26; see Jer. 1:10); in Exodus through Malachi, where exile precedes return; and in Isaiah 65, where the old fallen creation precedes the new restored creation. The pattern established throughout the Bible, from Genesis to Revelation, sets forth the remarkable principle that critiquing precedes energizing, that challenging injustice produces hope (Jer. 31:27-28), and that hope will not disappoint us (Rom. 5:5).

The alternative consciousness imagined by John of Patmos provides a model for energizing. It is the task of the prophet to express new realities against the more visible ones of the old order. Energizing is closely linked to hope. The message of Revelation, its emphasis throughout that makes this book an apt capstone of the biblical canon, is the gospel itself, as summarized by Paul to the Roman Christians in preparation for that community's tribulation and even his own imminent death there at the hands of the emperor Nero: "If God is for us, who is against us? . . . Who will separate us from the love of Christ? Will hardship, or distress, or persecution, or famine, or nakedness, or peril, or sword? . . . No, in all these things we are more than conquerors through him who loved us. For I am convinced that neither death, nor life, nor angels, nor rulers, nor things present, nor things to come, nor powers, nor height, nor depth, nor anything else in all creation, will be able to separate us from the love of God in Christ Jesus our Lord" (Rom. 8: 31, 35, 37–39).

In the end, God's love wins; that's the gospel. And that love is exemplified on the cross. The key to Revelation is that a slain Lamb has "conquered," the victim becoming the victor. From beginning to end, John's vision teaches a "theology of the cross," of God's power made manifest in weakness. Evil is defeated not by overwhelming force or violence but by Christ's suffering love on the cross.

WHY WAS REVELATION WRITTEN?

In order to understand the purpose of Revelation, we need to note that the book was not written to satisfy idle curiosity about the future or to provide a blueprint for the future. What, then, was John's intent? The following guidelines indicate that Revelation was written:

- to challenge the churches of Asia to greater faithfulness and to repent for past failure;
- to comfort and encourage those who were undergoing persecution and personal distress on account of their faith, and who were pondering the delay of Christ's promised return;
- to disclose the person and work of Christ and to remind believers that the future belongs to Jesus Christ and not to emperors or other temporal authorities;
- to critique and expose the absolutizing of political and military power embodied in the Roman imperial cult;

- to provide Christians with a philosophy or perspective (but not a chronology) of history.

While the first four principles seem largely self-explanatory, the fifth needs clarification. In a sense, Revelation is like great art. When viewers enter an art gallery, for example, they don't go to see the familiar world with conventional eyes. They wish to be guided by the perspective of the artist, to see aspects of the world in a new light. When Van Gogh painted the night sky, light did not merely shimmer; it exploded. He used colors in an extreme way—blue that was too intense, gold that was too bright—in order to provide a perspective on the night, so that one could see the familiar in new ways. When Picasso painted a person, it was as if he had created a picture of a person with eyes and ears, arms and legs, and then shattered the picture into a dozen pieces before reassembling them in a collage. All the pieces are there, but disjointed. We normally do not see people like that, but the artist has shown us a way of seeing the fragmentation we might otherwise have missed. The painting provides a new perspective, a new way of seeing. Something like that is going on in Revelation.

If we are looking for something that merely describes the world, then we need to look elsewhere. But if what we want is perspective, one that startles and challenges, then Revelation is very much what we want. The writer uses wild colors and fantastic images that shape the way we see the power of evil, the nature of hope, the character of God, and the character of the world. The scenes are unsettling and uplifting, disturbing and encouraging, sorrowful and joyous. And all of this allows the readers of Revelation to see with new eyes the world in which they live.

Since ancient times people have tried to turn Revelation into a roadmap for the end of the world, and thus far all of those expectations have been wrong. Others, thankfully, have learned from their mistakes and have come to realize that Revelation can best be read for what it might have to say about spiritual life in the present. The book opens up a transcendent world in which the presence of God is vivid and palpable, inviting people to consider what it means to live in God's presence and how that shapes a way of life.

APOCALYPTIC PERSPECTIVES IN THE BIBLE: JEWISH AND CHRISTIAN

The book of Revelation belongs to a literary genre called apocalyptic. Apocalyptic literature is written for people who desire insight into the meaning of life. Such writings revolve around two mysteries, two basic problems posed by people everywhere, even by those who don't identify with any religious tradition: the problem of evil and the nature of hope. To be human is to consider such problems, and in so doing to recognize that one is not so much solving them as exploring mysteries. And the greatest mystery, which prompted the prophets of Israel and Judah as well as "the Prophet of Patmos," was the mystery of God. When John recounts his own vision of God, he weaves together images of the heavenly throne and the six-winged seraphs from the book of Isaiah (6:1–3) with a description of the crystal dome and the mysterious four creatures from the book of Ezekiel (chapters 1 and 10).

In order to better understand the apocalyptic worldview, how it originated and why it was so important in the ancient world, we need to understand how the Hebrew prophets dealt with themes of evil and hope. When we think of the prophetic writings and the problem of evil, it is helpful to think in terms of three concentric circles:[3]

- At the center the prophets address the evils within the people of Israel (including violence, abuse of power, and other forms of social, political, and economic injustice);
- Beyond this inner circle we find a wider one, which takes into account the evils of other nations;
- Finally there is an outer circle of concern, where the prophets speak in cosmic terms of universal suffering and a curse that affects the inhabitants of earth and even earth itself.

Having addressed evil and warned of its consequences, the prophets provide messages of hope, more sweeping in scope than the warnings. If we continue the pattern of concentric circles, we start with the center, where the prophets offer promises of hope to their own people. Then the prophets move outward, offering hope for the nations. The prophetic hope extends outward yet again, offering hope for the transformation of the whole earth, a promise that includes overcoming death itself. Isaiah 2:2–4; 25:8; 65:17, 19 and Ezekiel 37:1–14 and 47:8–12 contain remarkable visions of hope for Israel, the nations, and the earth itself.

It is instructive to note that these prophetic themes helped shape the book of Revelation. Like the Old Testament prophets, John starts at the center. "He calls for repentance among his own people, the members of the Christian community, and he also gives them hope for life in the New Jerusalem. Then the author moves outward to the nations. He pictures a battle in which the nations are defeated, and yet he gives them hope for a place in

---

3. Koester, *Apocalypse*, lecture 2, "Apocalyptic Worldview in Judaism," 16, 27–29.

God's city as well. And finally the author goes out still further and speaks of death being overcome and the heavens and earth being made new."[4] The contours of the expanding prophetic tradition have become John's.

While the themes of evil and hope in the prophetic writings were composed between the eighth and the fifth centuries BC, the apocalyptic tradition emerged in Jewish circles during the centuries that followed. The two centuries before and after Christ can be described as a time of apocalyptic fervor across the Mediterranean world, during which period there appeared a considerable number of Jewish and Christian writings that belong to the category of apocalyptic literature. Though Jewish apocalyptic literature is said to begin with the book of Daniel, apocalyptic tendencies can be seen earlier, in passages such as Isaiah 24–27, Ezekiel 38–39, and Zechariah 9–14, where there are frequent references to the approaching "Day of the Lord." Important Jewish apocalyptic writings outside the Old Testament include the book of Enoch, the Apocalypse of Baruch, the Fourth Book of Ezra, the Ascension of Isaiah, the Apocalypse of Zephaniah, and parts of the Sibylline Oracles. The first-century Jewish community that wrote the Dead Sea Scrolls also wrote and preserved apocalypses.

One feature in particular distinguishes the apocalyptic tradition from the older prophetic tradition: a sharp dualistic contrast between the power of good and the power of evil, between people who side with goodness and those who side with wickedness. Apocalyptic thinking views history as consisting of two ages, the present, in which evil is operative, and the coming one, when only goodness will prevail. According to the apocalyptic mindset, evil is so great that humans cannot eliminate it; only God can do so. Divine intervention (often called the "Day of the Lord") is imminent, at which time the world will be judged, the righteous vindicated, and all things set right. While the prophetic tradition spoke of good and evil largely in human terms, the apocalyptic tradition tended to view evil in cosmic terms, as a demonic force operative in the world.

From a modern perspective, we are likely to think of the forces in our environment in psychological terms, as forces within ourselves, or in social terms, as destructive patterns that can influence entire groups. But for those who think of the world in apocalyptic terms, evil is cosmic, and humans cannot be insulated from it or remain neutral; one is on the side either of good or of evil. According to this perspective, evil cannot be defeated gradually or progressively in history but only in the future and only by God. During the apocalyptic period, the classic scenario expected God to act in a decisive way to end the present evil age by defeating the powers of evil,

---

4. Ibid., 29–30.

thereby inaugurating a new and different era, accompanied by the resurrection of the dead. The emergence of many Jewish sects during this period, including the birth of Christianity, is directly attributable to the apocalyptic mindset.

For early Christians, the legacy of Jesus redefined the paradigm. It was no longer a straightforward movement from the present age into the new age. Instead, the new age began before the old age was fully gone. And Christians found themselves at the juncture of the two. As they looked back, they believed that the world had really been changed by the coming of Jesus. In their eyes, his life, death, and resurrection had been God's way of intervening in the world. The result was that conditions were no longer the same. Yet when they looked at the present, they realized that the powers of sin and death were still operative. Though Jesus was believed to have risen from the dead, the general resurrection remained a future hope. They lived between these two realities: the new age had begun in Jesus but the old age had not fully gone away. This basic shift in thinking is present in the Gospels, where the kingdom of God is seen as existing in the present, but only embryonically. While the end of the current evil age is anticipated in the near future, certain conditions must be fulfilled, including the preaching of the gospel to the nations (Mark 13:10; Matt. 10:18 and 24:14). During the first century, as the Christian movement expands, the apocalyptic tension eases considerably. This is already evident in Luke's Gospel, where all the predictions about the end are worded differently from those in Mark and Matthew. In Luke, Jesus does not envisage the end of the age happening immediately. In the book of Acts, that idea is made abundantly clear as well, for the church must first spread to Rome and beyond, and that expansion would take time.

The Gospel of John tones down the apocalyptic message even further, moving beyond the other Gospels in seeing the promise of the future as a reality in the present. For John, eternal life is not a future event. The author understands that people were created for relationship with God and with other people. And when those relationships have been damaged, people are not fully alive. According to John's Gospel, the coming of Jesus is the apocalyptic event that makes the promise of resurrection a present reality. The way John does this is by identifying love as the center of Jesus' legacy. According to John, Jesus came in order to convey the fullness of divine love to the world. And Jesus' willingness to die was the most radical form that divine love takes. When the reality of divine love evokes a response of faith in humans, their relationship with God is restored. And from John's perspective, that restoration of relationship is where eternal life begins. It is a life that begins now, and it continues beyond the death of the body. The future hope is still there, but the apocalyptic drama is being played out now, as divine love evokes faith in people. Whereas Jewish apocalyptists maintained a dualistic view of the world, in John's Gospel this dualism has a spatial dimension (this world and the world that is above) but not a temporal one (this age and the future age). John, in short, presents a "de-apocalypticized version of Jesus' teaching."[5]

The apocalyptic tension between the present and the future profoundly shaped the work of Paul. At some points in his letters Paul looks back and insists that the new age truly began in Jesus, for "everything has become new" (2 Cor. 5:17). The power of sin and death is defeated on the cross and through the resurrection. Elsewhere he looks ahead and says that though the new age has already begun, the benefits are not fully present (1 Cor. 13:9–12). For Paul, death is the great adversary. By death he means not only a person's last breath but also suffering culminating in the cessation of life. The apocalyptic battle that God is waging in Christ must continue until death itself has been eliminated, which will occur in the final resurrection of the dead. For Paul, God will destroy the power of death through the gift of life. That is the essence of Paul's apocalyptic hope: a vision in which death is swallowed up in the victory that comes through life (1 Cor. 15:54–57).

Revelation looks forward to a future intervention of God in human affairs. But its understanding of this intervention is different from that of other apocalyptists, who could make little or no sense of their own present experience. To them, history was a meaningless enigma, and the sooner its course was stopped, the better. This view had not been that of the Old Testament prophets. Though some of the prophets had looked forward to the coming of a "Day of the Lord," when God would intervene in a final and decisive way in the affairs of the world, they believed that this event would be the continuation of what God was already doing. For them, the God who would inaugurate a new world order in the future was also the God who could be known here and now in the events of human life.

Like the Old Testament, the book of Revelation makes a clear link between what God is doing in history now and what God will do in the future. Indeed, the entire meaning of God's plan for the future of humanity is to be found in the life, death, and resurrection of Jesus. Revelation does not slavishly follow the pattern of the Jewish apocalyptic books. It presents a distinctive and positive Christian explanation of the presence of evil in human affairs. Its message is expressed through conventional language and in vivid Old Testament imagery, but its content goes beyond the literary form of apocalyptic writing.

---

5. Ehrman, *Brief Introduction*, 126.

METHODS OF INTERPRETATION

While Revelation can be viewed in a number of ways, there are four main schools of interpretation. I will describe each approach and conclude with an evaluation of each view.

1. *Preterist Approach*: This view, sometimes called the "contemporary-historical" approach because it emphasizes John and his contemporaries, stresses the importance of the original setting. This method is followed by practically every modern biblical scholar, of all theological persuasions. This approach applies the same historical method to Revelation that scholars use for the preceding books of the New Testament, attempting to determine the meaning of a text in its original historical context before determining its current meaning and application. This view assumes that John had a relevant message to the churches of his day, that they understood the message, and that the modern interpreter should not accept any interpretation of the book that its first readers would not have understood. It represents a corrective to unbridled futuristic speculation.

Early Christians were hoping for divine intervention that in their day would bring the anticipated kingdom of God to earth and end the hated Roman system of domination. But this expectation resulted in frustrated hope, for the eternal kingdom did not come as expected. Over time, other schools of interpretation arose.

2. *Idealist Approach*: This view, also labeled "poetic," "spiritual," or "non-historical," represents the eternal conflict of good and evil. This approach underscores the general promise of God to be with his people always. The imagery is taken from apocalyptic views of the first century and from the general language of myth. The value of this approach is that it allows Revelation to speak universal human symbols to people in every time and place. It minimizes, however, the specific historical references known to the original audience and does not allow for concrete significance, thereby denying its character as a real letter.

3. *Historicist Approach*: This view, also called "church-historical," "world-historical," or "chronological," approaches the book as a symbolic presentation of the entire course of church history, from the first century to the end of history. Chapters 2–3 are regarded as addressing the church of John's own time, but the visions of chapters 4–22 are interpreted as predicting all future history. In practice this meant that each interpreter saw John as predicting the course of history down to his or her own time, which was generally viewed to be the last period predicted by Revelation. Since this approach flourished in Europe, Revelation was understood to predict the course of European history, primarily church history. The value of this

approach is that it emphasizes the prophetic nature of Revelation and allows for specific fulfillment. It also affirms God's activity throughout history and maintains God's sovereignty over history. But this view eliminates any real meaning for the first audience and is highly parochial. It also misunderstands prophecy by reducing it to prediction. In addition, it allegorizes Revelation, subjecting it to far-fetched spiritualization of historical events. Finally, the variety of interpretations produced by this method cancel each other out, thus invalidating the approach.

4. *Futurist Approach*: This view, also called "dispensationalist" and "premillennialist," considers Revelation to be predictive, but it differs from the preceding approach in two important ways: (a) the seven churches of chapters 2 and 3 are no longer real churches in first-century Asia but represent seven consecutive stages of church history, from the apostolic church (Ephesus) to the apostate church of the last days (Laodicea); (b) the visions of chapters 4 through 22 are yet to be fulfilled. These events will take place in the last few years of world history, in the period immediately preceding the return of Christ. Advocates of this position see themselves as living in the eleventh hour of history, at the start of the final countdown.

This interpretation is correct insofar as it recognizes that Revelation deals with God's activity throughout history. Among its major problems is that it transfers the context of Revelation from the first century to that of the interpreter's lifetime, thus making the book meaningless to its original audience. It takes a hyperliteralistic approach to Revelation, misconstruing the nature of prophecy and the imagery of apocalyptic literature in general, and it generally supports a sectarian understanding of Christianity. This view is the most recent of the four types of interpretation, having been devised by a group of fundamentalist ministers during the late nineteenth century, notably John Nelson Darby in England, and then popularized by the American lawyer Charles Ingersoll Scofield in his Scofield Reference Bible. Despite lacking a theological education, Scofield founded in Dallas, Texas a nondenominational Bible School that continued after his death as Dallas Theological Seminary, which became a major center for the dissemination of this dispensational view.[6] This interpretation has become quite popular in the media and among evangelicals today. It is a dangerous approach, however, particularly when it is associated with current events and tied in to America's role in the Middle East, since it often advocates the necessity of a nuclear war as part of God's plan "predicted" in Revelation.

6. Dispensationalists have developed various schemes to support their belief that God relates to humans in different ways during history. This system of interpretation divides biblical history into a series of covenants known as "dispensations," a concept discussed in chapter 9 (see essay 9, "Eschatological Approaches to Revelation").

OUTLINE OF THE BOOK OF REVELATION

The focus of Revelation is the return of Christ and the establishment of God's kingdom on earth at the end of time. Corresponding to this, the structure of the book involves a series of parallel yet ever-progressing sections. This method, known as "progressive parallelism," brings before the reader, in spiraling form, the struggle of the church and its victory over the world in the providence of God. Many commentators divide the book into seven of these sections, though only four are clearly marked.[7] The following pattern has been noted in Revelation, although one cannot confirm that this was John's intention: seven seals (6:1—8:1); seven trumpets (8:2—11:19); seven visions of the dragon and his kingdom (12:1—13:18); seven visions of the coming of the Lamb of God (14:1-20); seven bowls of God's anger against evil (15:1—16:21); seven visions of the fall of "Babylon" (17:1—19:10); and seven visions of the end (19:11—21:4).[8] However many repetitive patterns one discovers, and however much recapitulation one discerns, these visions present a kaleidoscopic picture of how God overcomes the powers of evil. It is the work not of a self-conscious theologian but of a great artist. Like a good artist, John depicts the same subject from a number of different perspectives in order to reinforce the overall impression that he wants to create. And like a good teacher, who knows that repetition is a helpful learning device, he repeats his messages from differing points of view.

Literary structure is the first and the most obvious approach to the study of any book. The clue to the order may appear in repeated phrases that introduce topics, comparisons, parallel sections, or, as in Revelation, visions. The book of Revelation contains a large number of repeated phrases, some of which are significant as marks of progressive thought. Many readers fail to realize that the author provides clues that are intended to lead the reader through the maze of figurative expression to an intelligible pattern of

---

7. The number seven, representing perfection or totality, is regularly found in apocalyptic literature. The Fourth Book of Ezra (Second Esdras), a Jewish apocalypse written about the same time as Revelation, contains a series of seven revelations, has seven ways that evil is punished, and seven ways the righteous rejoice. Typical of apocalyptists, who utilize numbers, animals, and other images figuratively, John is fond of sevens; he mentions seven golden lampstands, seven churches, seven stars, seven flaming torches, seven spirits of God, seven eyes, seven seals, seven angels, seven trumpets, seven thunders, seven heads on the dragon, seven plagues, seven bowls, seven mountains, seven kings, seven beatitudes, seven references to the altar, seven affirmations of the return of Christ, seven categories of people (6:15), and sevenfold praise presented to the Lamb (5:12).

8. Drane, *New Testament*, 442.

teaching. The first and clearest of these is the phrase "in the Spirit," which occurs in four places:

- 1:10   I was in the Spirit on the Lord's day
- 4:2   At once I was in the Spirit
- 17:3   So he carried me away in the Spirit
- 21:10 And in the Spirit he carried me away

Each occurrence of this phrase locates the seer in a different place, and each signals the reception of a new vision. Each vision can be analyzed according to its geographical setting, its passage in the book, and its content.

Setting	Passage	Content of the Vision
Isle (Patmos)	1:9—3:22	Vision of Christ: the letters to the seven churches (the church imperfect in the world)
Heaven	4:1—16:21	Vision of Judgment: seven seals, trumpets, and bowls (process of world judgment)
Wilderness	17:1—21:8	Climax of judgment and of redemption (collapse of godless Babylon)
High Mountain	21:9—22:5	Advent of the City of God (the church perfected in the world)

The method I follow utilizes the concept of progressive parallelism, but it divides the book into five parallel sections rather than seven, surrounded by two visions of the church.

A. Prologue (1:1-8)

B. Church Imperfect in the World (1:9—3:22)

C. Five Parallel Sections

    1. Scroll with Seven Seals (4:1—8:5)

    2. Seven Trumpets (8:6—11:19)

    3. Seven Actors (12:1—14:20)

    4. Seven Bowls (15:1—16:21)

    5. Seven Judgments (17:1—21:8)

D. Church Perfected in the World (21:9—22:5)

E. Epilogue (22:6-21)

Three things are said to progress, increase, and become climactic in Revelation: (a) the severity of evil, (b) the severity of judgments, and (c) the perfecting of the faithful church.

GUIDING PRINCIPLES OF THIS STUDY

The following principles will guide this study:

1. *Keep in mind the historical context.* If we want to understand Revelation, we must recognize that it was not written to us. As a letter, Revelation contains a particular message to a particular situation and not a collection of "general principles" or "universal ideas." It must be read in terms of the original hearer-readers and their situation.

2. *Do not read Revelation as encoded message.* It has sometimes been suggested that in view of the political situation under which Revelation was written, John wrote his message in code so that Christians but not the Roman authorities could understand it. This view is untenable on various counts: (a) Only a fraction of the visionary material deals with Rome, yet all the visions are expressed in symbolic language; (b) the references to Rome are transparent (e.g. 17:9, 18), so that only the dullest Romans would be fooled; (c) there are many undisguised statements that could be taken as subversive by the Romans—including references to God or Christ as king (11:15) as well as references to Christians having a kingdom (1:6); (d) unlike a code, John's symbols are traditional and widespread.

We should not picture the original readers as individually pouring over the pages of the document or as entrusting its decipherment to a decoding specialist or subcommittee within the congregation. John used symbols in order to communicate what could not be expressed in any other way, not to conceal things that could be said more directly.[9] Encoded language is a kind of literal language; all one needs is the key. Revelation is not code language. It does not so much conceal meaning as provide perspective.

3. *Always look beyond the literal approach.* Revelation's language, akin to poetry, is pictorial and polyvalent—expressive and evocative. It does not appeal to logic but to the emotions, using symbols that are tensive, not referential. Attempts to express Revelation's images and metaphors in factual language rob them of their power of persuasion.

The distinction between "steno symbols" and "tensive symbols," made popular by Philip Wheelwright, or between "sign" and "symbol," suggested by Paul Tillich, is instructive. "Sign" language, in our culture, is represented, for example, by traffic signs, which convey precise information. When a traffic light is red, the meaning is straightforward and unambiguous. Traffic lights function as "steno symbols" in that they do not produce any tension in the mind. Tensive symbols, on the other hand, create tension in the mind. John's language is not the language of signs but of symbols, which are

---

9. Boring, *Revelation*, 54–55.

evocative. Unlike "signs," John's symbols are polyvalent: they *increase* tension, suggesting images and overtones of meaning that cannot be reduced to one level of meaning. As a mythopoetic work, Revelation is "not like a window to the world but is more like an onion or a rose with layers and layers of meaning . . . One could liken Revelation's symbolic narrative function to a prism refracting rich meaning in different and multiple ways."[10]

Much that is contained in Revelation is best perceived by the ear and the imagination. The book is unique in appealing primarily to our imagination—not, however, a loose or reckless imagination, but a disciplined one. The book contains a series of word pictures that convey an overall impression. Many of the details of these pictures are intended to contribute to that total impression, and are not to be allegorized or interpreted literally.

Ecstatic experience of various kinds is generally an aspect of human religion, and "visions and revelations" seem to have been quite common among the prophetic figures in the early church, as Paul and the author of Acts note (1 Cor. 14; 2 Cor. 12:1–10; Acts 10:1–23; 22:17; 27:21–26). While John was one of those early Christian prophets who experienced visions and revelations, we should not take this to mean that Revelation is simply the "reporting" of what he "saw" or "heard" in his visions. As Eugene Boring states in his commentary on Revelation: "The images from the Scripture and John's religious tradition that resided in his imagination were already active in the revelatory experience itself, providing the raw materials that were reshaped by his visionary experience. In later reflection and composition he used all the resources of his tradition and his creative literary imagination to express the visions to his hearer-readers, painting them in colors drawn from the rich palate already prepared in the Bible and other prophetic and apocalyptic tradition. In their present form the visions are literary compositions based on John's visionary experience, not merely descriptive reports of what he 'actually' saw and heard."[11]

4. *Be aware of hyperbole.* John's symbolic language includes a tendency toward hyperbole, a feature of prophetic discourse in general and of apocalyptic literature in particular. Jesus, along with his Jewish contemporaries, delighted in sharp contrasts and extreme statements. Teachings about a log in someone's eye (Matt. 7:3–5) or about hating one's family in order to follow Jesus (Luke 14:26) must be seen in the light of the Near-Eastern characteristic of exaggeration and are not intended to be taken literally. Like his Semitic counterparts, John combines contextual specificity with eschatological hyperbole. For example, in speaking about the power, dominion,

---

10. Schüsler Fiorenza, *Revelation*, 19.
11. Boring, *Revelation*, 27.

and worship of the beast in chapter 13 or about the mission and witness of the church, he consistently uses universal language. The church is drawn from *every* nation (5:9) and constitutes an *innumerable* multitude (7:9); its witness, symbolized by the angel's proclamation of the eternal gospel, goes out to *all* nations (14:6); the expected period of trial under the rule of the beast is coming on the *whole* world (3:10); the beast has authority over *every* nation and is worshipped by *all* the inhabitants of the earth (13:7-8); the second beast enforces his worship by a system of totalitarian control of economic life (13:12-17), which far exceeds the realities or possibilities of the first century; the dragon, the beast, and the false prophet assemble the kings of the *whole* world for the final battle (16:14); and Babylon deceives *all* the nations (14:8; 18:3, 23). These references depict the impending conflict between the church and the beast in terms that are eschatologically universal rather than historically realistically.

This does not mean that John predicts, in some distant future, a universal, totalitarian, anti-Christian state. The hyperbole is of the same kind as when John writes *as though* all Christians are to suffer martyrdom (cf. 6:9-11; 7:14; 11:7-10; 12:11; 14:1-5). This is how Christians conquer in Revelation, through faithful witness unto death, viewed as the continuation of Christ's sacrificial work by his followers. Those who follow the Lamb resemble the one they follow "wherever he goes" (14:4). The hyperbole makes clear what is at stake in the conflict between the church and the evil Empire. The beast/Babylon represents, in a thousand other historical forms, any society that usurps ultimate power before the coming of God's eschatological reign. Hyperbole gives these symbols intrinsic power to reach as far as the End. Thus Revelation, in its predictive element, found fulfillment in its own immediate future and also finds a continuing relevance that transcends its original context.

5. *Read Revelation as a pastoral letter.* John's letter should be read as a pastoral letter, not as a theological treatise. In a treatise or book the author is a particular person, but the readers are unknown to the author or to one another. The distinctive aspect about a real letter is that both the author and the readers are particular persons. A real letter presupposes the particular situation of the readers and addresses it specifically. Revelation is a letter to Christians John knew and for whom he felt a pastoral responsibility. The letter was intended to be read by a worship leader to a community gathered for praise and prayer.

The imagery of Revelation, which seems bizarre by modern standards, is mostly taken from the tradition of images familiar to first-century Christians who heard the Bible read in worship services, much like the tradition of Jewish worshippers who gathered in synagogues to hear their scriptures read during worship. In keeping with this tradition, contemporary students of Revelation might wish to gather in church, sing a hymn of praise, join in prayer, and then listen as a liturgist reads the book of Revelation in its entirety.[12] Better yet, members of one congregation might wish to read Revelation from the perspective of Christians in other cultures and with people who have been marginalized and have found hope in this book.

6. *Embrace the message of hope instead of fear.* In Revelation, the outcome of history is assured: Jesus has already won the victory through his death and resurrection. Because God reigns, hope is always near. This letter was not written to terrify people but to awaken them, to encourage them, and to sustain their hope when things seemed bleakest. Hope is the most important message of Revelation. Readers must always take into consideration the goal in 21:5, which acts as a compass pointing to the book's "true north": "I am making all things new." In Revelation, these are the *only* words spoken directly by the one sitting on the throne. This is where the Bible's storyline is headed, and it is incumbent upon people of faith to discern that the arc of history is bent toward hope.

7. *Read Revelation canonically.* Though the Bible is a "library of books," with a variety of theologies and conflicting points of view, it contains a unified story. Biblical theologians see the Bible as a narrative drama, with God as the main character. While scholars disagree on the number of episodes in the biblical drama or on what to call them, the following headings adequately describe the plot: Creation, Covenant, Christ, Church, and Consummation.[13] The book of Revelation brings the Christian canon to a close, figuratively and literally, since its place in the Bible and its message is associated with the consummation of history: "The kingdom of the world has become the kingdom of our Lord and of his Christ, and he shall reign for ever and ever" (11:15). In vivid pictures the book of Revelation establishes God's just rule throughout history, depicting the triumphant finale of the biblical drama with scenes of the last battle and the last judgment.

Revelation, however, is more than simply the concluding act in the biblical drama. The book should be viewed, not merely as a dramatic finale or a bizarre appendix to the biblical narrative, but as an appropriate capstone to scripture, in harmony with key biblical themes and encompassing each of the Bible's principal headings. In this sense, Revelation may be described as a Bible in miniature.

---

12. See essay 3, "The Centrality of Worship and Doxology in Revelation."
13. Boring, *Revelation*, 1–2.

Assignment

The book of Revelation should be approached as one would a work of art. If one seeks to appreciate a symphony, for example, one must listen to the entire work in order to grasp the full impact of its total composition—its musical forms, motifs, tonal colors, and relationships. Only after one has listened to the work as a whole can one analyze the elements and details of its composition and study the techniques employed by its composer. Likewise, Revelation can be fully appreciated only when analyzed in its entirety, because each vision and symbol takes its import in relation to Revelation's overall symbolic configuration.

Read through Revelation in its entirety, beginning with the vision of the New Jerusalem in Revelation 21–22. The entire journey through Revelation leads to this vision of heaven coming down to earth, where God dwells in our midst. The promise of the renewed earth is what sustains readers throughout the long journey of this book. As you read this climactic passage, meditate on the images of the tree of life, the river of life, and the city of God. Hold these images and promises as you read the remainder of the book, beginning with chapter 1.

Questions to Ponder

1. Having read Revelation, what seems to be its primary message?
2. Do you find an underlying message that has practical value in your present circumstances?
3. Which school of interpretation to the book of Revelation best represents your approach at the start of this study? Does this view leave you with any questions you wish to pursue?
4. Of the seven guiding principles given for this study, which do you find most helpful? Why?
5. Some apocalyptic writings understand evil to be a cosmic power that works in the world. Some identify the principal agent of evil as a supernatural being. Why might early readers of apocalyptic literature have found it helpful to conceptualize evil in this way? What problems arise from this approach?

PART I

Christ's Message to the Church
Addressing Complacency

Chapter 1

A Vision of Christ (Revelation 1)

Summary: In Revelation 1 the author introduces himself and explains his purpose in writing this book. He has seen a vision of the living Christ. He has an urgent message to communicate to seven churches in the Roman province of Asia (a coastal Roman province now located in western Turkey). That message is a call for them to be witnesses for Christ in every aspect of their lives.

Assignment: Read chapter 1 of Revelation

Key Passage: Revelation 1:13

Central Theme: The presence of Christ in the midst of the churches

Learning Objectives

Participants will examine:
1. Three different kinds of biblical writing in Revelation
2. The original audience of Revelation
3. John of Patmos and why he wrote
4. The nonliteral nature of symbols
5. The Christology of Revelation

OUTLINE TO REVELATION 1:1–20

I. Introduction 1:1–3

II. Salutation 1:4–8

III. Preface to Vision of Christ 1:9–11

IV. A Vision of Christ 1:12–20

ANALYSIS OF REVELATION 1:1–20

Most of us have learned how to read different kinds of writing. We know what to expect of a newspaper's editorial pages or its comics, and we know how they differ from the news sections or the crossword puzzle. We know the differences between poetry and prose and between a novel and a textbook. The Bible also contains different types of literature. Some books are narratives; some are poetry, others are letters. Some draw on more than one genre or type of writing. Knowing what to expect from each type of literature helps us understand how to read each book with deeper insight.

What Kind of Book Is Revelation?

To get our bearings, we need to consider the background of Revelation. We need to know what lies behind it, where this writing came from, and what it was intended to do. According to the first three verses of Revelation, three types of writing are utilized in this work: apocalypse, prophecy, and letter. Although the literary genre is clearly apocalyptic, all three styles of writing seem to characterize the book as a whole.

1. *Apocalypse*: When I ask my students what comes to mind when they hear the word "apocalypse," they often mention disaster, the end of the world, or the collapse of civilization. But when we examine its meaning in the Bible, we find that the term meant something quite different. The word "apocalypse" is a rendering of the Greek word *apokalypsis*. This is the first word in the original Greek version of the book of Revelation. The author is here using the word in its ordinary meaning: an apocalypse is a disclosure, a type of literature that provides insight and perspective. That is why the word is often translated in English as "revelation," since a revelation is an act of disclosure, a way of seeing. That's what the author wants to provide his audience in this last book of the Bible: a way of seeing.

The book of Revelation is the only book in the Bible that calls itself an apocalypse. As a literary genre, apocalypses were written in order to unveil or reveal some deep truth about the world. As Brian Blount explains, Revelation is "a truth that enables its hearers and readers to see the present in a new light. But that truth is so powerful, so overwhelming, that John's words cannot properly convey it. He therefore appeals to symbols and codes that must bear the weight his language cannot."[1]

Such language may not be familiar to us, but when Revelation was written, apocalypse was a popular type of literature for Jews, Christians, and others. Often written at a time of crisis, apocalypses typically used exaggerated imagery to heighten the sense of urgency and to call readers to action. In the case of Revelation, this vivid language also heightens the sense of hope.

Ancient readers had a high regard for apocalypses and the visionaries who wrote them. They were familiar with their fantastic imagery and mysterious symbolism. They loved the dramatic visionary journeys and were drawn to the way apocalypses pulled back the curtain of everyday life to reveal a deeper spiritual reality—God's reality. Apocalypses employed mysterious numbers, colors, and terrifying creatures. But Revelation, unlike apocalypses such as Daniel, is not a secret message to be sealed up until the end (contrast Dan. 12:4). Instead, Revelation is to be "read aloud" in the seven communities of Asia Minor (Rev. 1:3).

2. *Prophecy*: In addition to being an apocalypse, Revelation also is prophecy. Unlike all other Jewish and Christian apocalyptic authors, John claims for his work a close affinity with the writings of the Hebrew prophets. Thus, against his one reference to the book as being an apocalypse, John speaks of it as prophecy in six places (1:3; 19:10; 22:7, 10, 18–19); he places himself in the category of "prophets" (22:9); he says his function is that of prophesying (10:11); and, like the prophets before him, he claims to hear God's Word directed to himself (1:2, 9).[2]

But prophecy, in this usage, is not a prediction of the future. When Revelation was written, the word "prophecy" referred to the writings of the prophets of the Hebrew scriptures. In the tradition of the biblical prophets, prophecy meant proclaiming God's message of salvation and judgment at a crucial moment in history. As preachers, prophets were social critics who spoke out boldly and without compromise against current disobedience and disbelief within the social, religious, and political establishment. Prophets opened people's eyes to see the world in terms of God's vision.

1. Blount, *Revelation*, 11.
2. Bowman, "Revelation," 59.

The prophecy revealed in Revelation functions in a similar way. Though some of the language sounds predictive (see Rev. 1:1, "to show . . . what must soon take place"), even this predictive language falls in the tradition of the biblical prophets. Often, such prophecy serves as a wake-up call, urging repentance to avoid dire consequences. John served as prophetic interpreter of events for his congregations in two ways: (a) he declared the meaning of the historical events through which they were living and Christian responsibility within them, and (b) he continued to probe the meaning of Jesus' life, death, and resurrection, providing new interpretations and new Christological titles that were meaningful ways to understand the significance of the Christ event in John's time.

The current pop eschatology misunderstanding of Revelation as a book of long-range predictions forecasting events in our own time is due not only to cultural misunderstanding of prophecy as prediction but to the fact that John does announce events in the future. The future he announces, however, is always either the immediate future of his first-century readers (e.g. 2:10) or the ultimate victory of God at the end of history (e.g. 21:1—22:5), which he perceived as near at hand. If John were really predicting events of our time, Revelation would have been meaningless to its first readers and would not have been a letter to them. While Revelation does contain a message for our time, it does not make predictions about our time.

If we derive our understanding of prophecy from the Hebrew scriptures, as John did, the essential nature of prophecy is clear. Israel believed that God communicated with his people directly by choosing certain individuals who were given their message by divine revelation. While the message they received may or may not contain predictions, it was prophecy because it came as a revelation from God.

3. *Letter*: John alone among apocalyptic writers has superimposed upon the apocalyptic nature of his book another structure—that of a letter. Failure to discern this dual literary character of John's work has led to much misinterpretation on the part of his interpreters. The first Christian writer to present his message in letter form is Paul, whose first extant letter (1 Thessalonians, written c. 50, some twenty years after Jesus' death) represents the earliest endeavor to give literary expression to the gospel message. John follows Paul's characteristic formulas closely, including in his apocalypse the fourfold pattern: (a) salutation (1:4a); (b) opening benediction (1:4b–5a); prayer or doxology (1:5b–6); and (d) closing benediction (22:21).

Some scholars suggest that the letter embraces only chapter 1 or, at most, chapters 1 through 3, but such an analysis destroys the book's literary structure and its doctrinal unity. As it now stands, the letter format encompasses the entire book, for it ends with the closing benediction at 22:21 and not at 3:22, as some propose. To conclude the letter at the end of chapter 3 would result in our having a letter prefixed to an apocalypse, a hybrid otherwise unknown in literature.

For Whom Was Revelation Written?

The fact that Revelation is a letter has important consequences for understanding its message. The nature of a letter is to have a particular audience. This letter was written to Christians in a specific place, time, and situation. Isolated on Patmos, a small island about seventy-five miles west of Ephesus, John could not visit the Christian communities that he knew and loved. Instead, he writes a pastoral letter, requesting that it be read aloud, presumably in its entirety (1:3). John did not write Revelation as the closing book of the Bible but rather composed a letter to Christians he knew and for whom he felt a pastoral responsibility. John dates his letter "on the Lord's day" (1:10), implying that it was not intended for private, silent reading but was meant to be read aloud during worship. The worship service is an important context for this book, anchoring it in the church's gathering for liturgy and the sacraments. Singing and worshipping are an important part of embarking on this apocalyptic journey of hope. Heeding that contextual proviso could have curbed much divisiveness, bloodshed, and prejudice perpetrated by literalistic zealots across the ages. The author states his intention clearly at the outset: readers and hearers alike are to be blessed by the text (1:3); anything short of that thwarts its intention.

A central concern of Revelation is to shape the identity of the churches John is addressing. They are to be a people of God, living in a different manner and by a different creed than those of the surrounding culture. The statement in 1:5b–6 brings forth a dedicatory response of thanksgiving for the benefits of life in Christ: (a) ongoing love ("him who loves us"), (b) deliverance from the power of sin ("freed us from our sins"), (c) shared power ("made us to be a kingdom"), and (d) shared glory ("priests serving his God and Father"). Divine love motivates the author's apocalyptic message of hope. The wonderful ideas of the "kingdom" and "priesthood" of all believers (this theme will recur in 5:10 and 20:6) are reminders of the exodus story, in which slaves were liberated so they might be a "priestly kingdom" (Exod. 19:6). Revelation urges us to think of ourselves as royalty and as priests in the service of God. We are not kings, for there is only one King, but we will reign with Christ forever.

Though Christians associate the foregoing references with the promise of heavenly reward, John would have understood such service as temporal and present. In Revelation John continually shapes the Christian community as a countercultural community. He teaches his parishioners about the dangers of serving the Roman kingdom while giving them a different identity, first and foremost as citizens under God's rule. By placing their allegiance in God they would be able to witness to the conviction that God's reign already is at work in the world. Like Jesus, who is introduced as the faithful witness (1:5), we too should be faithful, in word and in deed. Witnessing can be verbal, but has more to do with lifestyle, priorities, and the choices we make. Witnessing calls for courage, especially under duress. Antipas, who is introduced as a faithful witness in the church of Pergamum, apparently was martyred for his faith (2:13). Likewise the two witnesses of Revelation 11:3–12 model faithful witnessing even to the point of death. For John's initial audience, simply attempting to be a Christian often led to hardship. John praises such witness, for he imagines that God's reign trumps that of Rome, and that Rome's unjust empire is coming to an end, an outcome he proclaims throughout every chapter of Revelation.

Who Wrote Revelation?

When the author introduces himself in the first chapter of Revelation as "I, John, your brother" (1:9), it is clear that he is well known to his audience. Since three letters of the New Testament and one Gospel are attributed to someone named John, it is sometimes assumed that all were penned by the same author, namely by the apostle John, the disciple of Jesus known as a son of Zebedee. This assumption is erroneous on all counts. The person we call John of Patmos makes no claim to be an apostle and seemingly distinguishes himself from the apostles (21:14). He recounts no stories or sayings from the ministry of Jesus and gives no indication that he had known Jesus during his earthly life. If this John is not the son of Zebedee, neither is he the author of the Gospel or the letters of John, as the differences in language, style, theology, and general point of view make clear. Although John writes in Greek to a Greek-speaking audience, his Greek is peculiar and full of grammatical irregularities. The nature of his writing style suggests that his native language was Hebrew or Aramaic. In all likelihood he was a Palestinian Christian prophet who had immigrated to Asia Minor, probably during or shortly after the Jewish war against Rome of 66 to 70. It is best to consider John of Patmos a wandering prophet who served as pastor or shepherd of the "seven churches" of the Roman province of Asia.

The debate about the precise relationship of the book of Revelation to the Gospel of John and the three letters attributed to John in the New

Testament is fostered not only by the fact that each is attributed to someone named John, but also by similarities among these writings, linguistically and theologically. In addition, the description given to the heretics opposed in 1 John seem to have a number of features in common with those mentioned in Revelation (chapters 2 and 3). One of the more plausible explanations is that toward the end of the first century there was at Ephesus a "Johannine school" of Christian thought organized around a man known as John the Elder, who may have been a disciple of John the apostle, and that perhaps different members of this group were responsible for the final form of the five books that now go under his name. If that is so, it would account for the similarities found in these works as well as for the obvious differences. The fact that the first of the seven letters to churches in Revelation (2:1–7) is addressed to Ephesus also seems significant. The books attributed to John may not have been written by the same person, but they came from the same world of thought and from the same geographical center.

When Was Revelation Written?

John wrote to his Christian flock while temporarily exiled from them on the island of Patmos on account of "the word of God and the testimony of Jesus" (1:9) that formed the subject of his preaching. Even as the identity of the author is uncertain, so also is the date of his apocalypse. Revelation was composed at some point between 69 and 96 to encourage fellow believers to remain faithful to Christ despite religious discrimination. Although some scholars have identified this persecution as originating from the emperor Nero (54–68), it is more likely that the book reflects the conditions prevailing during the latter years of the emperor Domitian (81–96). The Christian movement was transitional and vulnerable during this period, trying to find its way forward in the generation between the death of its apostolic leaders and the emergence of a firm structure and identity.

In the aftermath of the disastrous war in Judea between Jewish rebels and the Romans, there was a large influx of Jewish and Jewish-Christian immigrants and refugees into Asia, where there had been an established Jewish community for generations. Partly as a result of this conflict, Judaism was undergoing a clarification of its own identity and a restructuring of its institutions. Previously, Jewish Christians had often understood themselves, and had been understood by both the secular and religious authorities, as members of the Jewish community. This relationship entitled them to the rights and protection of a sanctioned religion in the eyes of the Roman law. After 70, the restructuring of Judaism led to conflicting claims about who was really a Jew. Christians in Asia were sometimes caught in these conflicts, reflected in Revelation. During this period increasing social and political pressures were brought to bear by governmental policies, creating tensions between Christians and other social groups, particularly the Jews, as well as tensions and conflicts within the church itself. The followers of Christ increasingly asked what it meant to be a Christian under these trying circumstances. John of Patmos chose the medium of a letter and the form of an apocalypse to craft his answer.

Prior to Domitian the state religion had not discriminated against the Christian faith. It is true that Nero had persecuted Christians, but his mad acts were restricted to Rome and had nothing to do with matters of faith or manner of worship. The first emperor who insisted on divine honors and tried to impose the idea of divine worship on his subjects is said to be Domitian, though no specific evidence for that has been found.[3] Temple inscriptions in the province of Asia make clear that by the nineties of the first century Christians in that region must have felt tremendous political, economic, and social pressure to openly venerate the emperor or face fearful consequences.

Another argument favoring the close of the first century as the time of the composition of Revelation is the fact that, according to 2:8–11, the church in Smyrna for a long time had persevered under trials. But according to Polycarp, the bishop of Smyrna in the first half of the second century, that church had not come into existence until after the time of Paul (that is, during the 60s).[4] Furthermore, in 3:17 the church in Laodicea is described as rich, though this church had been almost completely destroyed by an earthquake in 69. These factors lead to the conclusion that the book of Revelation was written toward the end of Domitian's reign, about 90 to 95.

What Did John See?

Apocalypses are about seeing, and in Revelation John is a seer—he sees deep truths others miss. John had never seen Jesus in the flesh, but he does see Jesus in a vision (1:12–20). We should note two things about this vision: (a) it is impressionistic in nature and (b) its details are drawn from the Hebrew scriptures. We should not take it literally, nor should we focus on the details,

---

3. The Roman historian Suetonius wrote that Domitian issued a decree insisting that everyone address him as *dominus et deus* ("lord and god"), but no specific evidence to that effect has been found. The cult of the Roman emperors was not so much imposed from the top down as it was developed from the bottom up, particularly in the province of Asia, where leading citizens and cities competed for imperial favor.

4. Mentioned in Polycarp's Letter to the Philippians, 11:3.

for to do so is to lose sight of the overall impression John wishes to convey. It appeals not to logic but to the imagination. The image is clearly inspired by the vision of God and of the Son of Man ("one like a human being") described in Daniel 7:9–14, although other details are taken from across the breadth of scripture. In this segment traditional imagery is applied to Jesus in strikingly new ways. In 1:12–16 John sees "one like the Son of Man, clothed with a long robe . . . His head and his hair were white as white wool, white as snow." What is remarkable about this picture is that two figures from Daniel 7—one like the Son of Man and the white-headed Ancient One (Ancient of Days)—are fused into one. There were Jewish precedents for referring to the Messiah as Son of God, and much of the imagery associated with the Son of Man was also associated with God, but fusing the two is highly exceptional.

The scene is overpowering in its grandeur as it presents Jesus as the transcendent ruler of the cosmos. It represents the conviction that Christ is the fulfillment of the entire scripture, as Paul maintains in 2 Corinthians 1:20: "For in [Christ] every one of God's promises is a 'Yes.'" Of the many details one could discuss from this image, two appear together in verse 16 and each is central to John's argument.

1. The picture of seven stars in Christ's right hand signifies both Christ's cosmic ability to secure and safeguard his people as well as the intimacy he discloses to the witnessing community, for the same hand that holds the stars touches John (1:17). The commission John receives comes from the one who holds seven stars in his hand. The seven stars are the heavenly counterparts of the seven golden lampstands, John's image for the empirical, earthly churches. The imagery of the lampstands is derived from Zechariah's vision (see Zechariah 4) of the seven-branched candelabra of Israel (known today as the menorah), a passage that would have been well known to anyone who had regularly attended the synagogue. John is here asserting that the church is the new Israel, but with this difference: whereas Israel was represented by a single menorah with seven lamps, the churches are represented by seven separate lampstands. The motif of the seven stars is not taken from scripture but from the realm of astrology, as employed by pagan religions and the imperial cult. John probably chose it as a challenge to the claims of both systems. The stars do not control our destiny and are not to be feared; Christ holds them in his hand. Secular rulers are equally powerless over us; their power belongs to the true cosmic ruler, Christ. In verse 20 we learn that the seven stars are "the angels of the seven churches." The word "angel" means messenger, and can be used of human as well as heavenly messengers. In this context the word "angel" is commonly taken as

a personification of church leadership or more likely the essential "spirit" or character of each church.

2. The other significant element from John's vision of Christ is the reference to the double-edged sword proceeding from Christ's mouth. This feature figures prominently in the message to the church in Pergamum (2:12, 16) and even more so in the militaristic vision of chapter 19, where the conquering Christ returns at the end to defeat his enemies, not with a literal sword, but with the sword of his mouth (19:15), his only weapon being his word, the Word of God which he himself is (19:13). The biblical background for this motif is the reference to the promised deliverer in Isaiah 11:4 and the servant of the Lord in Isaiah 49:2, where unrighteousness is challenged, evil defeated, and redemption enacted by the spoken word. John's Lord is not aloof; he will be there at the end for he has already preceded his followers through his death and resurrection. Through his own experience he has overcome all enemies: "Do not be afraid; I am the first and the last, and the living one. I was dead, and see, I am alive forever and ever; and I have the keys of Death and of Hades" (1:17–18). Christians are not promised that if they are faithful they will be spared the injustices of life or of death. Rather, in and through death they are met by the one who has conquered death and the grave (Hades to the Greeks and Sheol to the Jews stood for the common grave) and abides forever as the living one.

The heavenly figure then explains that the lampstands among which he walks are the seven churches. The church is pictured as having a mission and is challenged to faithfulness in discharging its mission, though it is not alone in carrying out its mission; Christ is present among the earthly congregations of his people (1:12–13, 20). John's immediate response was one of dread at the awesome mystery he experiences, but the hand that holds the stars touches him and grants him a mission. Christ appears, not to startle or to frighten, but to communicate a message: "Now write what you have seen, what is, and what is to take place after this" (1:19). The temporal references depict the present situation (chapters 2–3) and the eschatological future that is already dawning (chapters 4–22).[5]

Essay 1: The Christology of Revelation

The confessional statement "Jesus is Lord," uttered by the first Christians concerning a penniless first-century preacher from Galilee, ranks among the most astounding claims professed by mortals of another mortal. The

---

5. Boring, *Revelation*, 83–85.

statement can be understood on two levels, politically and religiously. As *a political claim*, Christians were affirming that their primary allegiance belonged to Jesus and not to the Roman emperor, government officials, tax collectors, bankers, businessmen, traders, the religious elite, or the military establishment. As noted earlier, historians traditionally attribute to Domitian the start of compulsive emperor worship. One of his decrees began: "Our Lord and God commands that this be done."[6] To the author of Revelation, such lords and gods were blasphemous and demonic beasts (Rev. 13:1-6). His book implies that Christ, as "King of kings and Lord of lords" (19:16), is the only emperor whom Christians can recognize. To say "Jesus is Lord" conveyed the notion of loyalty, directly challenging allegiance to Rome and to all temporal authorities. Such a claim had social, political, and economic implications, for it signified disloyalty to the state and to the Roman gods who guaranteed the state's wellbeing.[7]

As *a religious claim*, Christians were affirming that Jesus Christ was the personification of God, the one in whom heaven and earth met. Looking at him, and contemplating his death and resurrection in particular, they believed they could see directly into God's world, understanding God's purpose in words previously unimagined.[8]

The expression "Jesus is Lord" belongs to the very earliest stratum of Christianity. In his writings Paul often used the phrase "the Lord Jesus Christ" in conjunction with the mention of God the Father (1 Thess. 1:1; 2 Cor. 13:14). In contrast to the many so-called gods and lords, there is for Christians but one God—the Father—and one Lord—Jesus Christ (1 Cor. 8:5-6). Paul, like the author of Acts, says that no one can say "Jesus is Lord" except by the Holy Spirit (1 Cor. 12:3). "Lord (*Kyrios*) is used in connection with the hope of Christ's return (Phil. 3:20; 4:5; 1 Thess. 3:13), and at the conclusion of 1 Corinthians Paul utters the Aramaic prayer: Maranatha, "Our Lord, come!" (16:22), a hope that is central to the author of Revelation (see 22:20: "Amen. Come, Lord Jesus").

While the author of Revelation adheres to a high Christology, later interpreters labeled his view unorthodox. According to Martin Luther, the book of Revelation neither teaches nor acknowledges the Christ of the Gospels. From that conviction, he declared Revelation to be uninspired by the Holy Spirit and deficient theologically. Fellow Reformer Ulrich Zwingli was equally hostile, pronouncing the book unbiblical. Perhaps this verdict

---

6. Suetonius, *Domitian*, 13.

7. The author of 1 Peter, who is much more friendly to the Roman Empire, exhorts his readers to honor the emperor but to fear God (2:17) and to sanctify Christ as Lord in their hearts (3:15).

8. Wright, *Revelation*, 3.

results from the violent imagery, not recognized as from the book's figurative nature. Revelation is not as vindictive as many have imagined, and its message need not be viewed as incongruous with the biblical message of forgiveness and reconciliation. John's Jesus may not be orthodox by later Chalcedonian standards (meaning Jesus as the second member of the Trinity), but his theology is theocentric and his Christology orthodox, certainly by first-century standards. Almost from the outset of his work he depicts the divine in threefold terms, as his salutation in 1:4–5 indicates. "It places Jesus Christ with God on the divine side of the distinction between the divine Giver of blessings and the creaturely recipients of blessing."[9] John may not have vocabulary equivalent to later Trinitarian theology, but he plays a central role in developing the Christology of the early church, as the following ideas indicate.

1. *Jesus is central throughout Revelation.* Even in those chapters where signs and symbols seem uppermost and where judgment and vindication eclipse all other interests, the person of Christ is still central. The structure of Revelation seems to bear that out. In each of the four main visions we find a portrait of Christ. The first vision presents him as Lord of the church, walking in the midst of the seven lampstands (1:12–17). The second vision reveals the Lamb on the throne, into whose authority has been committed the judgment and rule of the entire world (5:1–14). In the third vision he is the Word of God, the invincible conqueror riding his horse in triumph over all his foes (19:11–16). The final vision places him at the very center of the new creation, the city of God (21:22—22:2).

2. For John, *Jesus is mediator of God's revelation.* He introduces his Christological approach in the prologue, where he specifies the revelatory chain: God, Christ, angel, prophet, church. The revelation is from Jesus, but it does not originate with Jesus. It begins with God, who is the source of all truth, though Christ is the definitive member of the revelatory chain. God's revelation, according to the writer of Revelation, is given to Jesus, who sent that revelation to John through an angel (1:1). At this time Jews and even Jewish Christians were particularly conscious of the transcendence of God, stressing the difference and the distance between themselves and God. In this regard they came to feel that direct communication between God and humans could take place only through an intermediary. In an earlier age it was possible to believe that Moses received the Law directly from God (Exodus 19 and 20), but twice in the New Testament it is said that the Law was given by angels (Acts 7:53; Gal. 3:19).

---

9. Bauckham, *Theology of Revelation*, 23–24.

What God has to say to the churches is mediated through Christ. But an angel stands between Jesus and John in the revelatory chain. That is significant. If Jesus were a mere mortal, or even a super mortal, as Moses was, the revelatory chain would have been: God, angel, Jesus, John. But John's Christology places Jesus next to God, prior even to angels. For John, as for the author of Hebrews, Jesus has become "as much superior to angels as the name he has inherited is more excellent than theirs" (Heb. 1:4).

3. *John's titles for Jesus are indicative of his high Christology.* The title of God in 1:4: "who is and who was and who is to come" denotes the eternal nature of God, who always exists, always existed in the past, and will continue to exist in the future. In 1:5 John's Christological approach is amplified by a threefold title: "the faithful witness, the firstborn of the dead, and the ruler of the kings of the earth." The titles appear to be a summary of Christ's work in chronological order: (a) first comes his earthly ministry, in which he was "the faithful witness," faithful in word and in deed, no matter the consequence; (b) "The firstborn of the dead" clearly refers to the resurrection of Christ; (c) "Ruler of the kings of the earth" recognizes Christ as the conqueror over evil and the establisher of God's rule on earth. The three titles relate also to the general structure of Revelation. "The faithful witness" describes Christ's relation to the churches (1:9—3:22); "the firstborn of the dead" describes his role as the arbiter of destiny, opening the seals and effecting redemption through his death and resurrection (5:1—8:1); and "ruler of the kings of the earth" is his title as he defeats his enemies and asserts his lasting influence over the earth (19:11—22:21).

The doxology addressed to Christ alone in 1:5b-6, one of three such doxologies in the New Testament (along with 2 Tim. 4:18 and 2 Peter 3:18), shows that John and his churches practiced the worship of Jesus. Doxologies were a Jewish form of praise to the one God. There could be no clearer way of ascribing to Jesus the worship due to God. In John's case this cannot be attributed to Gentile Christian carelessness but "must be regarded as a development internal to the tradition of Jewish monotheism, by which Jewish Christians implicitly included Jesus in the reality of the one God."[10]

In 1:8 God says that he is the Alpha and the Omega and again in 21:6, where he adds, "the beginning and the end." The identical expression is found in 22:13, with the insertion "the first and the last." All three expressions mean much the same. If they apply to Christ, as surely they must in 22:13, then they set Christ apart from all created beings, since none other than God could share in these titles. As a way of stating unambiguously that Jesus Christ belongs to the fullness of the eternal being of God, this

---

10. Ibid., 61.

surpasses anything in the New Testament. Here we see the developing Christology of early Christianity taking shape. Christian prophets such as John played an important role in this process.

4. The vision of Christ in 1:12–20 makes clear that *the messianic office of Jesus includes the prophetic, the priestly, and the kingly functions*. These are not new or arbitrarily created by John but adapted by him from theocratic roles performed by Israel. The "long robe" is his priestly garment, while the "golden sash" is the royal emblem of the king. His voice "like the sound of many waters" and the "two-edged sword" proceeding from his mouth represent his prophetic function. The dazzling white hair is taken from the "Ancient One," the vision of God in Daniel 7:9. The language is pre-conceptual and the imagery impressionistic: "John's monotheism and theocentrism save him from the danger of identifying God and Jesus, or making them competitors, so he does not hesitate to use God-language of Jesus. The use of such language is an expression of his conviction that 'God' is to be defined as 'the one who has revealed himself definitively in Jesus.' On the other hand, the 'feet . . . like burnished bronze' and the 'voice . . . like the sound of many waters' are taken from the description of the heavenly messenger in Daniel 10:6 (cf. Ezek. 43:2). Since John is not thinking metaphysically, this combining of angel-language and God-language in his portrayal of Jesus is not problematical."[11]

5. For John, *Jesus is endowed with the sevenfold spirit of God*. The salutation in 1:4 provides a tripartite formula not yet fully Trinitarian; the "seven spirits" are the seven angelic beings said by John to be under the authority of both God and Christ (3:1; 4:5; 5:6). While John never uses the expression "the Holy Spirit" in his book, he does refer to "the Spirit" (see, for example, 2:7 and 17), so he clearly knows of the Spirit of God. In this sense "the seven spirits" may be said to represent the fullness of the Spirit of God. Possibly John had in mind the sevenfold spirit with which the Messiah was to be endowed (Isa. 11:2; six qualities are listed in the Hebrew text, but a seventh is added in the Greek translation known as the Septuagint). In Rev. 5:6 Jesus is introduced as the Lamb, and in this role he has seven horns (fullness of power) and seven eyes (fullness of insight), "which are the seven spirits of God sent out into all the earth." The seven eyes of the Lamb are the seven spirits of God. John wants his audience to grasp how close the relationship is between Christ, God, and the Spirit. "What God does for humanity through the Lamb is not a three-party transaction (God, Jesus, and humanity) but a two-party transaction: God and humanity."[12]

---

11. Boring, *Revelation*, 83.
12. Ibid., 110.

6. *John regularly depicts Jesus jointly with God in scenes of heavenly power, praise, and glory.* At times, as in the initial throne room scene in 4:3, the figure seated on the throne is not identified. In traditional Jewish imagery the final judge is of course God, though in some later apocalyptic traditions the heavenly "Son of Man" was authorized by God to judge as his representative. By failing to specify the figure on the heavenly throne as well as on the great white throne on the day of judgment (20:11), John is able to avoid the necessity of distinguishing between God and Christ; "God or Christ" is not a possibility in his thought. Like other New Testament authors, John believes that the glory of God has been seen in the face of Jesus Christ (cf. 2 Cor. 4:6). He therefore portrays Christ at his first appearance with all the attributes of deity (1:12-16). In the seventh trumpet scene the kingdoms of the world become the "kingdom of our Lord and of his Messiah" (11:15). Such a blurring of these figures can be seen elsewhere in his imagery and theology. For example, the "Lamb" is never an independent figure, but always Lamb-as-representative-of-God; likewise, God is never a figure defined apart from Christ, but always God-who-defines-himself-by-Christ. John refuses to parcel out the roles of judge and savior between God and the Lamb. He does not and cannot have a judgmental God who is enhanced by a compassionate Christ.[13]

7. *Jesus, for John, is the act of God for our salvation*; Jesus is not primarily sage, miracle worker, or demigod, but one who died at the hands of the Romans, not as a tragic victim but as cosmic redeemer. As "God" is defined by "Christ" and "Christ" is defined by "Jesus," so "Jesus" is defined by "dying on our behalf" (1:5b; 5:9). In Jesus, God has defined himself as the one who suffers for others, whose suffering love is the instrument of the creation's redemption.[14]

8. To safeguard Christ's connection with the church, yet without detracting from the uniqueness of Jesus, *John presents a "shared" Christology*, attributing functions (1:12-16) and titles of Jesus (1:5) to the church. For example, the title for Jesus, "the faithful witness," is used of Antipas of Pergamum (2:13), a Christian who had died for his faith; faithful Christians may expect to experience the resurrection that Christ as the "firstborn of the dead" has already experienced; Christ as the "ruler of kings" has a kingship, but so do Christians (1:6). Throughout Revelation John takes up Israel's predicates and applies them to Jesus as well as to the church.

Christian existence for John entails sharing the ministry of Christ. In Revelation, "Christ" is less a title of deity and more the office of God's

---

13. Ibid., 211-12.
14. Ibid., 65-66.

Messiah as prophet, priest, and king. Christians share in this messianic ministry; in 1:6 Christians have a priestly function and in 11:1–13 the church is a prophetic as well as a royal and priestly community. As a prophetic community the church mediates the word of God made known to the world in Jesus. As a priestly community the church mediates to the world God's reconciliation of the world in Jesus. As a royal community the church represents the rule of God as already present in the world. All these affirmations demonstrate the fragmentary but real existence of the messianic ministry as already present in the church. In Revelation, "the meaning of discipleship corresponds to one's idea of Christ."[15] For example, "conquering" is a key word in Revelation's Christology as well as in understanding of the Christian life. As Jesus' work on earth can be summarized by saying that he "overcame" or "conquered" (3:21; 5:5), so the faithful Christian life can be summarized as "conquering" or "overcoming" (2:7, 11, 17, 26; 3:5, 12, 21).

Questions to Ponder

1. What verse, passage, or theme stands out for you as the key to chapter 1 of Revelation? Support your answer.

2. In Revelation 1:6 readers are urged to think of themselves as royalty and as priests. How might these influence your self-image and your lifestyle?

3. What does the confession "Jesus is Lord" mean to you? How different is this understanding from what it might have meant to the first Christians?

4. What message of hope do you find in chapter 1 of Revelation?

---

15. Ibid., 78

Chapter 2

A Vision of the Church Imperfect (Revelation 2–3)

Summary: In Revelation 2 and 3 John addresses letters to early Christian communities. These seven churches faced challenges unique to each local situation. They grappled with issues such as compromise with the dominant culture, questions of poverty and wealth, relations with fellow believers, and interactions with Jewish communities. John's letters are like performance reviews, examining the strengths and weaknesses of each church. John's goal is to persuade Christians not to blend in with their culture but to remain faithful witnesses to Jesus. To those who persevere, John offers hope.

Assignment: Read chapters 2 and 3 of Revelation

Key Passage: Revelation 3:19–20

Central Theme: The importance of remaining faithful to Christ

Learning Objectives

Participants will examine:
1. John's stereotypical literary format
2. The internal and external situation of the seven churches of Asia
3. Lessons they can learn from these ancient church struggles
4. The relation between rival Christian groups within the churches of Asia

OUTLINE TO REVELATION 2:1—3:22

I. Message to the church in Ephesus 2:1–7

II. Message to the church in Smyrna 2:8–11

III. Message to the church in Pergamum 2:12–17

IV. Message to the church in Thyatira 2:18–29

V. Message to the church in Sardis 3:1–6

VI. Message to the church in Philadelphia 3:7–13

VII. Message to the church in Laodicea 3:14–22

THE SOCIAL CONTEXT OF REVELATION: CHRISTIAN LIFE AS DEPICTED IN THE SEVEN CHURCHES

The picture we get from the seven letters shows that the Christians in Asia were struggling with a variety of issues: persecution, false teaching in their midst, and loss of religious fervency, possibly because of the passing of time and the hardships imposed upon them as Christians. Here we will briefly examine the issue of persecution, assimilation, and complacency. Essay 2 examines the issue of false teachers, which is related to the larger dimension of rival groups within the churches of Asia.

1. First is the issue of *persecution*, since some of John's readers had to deal with open hostility in their communities. Elsewhere in Revelation we read of extensive persecutions (7:14) and Christian martyrdoms (6:9). John directs his anger against the political and economic institutions of his day, especially the Roman Empire, which was responsible for the oppression and suffering of the people of God. In his view, this government would not survive, since God was about to destroy it. In short, Christianity as experienced by John was an oppressed and persecuted religion. We can understand John's fervor, particularly if he actually wrote the book while in exile from his homeland because of his Christian witness (1:9). The churches of his world had suffered from economic exploitation and some Christians had been martyred (2:13), but God was going to put an end to it all, and he would do so soon.

Current scholarship affirms that whatever persecution Christians were enduring in Asia toward the end of the first century, it was not systematic and it was not imposed from the top down. The early chapters of Revelation indicate that persecution was actually local and sporadic. It started when local people became suspicious of Christians, who did not always fit in to the wider society. They worshipped only one God, rather than the many gods and goddesses worshipped by the Greeks and Romans. Yet they also worshipped a crucified Messiah named Jesus, which meant they no longer fit into local Jewish communities. And that created another set of tensions.

2. The second major issue facing the Asian churches was *assimilation*. Some Christians may have faced open hostility, but others had to deal with more subtle pressures to conform. Could they remain true to their convictions while interacting socially with those who did not share their faith? The cities of Asia Minor had local religious festivals that were major social events. These included banquets, often held at pagan temples, and attendance brought honor to the god or goddess associated with the temple. In addition, the food at these events would have been viewed sacramentally, meaning that Christians invited to such gatherings were faced with the dilemma of compromising their convictions if they accepted or alienating their friends or business associates if they refused.

3. The issue of *complacency* appears several times in the opening chapters of Revelation, but it is most evident in the message to the church at Laodicea. Christians there and elsewhere were apparently thriving in the Roman economy. The *Pax Romana*, the great era of Roman peace and prosperity (19 BC–AD 181), had enhanced the possibilities for trade and commerce on an ever-widening scale. As local markets expanded into regional and international markets, local trade flourished. According to Revelation, some Christians had become wealthy in this climate and were content to maintain their faith so long as it did not become too intense or make too many demands.

The compromises required to stay within the mainstream of social and economic life in Asia Minor may have seemed innocent enough when taken on their own, but the visions of Revelation highlight the contrast between good and evil much more emphatically.[1]

ANALYSIS OF REVELATION 2:1—3:22

Chapters 2 and 3 of Revelation contain seven messages to the seven churches that John received in a vision from Jesus while he was on the island of Patmos. The letters are integrally related to the vision of Christ in chapter 1 (1:5 and 9–20) and cannot be interpreted apart from that passage. While the letters are addressed to specific churches, John informs us that the message extends to all the churches (1:4; 2:7). All the promises and all

---

1. The material in this segment is adapted from Koester, *Apocalypse*, lecture 5: "Issues Facing Revelation's First Readers," 76–86.

the warnings are for all the churches in Asia, and, by implication, for all churches throughout history, including the current church. This conclusion is confirmed by the refrain found in each of the seven messages: "Let anyone who has an ear listen to what the Spirit is saying to the churches." While the letters share the same apocalyptic perspective as the rest of Revelation, they also prepare us for the visions to follow. It is important that John's hearers examine their own situation before they launch into the more transcendent visionary world of the later chapters.

The churches to which the letters are addressed are named in a specific order, forming a circular route along the main trade roads beginning with Ephesus and moving north to Pergamum, then southeast to Laodicea and presumably back to Ephesus. Each letter was probably intended to be read by the other churches listed, implying that each was affected by the other as one member of the body is related to the rest. The place of these letters in the Christian canon means that the topics have relevance to the church at all times and in all places.

Each letter is addressed to the "angel" or "messenger" of the church. This does not refer to an actual angelic being or to a specific leader within the congregation but to the corporate spirit (the essence or character) of each congregation. The letters follow a fourfold pattern: (1) a quality of Christ (taken from chapter 1); (2) praise for the church; (3) censure or blame for the church; and (4) a promise for the church. Some interpreters expand the pattern to include seven elements:

1. The Commission: "To the angel of the church in _____ write";
2. The Character: "These are the words of" followed by an allusion to the vision of Christ in chapter 1;
3. The Commendation: "I know" followed by a commendation [not in the case of Laodicea];
4. The Condemnation: "But I have this against you" followed by a list of criticisms [not in the case of Smyrna or Philadelphia];
5. The Correction: various injunctions appear, couched in the imperative mood;
6. The Call: "Let anyone who has an ear listen to what the Spirit is saying to the churches." [This exhortation is uniform in all seven letters, but in the last four it takes the seventh rather than the sixth place in order];
7. The Challenge: "To everyone who conquers"; each letter has a promise for the one who rises above the temptations and perils besetting the particular church.

A further pattern can be discerned: churches 1 and 7 are in grave danger, churches 2 and 6 are in excellent shape, and churches 3, 4, and 5 are middling, neither very good nor very bad.[2]

First and Seventh Churches—Ephesus (2:1–7) and Laodicea (3:14–22): Rekindling the First Love

The churches at Ephesus and Laodicea are in grave danger and both congregations are urged to repent. Their faults, however, are diametrically opposite, for while the Ephesians are accused of moral extremism, the Laodiceans are indicted for religious complacency.

Ephesus was the most significant of the seven cities. Its seaport, the most important in Asia Minor, made Ephesus a prosperous metropolis. Through this city passed most of the trade and travel between East and West. Ephesus was a major religious center, longtime home to the Mother Goddess, later identified with the Greek goddess Artemis. Her temple was one of the wonders of the ancient world and the object of intense civic pride. The Christian church at Ephesus was also the most prestigious of the seven, having been associated with the ministries of numerous early Christian leaders, including Paul and John the Apostle. It was the reputed home of the Johannine "school" and was the closest city to Patmos, from where John was writing.

Under the scrutiny of Christ their Lord, who knows what goes on among his people and is intimately aware of their faults and merits because he walks with them (2:1), the Ephesians at first show up well. They are commended for their deeds, their hard work, and their perseverance. They have strenuously resisted all threats to the purity of their faith, both from without and from within. From outside have come people claiming to be apostles, not in the sense of belonging to the group known as the Twelve (the original band of Jesus' disciples) but rather to that wider group of apostles that included James the Just, Barnabas, Silas, and Paul. The internal threat came from the Nicolaitans, a group similar to the Balaamites (2:14–15) at Pergamum and to the followers of the false prophet branded "Jezebel" at Thyatira (2:20). These dissidents were not seeking to destroy Christianity but to modernize and improve it, something John did not approve (for further elaboration see essay 2 at the end of the chapter).

The one charge against the Ephesians is that their intolerance of dissent "had bred an inquisitorial spirit which left no room for love. They had set out to be defenders of the faith, arming themselves with the heroic virtues

---

2. Morris, *Revelation*, 58.

of truth and courage, only to discover that in the battle they had lost the one quality without which all others are worthless."[3] You have "abandoned the love you had at first," Christ informs them (2:4). It is not clear whether this is love for Christ or for humanity at large, though at some level these identities merge (1 John 4:20–21). The Ephesians had yielded to the temptation, ever present to loyal Christians, to put all their emphasis on sound teaching. In the process they had lost love, without which all else is nothing. The way to restoration involves three steps (1:4): (a) they should *remember* their first state; (b) they should *repent* (presumably of their arrogant attitude); and (c) they should *repeat* the works that issued from their first love. "Love," in the early Christian sense, is something you do, providing hospitality and practical need to those in help. Love was the chief mark of the early church. No other non-ethnic group had ever behaved like this.

The call to repentance is followed by a promise to those who "conquer." John is fond of this verb (he uses it seventeen times), which can also mean "overcome." The author has taken a militaristic term of the Roman Empire and given it a spiritual meaning, one that would have surprised Christians of his day. John introduces this mysterious, almost numinous, reference to victory over and over in Revelation without any attempt at definition, for it is the purpose of the entire book to define the term. Only slowly does the character of Christian conquest take shape as we read; it is always related to the victory of Christ (2:26; 3:21). Jesus himself won the victory through his suffering, and so must his people. The person who "conquers," in sum, is the Christian in whom Christ wins afresh the victory of Calvary with the weapons of love (7:14; 12:11; 15:2). John seems to use the word "conquer" in much the same way Paul does in Romans 8:37: "in all these things we are more than conquerors through [Christ] who loved us." As we journey deeper into the story of Revelation, the meaning of the Greek word for conquer, *nike*, will unfold in amazing ways—for Jesus and for us.

The seventh church, that of *Laodicea* (3:14–22), receives the harshest performance review but also the most wonderful promise. The city of Laodicea, located at the juncture of three major trade routes, was very prosperous, a benefit shared by the members of that congregation. They were rich and felt secure in their wealth, but their security resulted in material comfort and spiritual complacency. To God these Christians are lukewarm, and for that, God is about to spit them from his mouth (3:16), as though they represented a disease.

This image, one of the most memorable in all scripture, is influenced by the one deficiency in Laodicea, the abundance of good water. The Lycus

---

3. Caird, *Revelation*, 31.

River, which flows through this region, sometimes dries up in the summer. Two other regional sources of water were available, a set of hot springs eleven miles to the north and a splendid source of water from alpine streams to the southeast. In the first century aqueducts existed to bring both the hot water and the cold water to Laodicea, but by the time the water arrived at its destination, the hot water was no longer hot and the cold water had become lukewarm. It is this remarkable feature of Laodicea—hot water that has cooled down and cold water that has heated up—that provides the background for apathy (neither one thing nor another), an attitude that renders its practitioners religiously poor, morally naked, and spiritually blind (3:17). These references correspond to the city's premiere industries: banking, textiles, and its medical school. The remedy for this threefold deficiency is in Christ. From him they should buy gold refined by fire, obtain clothing for their nakedness, and procure salve for their eyes (3:18). Apart from Christ, who alone gives real sight (cf. John 9:39), they lack insight and cannot "see" their situation. God calls the members of this church to anoint their eyes that they may regain their sight, their spiritual wisdom and imagination.

The call to repentance in verses 19 and 20 is unlike anything that appears in the remaining letters. To the plea for repentance (3:19), two new concepts are added, both having to do with Christ's love. The first we might describe as "tough love": "I reprove and discipline those whom I love" (3:19) and the second is of unconditional love: "Listen! I am standing at the door, knocking" (3:20). The image is vivid; Christ promises to enter in to anyone who opens the door and to provide enduring fellowship.

The word of Jesus that closes this section (3:21) provides a striking summary of Revelation's theological perspective: (1) God rules from the throne (note the vision of the throne room that begins chapter 4); (2) Christ "shares" the throne with God in the present, for the God who rules is the God who represents himself in Jesus; and (3) Christians will share this same throne, which is attained by "conquering," just as Jesus attained the throne by giving his life for others (Revelation 5 presents this in powerful imagery).

Second and Sixth Churches—Smyrna (2:8-11) and Philadelphia (3:7-13): Modeling Faithfulness

Both churches win heartfelt praise and no blame. The church at Smyrna was economically poor and the church in Philadelphia was powerless. In John's time Christians in Smyrna and Philadelphia were suffering opposition from their neighbors, socially and economically, and were being marginalized. These two letters also introduce another difficult issue, the question of the relationship of Christians to Judaism. We cannot know the extent of conflict between these two groups, or whether the damaging references to Jews here should be taken literally or metaphorically, but in both cases the opponents are labeled "the synagogue of Satan" (2:9; 3:9).

The city of *Smyrna* had a long and honorable history. Founded a millennium before Christ as a Greek colony, in the second century BC it became an ally of Rome, and from that time it prospered. Smyrna, touted as the birthplace of Homer, was one of the greatest cities in Asia. It enjoyed many natural advantages, including an excellent harbor at the head of a well-protected gulf. Rebuilt around 290 BC to a comprehensive plan, Smyrna was one of the few planned cities of antiquity. Many writers comment on its beauty. It was one of the first cities to worship the Roman emperor and it won the honor of erecting a temple to him in the reign of Tiberius.

In appealing to the church, the aspect of Christ that John stresses is his resurrection, very appropriate in a city that had been destroyed by an earthquake and now lived once again. The identification of Christ as one who "was dead and came to life" (2:8) would have reminded the Smyrnans that Jesus himself experienced suffering and death and thus is able to walk alongside them in their current experiences of poverty and exclusion. Christ's knowledge of the church is concerned with the suffering of its members, suffering that had economic and social consequences. The poverty of the Christians was certainly due to social class, since many belonged to the lower classes of society or were slaves, but also to local antagonism. If they publicly rejected emperor worship and did not attend pagan festivals, they could lose their jobs and be socially excluded. The poverty of the Christians could also have resulted from mob violence and looting (cf. Heb. 10:34), factors that often accompanied an antagonistic environment.

Some opposition might also have come from the Jewish population (2:9), numerous and influential in Smyrna. Christians in other cities of Asia Minor had long been familiar with Jewish resentment, occasioned by the conversion of Jews and "God-fearers" to Christianity, but at Smyrna and Philadelphia it was apparently more extreme. The author of Revelation, though a Christian, was clearly also a Jew. He was deeply saturated in the Hebrew scriptures and identified strongly with the traditions of Israel, so his criticism of Judaism in these letters should be viewed as a dispute within different branches of the Jewish family rather than as anti-Semitic. The earliest Christians were Jewish, and John seems to be deeply commitment to his heritage.

John prepares Christians for duress by recognizing the attack as the work of the devil (2:10), which can be interpreted as a reference to the Roman Empire as well as to Jewish antagonists, and by affirming that Satan's work is subject to God's control. He encourages faithfulness ("Be faithful unto death, and I will give you the crown of life," an obvious reference to the victory wreath given the winner of an athletic contest) and promises spiritual immunity to those who overcome. Victorious Christians will not experience the second death (2:11), also called "the lake of fire," the antithesis to eternal life (20:6, 14; 21:8).

Philadelphia, called "the gateway to the East," was the youngest of the seven cities. It was founded c. 140 BC by Attalus II Philadelphus of Pergamum as a center of propaganda for Greek language and Greek culture to the bordering regions of Lydia and Phrygia. The city was prosperous, partly from its strategic location, although its location on a seismic fault-line made it subject to earthquakes. In AD 17 it was destroyed by a great earthquake, as also were Sardis and ten other cities. In Philadelphia, rebuilt with generous assistance from Tiberius, the church was evidently small (3:8), though spiritually faithful and strong. Its enemies came from outside, not within, for there is no mention of factions or heresy. This church had much in common with that at Smyrna: both receive only praise; both suffered from those who falsely called themselves Jews; both experienced discrimination; both are assured that the opposition was satanic; and both are promised a crown.

The church is greeted by one who has "the key of David." The reference is to Isaiah 22:22, where the key of the house of David is entrusted to the steward Eliakim as a symbol of his complete control over the royal household and of his authority to grant or refuse access to the king's presence. The writer does not tell us what it is that Christ shuts and opens. Most likely this key grants access to the city of David, viewed by John to represent the heavenly Jerusalem, access to which Christ alone grants or withholds. It is quite likely this city and the key to the messianic kingdom that John envisions here.

Jesus' message is full of encouragement and praise for these beleaguered congregations. Three promises are made in the commendation: (1) the first, connected with the characterization of Christ in verse 7, guarantees the opportunity for Christian witness; (2) the second promises the humiliation of the church's enemies; and (3) the third promises preservation from the hour of trial that is to come. The Greek preposition *ek* in "from the hour of trial" can mean "from" or "through," so Christians are not necessarily promised exemption from such events. The purpose of the trial is to test the world. We need not take this as a reference to the final crisis of history, since the letters are pastoral and practical and not prophetic or sensational in nature. Whatever ordeal John has in mind, he stresses local implications. Since the reference is to a test and not to judgment or punishment, we can view this event as an expression of compassion, for God is gracious in providing extended opportunities for repentance.

Christians in Philadelphia are promised that they will be named "pillars" in God's future temple. Imagine the effect, in a city that experienced numerous earthquakes and collapsed temples, for Christians to be told they would be pillars in God's temple. The first Christians, particularly the Jerusalem leaders, were sometimes called "pillars" (Gal. 2:9), but in this case it is ordinary Christians in Philadelphia, far away from Jerusalem, who are to be "pillars" in the new temple. They are the ones who will bear with Jesus the new name of King and Lord.

Third, Fourth, and Fifth Churches—Pergamum (2:12–17), Thyatira (2:18–29), and Sardis (3:1–6): Overcoming Complacency

A less-than-positive performance review applies to the three middle letters, for the congregants are indeed average ("middling"). Two of the three churches receive praise (Sardis does not), but all receive blame for tolerating complacency, compromise, or, in the case of Sardis, for lack of maturity.

Pergamum was never important until it became the capital of the Attalids, an independent kingdom after Alexander the Great. The last king of the Attalid dynasty bequeathed the city to Rome in 133 BC, when it became the official capital of the province of Asia and the seat of imperial authority. Located about fifteen miles inland, the city consisted of a fertile meadow with an eagle's nest-like natural acropolis over one thousand feet high at its center. In Hellenistic times the Attalids made Pergamum one of the most important and beautiful of all Greek cities. A prosperous economy led to a massive building project whose monumental structures rivaled those of Athens. The acropolis is one of the most outstanding examples of city planning in that era. The Pergamene kings built the city upon leveled natural terraces. The summit was carefully selected for the royal palaces. On the second level, below the summit, stood the temple to Athena, the library (second in size only to the library of Alexandria in Egypt), and the temple of Trajan. On the third level from the summit stood the altar to Zeus and a huge amphitheater, the steepest in the world. The amphitheater sloped down to the fourth terrace, which included the agora (marketplace), the stoa, a column-lined promenade that looked out over the plain below, the gymnasium, and the Temple of Demeter. A mile away, on the plain below the acropolis, stood the Asclepion, the center of the cult of Asclepius, the god of healing, and the most famous hospital in the world. People from all over the world came in search of physical, mental, and spiritual healing to this "Lourdes of the ancient world." Pergamum was also a center of emperor worship, with a temple dedicated to Rome as early as 29 BC. In due course it added a second and a third temple in honor of the emperor.

John depicts Pergamum as the place "where Satan's throne is" (2:13). Some see an allusion to the serpent, the symbol of Asclepius, but since the cult of this god thrived in centers like Epidaurus, it is unlikely that this is the meaning. Another suggestion is that the great altar of Zeus is meant, but Zeus was highly honored elsewhere. Since Pergamum was a religious as well as an administrative center, the focal point of the emperor cult for the whole province of Asia, and as Rome was a source of persecution to the Christians, we can be certain that this is primarily what John has in mind here. The reference to the martyrdom of Antipas in 2:13 points to a specific incident rather than to continuing persecution of Christians at Pergamum.

The blame given to this church suggests moral and spiritual laxity. The church is condemned for following the teachings of Balaam (2:14), a reference to an Old Testament seer who was hired by the king of Moab to find a way to defeat the people of Israel who had left Egypt and were passing through Moab on their journey to the Promised Land. Balaam enticed the Israelites to compromise by inducing them to worship idols and participate in pagan practices. Two points are singled out, the eating of food sacrificed to idols and sexual immorality. It is possible that the former refers to meat that had first been offered to idols and then sold on the open market—since all meat sold in the city markets would first have been sacrificed to pagan gods—and the latter to sexual sin in general. But it is more likely that both refer to idolatrous practices. Feasting on sacrificial meat and licentious conduct were usual accompaniments of the worship of idols, both in Old and New Testament times. At the time Revelation was written, Asia's great cities vied with one another to demonstrate their patriotism to Rome by building temples, sponsoring parades, and hosting official games and festivals. John wanted his readers to avoid the "fornication" of any act that worshipped the empire. For John, worship belongs to God alone.

The letter to *Thyatira* is the only one that refers to "all the churches" (2:23), reminding us that despite the many local allusions found in these letters, the overall message is for the church at large. Occurring in the middle of the group of seven letters, and written to the church in the smallest and least important of the cities, it is the longest of the letters. Very little is known about Thyatira, where the Christian church may have been small. Thyatira appears to have been a commercial center, with many trade guilds. In Acts 16:14 we read that Lydia came from this city and was a "dealer in purple cloth." The town was famous for its wool dyeing, which may explain Lydia's occupation. This is the only letter, indeed the only place in Revelation, to use the title "the Son of God" for Jesus (2:18). Christians in this city are commended for their works, explained as a series of praiseworthy qualities: love, faith, service, and patient endurance. There is progress in the life of this church, which forms a contrast to Ephesus, where the church has been blamed for having slipped backward. There is much to commend at Thyatira.

But like the Christians at Pergamum, there is religious and cultural compromise. The city's many trade guilds may have included Christians who wanted to participate in civic life. John condemns a rival leader for permitting Christians to eat meat that has been sacrificed to pagan gods (2:20). Here the rival is a woman; she has many followers, whom John calls "her children." Because he disagrees with her openness to Roman culture, John labels this prophet "Jezebel," a pejorative link to the queen of Israel and wife of King Ahab who promoted pagan worship (1 Kgs. 18:19). John uses sexual innuendo and shocking threats to vilify this woman. As in Pergamum, the activity that John condemns probably is not sexual at all. It is idolatry—worship of the emperor and compromise with its culture. The allusion to "the deep things of Satan" shows that what may have been an aberrant teaching in the church at Pergamum has become more virulent at Thyatira. In John's view, there were too many everyday cultural practices in the Roman Empire that could result in idolatry. It was best to resist such practices, even if ostracism and economic hardship resulted.

It is interesting to contrast Revelation with the writings of the apostle Paul on the issue of food offered to idols. Paul confronted the problem a generation earlier in his letter to Christians in Corinth (see 1 Cor. 10:25–30) and did not forbid this practice, particularly when unbelievers invited Christians to dine with them. In Romans 14:1–12 Paul notes the existence of two groups in the church, those who "are weak in faith," including vegetarians and others who have scruples about eating practices, and those who side with himself, who "believe in eating anything." He affirms that individual Christians should refrain from judging one another on matters such as these, since one is ultimately accountable only to God. (The topic of John's opponents in the churches of Asia and their relation to Pauline Christians is taken up in essay 2 below.)

The church at *Sardis*, like the church at Laodicea, receives no praise, only blame. The call to the lethargic church at Sardis is to "wake up" (3:2–3) from its spiritual death before it is too late. Situated at the junction of five roads, Sardis was an active commercial city. It had been the capital of Croesus, proverbial for his wealth. The city's inherited prosperity, easily gained, seems to have contributed to its laxity. It was captured by Cyrus the Persian (549 BC) and by Antiochus (218 BC), both times because of its lack of vigilance. The city was built on a hill so steep that its defenses seemed impregnable. On both occasions enemy troops scaled the precipice by night and found that the overconfident Sardians had set no guard. The invaders plundered the city and left it deserted. The terrible earthquake of AD 17 also ravished the city. John's comment in 3:1 acknowledges the similarities between the church's image and the city's heritage: "you have a name of being alive, but you are dead."

John does not mention anything like the oppression at Smyrna and Pergamum or the dissension caused by the Nicolaitans. It may be that this church had not suffered disturbance from without and that its troubles stemmed from its comparatively sheltered existence. The temptation for the sheltered is to take things easy, and this leads to slackness. Whereas the churches at Pergamum and Thyatira had a few members who adopted worldly standards, at Sardis the faulty congregants are a majority. Only a few "have not soiled their clothes" (3:4); the rest need to "wake up," not in the sense of a one-time awakening but more in the sense of ongoing vigilance. Such a message must have struck home to those in a city that twice had been captured owing to its failure to be watchful. Lack of spiritual vigilance may likewise be costly. All was not yet lost, but unless the ember is fanned into flame, all would be lost.

Unlike many of its neighbors, this church was left undisturbed by opponents. The reason may well be its lack of aggressive and positive Christianity. "Small wonder that neither controversy nor persecution has disturbed this church's superficial prosperity. Content with mediocrity, lacking both the enthusiasm to entertain a heresy and the depth of conviction which provokes intolerance, it was too innocuous to be worth persecution."[4]

The promise to the few who remained faithful is that they would be clothed in white robes (a symbol of purity and of victory) and that their names would not be blotted "out of the book of life" (3:5). All ancient cities kept a civic register in which the names of the citizens were inscribed, and the book of life is the register of citizens of the heavenly city (21:27). But it is more than that, for the names it contains were inscribed "from the foundation of the world" (17:8). If a person is a citizen of the New Jerusalem, it is due to divine initiative and not human effort. Furthermore, if Jesus vouches for anyone, that person is accepted (Luke 12:8). The final chord struck in this message to the needy church of Sardis is one of hope and encouragement.

---

4. Ibid., 48.

We Are All of the Above

It is possible, though not very comfortable, to see ourselves and our churches in these letters. The diversity of these ancient churches and the challenges they faced can provide insight into our churches today. We might fit the profile of the church at Ephesus—so fixed on pure doctrine and theological correctness that we risk losing our "first love." If so, the challenge is to rekindle our love for one another, for our neighbors, and for God. Perhaps we identify with the beleaguered churches in Smyrna and Philadelphia. When we feel utterly marginalized, poverty-stricken, or powerless, Jesus' praise and promises bring a comforting message and a sense of true hope. One of main goals of Revelation is to comfort the afflicted. Revelation also afflicts the comfortable. Four overly complacent churches are told to repent, and five churches experience sharp rebuke. These rebukes are wake-up calls.

Essay 2: Internal Conflicts in Early Christianity (As Viewed from the Perspective of the Seven Letters of Revelation)

Traditional scholarship on Revelation tends to limit the antagonists in the seven churches in the Roman province of Asia (and by implication competitors of John of Patmos) to (a) spiteful Jews, (b) apostate Christians, or (c) pagan Romans. Studies indicate that the list should include fellow Christians in the Pauline (apostolic) tradition, the ecclesiastical system of authority that culminated in institutional Christianity.[5] In his conflict with Pauline Christianity, John of Patmos represents an important tradition within early Christianity that eventually was superseded by or incorporated into institutional Christianity.

---

5. Ferdinand Christian Bauer (1792–1860), professor of theology at the University of Tubingen, regarded the early church as a battleground for conflicting theological viewpoints. In a volume published posthumously, *The Church History of the First Three Centuries* (1863), he wrote that John of Patmos was a Judaizer who wrote Revelation in opposition to Paul. In this regard he was followed by Ernst Renan, the French scholar of religion, who argued that John was "the most ardent of the Judaizing Christians," *Antichrist* (1897); cited in Wainwright, *Apocalypse*, 129.

Apostles and Prophets: A Clash of Traditions in the New Testament Period

According to Paul (1 Cor. 12:28), God appointed as leaders "apostles first, prophets second." The term "apostle" in the later Christian tradition came to represent an ecclesiastical system of authority headed by bishops, priests, and deacons. By the fourth century, this position became dominant in western Christianity. Many people are not aware that only sixty years after Jesus' death, John of Patmos challenged the way early Christians, including many of Paul's followers, were interpreting Christ's message. John represented a prophetic tradition that claimed authority directly from God, without additional human (ecclesiastical) mediation. All apostles are not true apostles, he declares in Revelation 2:2, and therefore should be judged by a higher, unmediated standard: "you have tested those who claim to be apostles but are not, and have found them false." Such a mystical, unmediated tradition, could and eventually did lead to power struggles within the emerging church, as reflected in (a) Gnosticism, which appealed to intuition and individual spirituality for truth, (b) Eastern Orthodoxy, which appealed to mystical understandings of worship and theology, and later in (c) the Protestant Reformation, a movement that appealed to scripture, the role of the Spirit, and the priesthood of every believer over the ecclesiastical authority and tradition of medieval Christendom.

John of Patmos writes as though his visions were sent directly from heaven, and for two thousand years many Christians have assumed that they were, since his is the only "book of revelation" in the New Testament. But John was competing with other "prophets" and church leaders and was angry that some of his hearers were also listening to them and heeding their messages.[6] At the start of Revelation he devotes a great deal of attention denouncing these competitors with vicious epithets. John declares that "the son of man" (1:13), who holds the church leaders in his hand and who stands in the midst of the churches (1:13, 2:1), ordered him to denounce these antagonists, whom he describes as:

- false apostles (2:2)
- Nicolaitans (2:6, 15)
- the synagogue of Satan, those who say they are Jews but are not (2:9 and 3:9)
- the man he calls Balaam (2:14)
- the false prophetess Jezebel (2:20–23), and

6. Pagels, *Revelations*, 39.

- specialists in the deep things of Satan (2:24)

Who are these antagonists? Biblical scholar Elaine Pagels, in her 2012 book *Revelations*, makes a strong case that these individuals are not Jewish antagonists or pagan Romans who are persecuting Christians but rather internal enemies, respected members of the various churches in Asia, to whom John is writing. They might well be Gentile converts or followers of the apostle Paul. It is interesting to note that John of Patmos never mentions Paul's name. Was he skeptical of Paul's teaching and did he feel threatened by those who accepted it?

Jews and Christians in the Book of Revelation

Although John's writings are in the New Testament, we should not assume that he saw himself as a "Christian." The first person we know who aggressively called himself "a Christian," to distinguish himself from "Jews," was the Syrian Ignatius of Antioch. Converted to Paul's message perhaps around 80 or 90 AD, Ignatius took Paul as the model for his own life.[7] Calling himself Christophoros ("Christ bearer"), he traveled through Asia Minor about fifteen years after John had been there and, like John, wrote letters to seven churches, including to congregations in Ephesus, Smyrna, and Philadelphia. Like John, Ignatius identified with people who suffered persecution. After declaring himself a Christian before a Roman magistrate, he was sentenced to die the death of a martyr, torn apart by wild animals in the Roman Coliseum around the year 110.

There is no doubt that John was a devoted follower of Jesus Christ, but he never actually uses the term "Christian"—probably because what we call Christianity had not yet become entirely separate from Judaism. Instead, like Peter, Paul, and other early followers of Jesus, John clearly saw himself as a Jew who had found the Messiah. Writing around 90, John expresses alarm at seeing God's "holy people" increasingly infiltrated by outsiders who had no regard for Israel's priority and religious distinctives.[8] John stood on the cusp of enormous change, one that eventually would transform the entire movement from a Jewish messianic sect into "Christianity," a new religion flooded with Gentiles. But since this had not yet happened—not, at least, among the groups John addressed in Asia Minor—he took his stand as a Jewish prophet charged to keep God's people holy, unpolluted by Roman culture. The following examples from chapters 2 and 3 of Revelation provide helpful perspective.

7. Ibid., 65.
8. Ibid., 46–47.

A Vision of the Church Imperfect (Revelation 2–3) 55

1. Some forty years after Paul clashed with early Jewish Christian leaders such as Peter and James (see Gal. 1:6–8; 2:11–16), John of Patmos met with groups of Jesus' followers throughout Asia Minor and was dismayed to discover considerable variation among them. He learned that some of these groups, perhaps predominantly Jewish, adhered closely to Jewish tradition and welcomed him as a respected prophet. He commended them, as he did those in the city of Philadelphia, whom he declared to be protected by Jesus, who "has the key of David."

2. The first church John addresses in Revelation is Ephesus, a center of Pauline teaching. When John chastises the Ephesian believers in 2:4 for having abandoned their first love, he may not be referring to the elements of the gospel as taught to them by Paul, their first Christian teacher, but to the fact that they had compromised essential elements of the Jewish faith.

3. When speaking of Balaam (2:14) and Jezebel (2:20), John alludes to evil prophets and false rulers in the Old Testament literature who led Israel to "practice fornication and to eat food sacrificed to idol," a formula expression that refers primarily to idolatry. Here John borrows the sexual metaphor for idolatry that prophets like Hosea and Jeremiah used when they reprimanded their people for "committing adultery" against God. When John charges that certain prophets and teachers are encouraging God's people to eat "unclean" food and engage in "unclean" sex, he is also taking up arguments that had broken out between Paul and followers of James and Peter about forty years earlier—an argument that John of Patmos continues with a second generation of Paul's followers. Those whom John says Jesus "hates" look very much like "Gentile followers of Jesus converted through Paul's teaching."[9] Twice John warns his followers in Asia Minor to beware of "blasphemers" among them, who "say they are Jews, and are not" (2:9, 3:9). When we step back from John's angry rhetoric, we can see that the very practices he denounces are those that Paul had recommended: (a) In 1 Corinthians 8:4 Paul had written that since "we know no idol in the world really exists," eating sacrificial meat could not do any harm. (b) In 1 Corinthians 7:10 Paul addresses "unclean" sexual relationships, like marriages between believers and unbelievers, advising his converts not to seek divorce. As a strictly observant Jew, John could have inferred that Paul had sanctioned mixed marriages, which he considered "uncleanness." The prophets John derisively calls by the biblical names of despised Gentile outsiders—Balaam and Jezebel—could be Gentile converts to Paul's teaching.

4. When we read about the "synagogue of Satan" (2:9; 3:9) it is easy to think that John is talking about actual Jews, an assumption that John had

---

9. Ibid., 54.

become a "Christian" by the time he wrote his book. Many people believe that Judaism came to an end around AD 70, when the Jerusalem Temple was destroyed, and that Judaism and Christianity would have been separated by the time John wrote Revelation. However, this belief may not be sound. If John knows the term "Christian," he never mentions it, much less applies it to himself. He seems, in fact, to consistently see himself as a Jew who acknowledges Jesus as Israel's Messiah rather than as someone who has converted to a new "religion."[10]

Roman magistrates may have been the first to coin the term Christian, around the year 112, when a governor in Asia Minor named Pliny ordered the arrest of some people whom he called "Christians." Despite the reference in the book of Acts that Jesus' followers "were first called Christians at Antioch" in Syria (Acts 11:26), this reference was probably not written earlier than 85 to 90 AD, by an author who displayed a clear bias to present the Christian movement in as positive a manner as possible and as a unified movement.

5. When John of Patmos traveled through Asia Minor, he found followers of Paul who apparently assumed that Gentile converts had become, in effect, the new "Israel," for this is what Paul had taught (Rom. 2:28–29; 9:6–8; Gal. 3:7–8; 6:15–16). John found these claims outrageous. John reassures those who really are Jews in Philadelphia that "I [Jesus] will make those of the synagogue of Satan, who say they are Jews and are not, but are lying—I will make them come and bow down before your feet, and they will learn that I have loved you" (3:9).

6. When John in the seven letters urges believers to "conquer," he means that they not accommodate or compromise with pagan culture (something Pauline Christians were presumably doing). Because John saw Rome as God's enemy, the latest incarnation of evil, he saw himself and those he hoped to influence as at war (culturally and spiritually) with Rome. Later, when John speaks of 144,000 men who "have not defiled themselves with women, for they are virgins" (14:4), he is referring to spiritual and cultural purity.

7. John, in the prophetic tradition, never mentions "bishops" at all. The only "apostles" he reveres are the twelve disciples of Jesus, whom he envisions in heaven. When he hears of certain people still alive who are promoting themselves as "apostles" in Ephesus (Rev. 2:2), he responds with alarm. Unlike John, who saw himself as a prophet, Ignatius of Antioch identified himself as a "supervisor" or bishop. Building on the tradition of Paul, he was the first person to actively promote this new system of leadership. Ignatius,

---

10. Ibid., 60–61.

for his part, knew of groups like John's, led by prophets, and fiercely campaigned against them. He is well known for his proclamation: "Pay attention to the bishop, the priests, and the deacons." Unlike John, who validated faith in Jesus from the Hebrew Bible, especially its prophetic books, Ignatius rarely cited passages from the Hebrew scriptures. For him, the primary authority was the letters of Paul and the Gospels. What mattered now, he declared, is Christianity, not Judaism.

Two hundred years later influential Christian leaders chose both traditions, Paul's and John's, and wrestled them into the same New Testament canon.[11]

Questions to Ponder

1. What verse, passage, or theme stands out for you as the key to chapters 2 and 3 of Revelation? Support your answer.
2. With which church or city in Revelation do you most relate? Why?
3. Do a performance review of your life based on your strengths and weaknesses. Identify specific ways where you can grow in character and in faithfulness to God. Do the same for your church, identifying specific ways in which it can grow in effectiveness.
4. What message of hope do you find in chapters 2 and 3 of Revelation?

---

11. Ibid., 71.

Chapter 3

A Vision of a Rightly Ordered Universe (Revelation 4–5)

Summary: In Revelation 4 and 5 John journeys to heaven, where he enters the throne room of the universe. Worship is central in heaven, and sacred song its primary vehicle. In his journey John sees in the hands of God a scroll, sealed with seven seals. The one worthy to reveal its contents is Jesus, the Lamb who was slain. Jesus offers a model of "Lamb power" that supersedes all earthly power structures. In light of God's gift of Jesus, all creation praises God.

Assignment: Read chapters 4 and 5 of Revelation

Key Passage: Revelation 5:12

Central Theme: True power is found in Jesus, the Lamb. Those who recognize that power join all creation in praising God.

Learning Objectives

Participants will examine:
1. The symbolic nature of Revelation's cosmological imagery
2. The meaning of the concept of heaven in Revelation
3. How Old Testament passages influenced John's vision of heaven
4. The symbol of Jesus as a Lamb
5. How Revelation has inspired church hymnody

A Vision of a Rightly Ordered Universe (Revelation 4–5)

OUTLINE TO REVELATION 4:1—5:14

I. The Holiness of God 4:1–11
    A. John's Visionary Transport to Heaven 4:1
    B. The Heavenly Throne Room 4:2–3
    C. The Twenty-Four Elders 4:4
    D. The Seven Spirits of God 4:5
    E. The Sea of Glass 4:6a
    F. The Four Living Creatures 4:6b–8
        1. The First Song 4:8b
        2. The Second Song 4:9–11
II. The Scroll and the Lamb 5:1–14
    A. The Scroll with Seven Seals 5:1–4
    B. Jesus as Lion 5:5
    C. Jesus as Lamb 5:6–14
        1. The First Song to the Lamb 5:8–10
        2. The Second Song to the Lamb 5:11–12
        3. The Third Song to the Lamb 5:13–14

JOHN'S HEAVENLY TRIP AS A JOURNEY TO PERSPECTIVE

The first three chapters of Revelation take place on earth. Chapter 4 begins a new section, a vision of John's heavenly journey that extends through chapter 18. He remains in heaven through the sea and trumpet vision of chapters 6–9. From chapter 10 on, John's standpoint sometimes appears to be back on earth, yet all is still seen from the transcendent perspective.

    Visionary journeys are a standard feature of many ancient apocalypses; such journeys, like science fiction writing of today, can involve both time and space travel. While apocalyptic writings seem strange to us, we must remember that they were quite familiar to John's original audience. John's readers knew not to take these visions literally, but to look for the deeper message they conveyed.

    The visions beginning in Revelation 4 assume a three-layered universe (heaven, earth, and under the earth; see 5:3 and 13), a model central to the second half of the book. This cosmology, while understandable to a first-century audience, does not work for us, nor was it central to John's perspective. Heaven and earth, in biblical theology, are not separated by a great gulf, as they are in popular conception. "Heaven," God's sphere of reality, is not far away but right here, close beside us, intersecting with our ordinary reality.[1]

In the book of Revelation "heaven" is the starting point for all revelation. "Heaven," for John, is not the place where God is preparing an eternal dwelling for humanity. John is not taken to heaven to avoid what is taking place on earth; quite the opposite. He is taken into God's throne room so that he can see "behind the scenes" and understand how things fit together. This perspective is vital to the message of Revelation and to the Bible as a whole. Going to heaven is not the goal of the religious life. It was not John's goal, and it should not be ours. John's cosmological perspective should be interpreted spiritually, not spatially. Going to "heaven," in John's vision, is less about cosmic geography and more about the place where God chooses to reveal himself, the place where heavenly realities are made plain. Heaven is the deeper dimension that offers God's perspective on what happens on earth, a new way of seeing that is beyond the control of earthly rulers.

In Revelation, every heavenly description that John provides corresponds to something on earth. John's Jewish-Christian readers would have recognized the Jewish temple in Revelation's description of heaven. In the temple, as in John's heaven, the menorah (seven golden lamp stands, 1:12) and the altar of incense (8:3–5) stood before the Holy of Holies. In the temple four carved cherubim adorned the walls, as the four living creatures minister before the throne in John's heaven. The twenty-four elders around the throne replicate the twenty-four priestly divisions that served in the temple in any given year. The "sea of glass, like crystal" (4:6) corresponds to the large bronze basin in the temple courtyard. At the center of Revelation's temple, as in Solomon's temple, was the Ark of the Covenant (11:19).

ANALYSIS OF REVELATION 4:1—5:14

The Holiness of God (Chapter 4:1-11)

The shift of perspective at 4:1 involves a new way of seeing the church. Revelation began with John on the earth, involved in the struggle of ordinary Christians to be loyal to Christ in their situation. The messages to the seven churches were often critical of the Christians in the churches of

---

1. Wright, *Revelation*, 42.

A Vision of a Rightly Ordered Universe (Revelation 4–5)

Asia. From 4:1 on Christians are idealized, as in 14:1–5. They are no longer distinguished into good, bad, and indifferent but are assumed to be faithful and obedient. Everything is now seen from the heavenly, eschatological perspective.

In Revelation 4:1 John hears anew the voice of one who spoke like a trumpet, the same voice he had heard in 1:10. It is the voice of the glorified Christ calling him to come up to heaven and promising to show him what must take place "after this." Scholars of the futurist school tend to interpret Revelation 4 through 22 as pertaining to the eschatological end time, and since that time has not yet arrived, these chapters are said to have little relevance to the present. This approach misunderstands John's perspective. While Revelation 4 signals a decisive turn to the future, John is referring to the short-term future of his own audience, not the age-long perspective from which later readers tend to see his prophecy. When John declares in his introduction that his book reveals what must "soon" take place (1:1) and that "the time is near" (1:3), he is thinking apocalyptically. That the end of history is near in the author's own time is a regular feature of apocalyptic thought. Major elements of earliest Christianity understood and expressed their new faith in apocalyptic terms, for they supposed they were the last generation. This way of thinking characterizes not only John's perspective in Revelation but also typifies the New Testament as a whole.[2]

What did John expect to happen "soon"? Generally speaking, his expectation was twofold: he believed that God would defeat evil, as embodied in the Roman Empire, and that Christians would be vindicated for their suffering when God's reign came on earth. Has John's expectation been fulfilled yet? Those who anticipate the "rapture" of true believers from this earth prior to final tribulation would say that all awaits future fulfillment. But such expectation is flawed, on biblical and historical grounds. While God's promised defeat of evil has not yet occurred in a final sense, four remarkable events have occurred through history that can be seen as fulfilling ancient Jewish and Christian hopes, at least in preliminary ways:

1. Through a stunning reversal, Christianity became the religion of the Roman Empire;
2. The Roman Empire collapsed (from internal and external causes);
3. The Jewish people became a nation once again, run democratically;
4. Christianity became the largest and most widespread of all religions.

---

2. Readers looking for additional clarification on this defining aspect of early Christian self-understanding are encouraged to read "Reflection: Interpreting the 'Near End' in Revelation" in Boring, *Revelation*, 68–74.

Like the Old Testament prophets, John is caught up into the heavenly court, where he overhears the divine council (cf. 1 Kgs. 22; Isa. 40; Jer. 23:18; Job 1:6). John's purpose in traveling to heaven is not to give his readers a picture of "heaven," for that is not what he sees. Rather he is taken to the throne room to obtain a perspective of the universe as governed by God. The central theological question of chapters 4 and 5 as well as of the entire book is: Who is the true Lord of the world? This theological question of power is addressed and elaborated with cosmological imagery and symbolic language. John sees a throne and it is clear that this throne represents the spiritual center of the entire universe. Like the Roman world, which had its own concentric circles of power, everything in heaven radiates outward. At the center of the Roman world was the emperor, who was surrounded by an inner circle of friends and admirers, which led the rest of society in praising the emperor and the traditional gods. John's picture of the heavenly throne room follows this model, but ultimate allegiance is to God, not to the emperor. And the two forms of rule are diametrically opposite. The throne image, found initially in 4:2–6, 9–10 and 5:1, 6–7, 11, 13, occurs again and again "like a keynote symbol throughout the whole book."[3] It indicates how decisive for the theological perspective of Revelation faith in God's sovereignty is over all things.

John, having seen God's sovereignty as already fully acknowledged in heaven (chapters 4 and 5), then sees how it must come to be acknowledged on earth. The three series of judgments that follow—the seven seal-openings, the seven trumpets, and the seven bowls—are connected with the vision of God's throne room, each series portrayed as in some way issuing from the throne room. For example, the four living creatures around the throne summon the four riders of the first four seal-openings (6:1, 3, 5, and 7). The seven trumpets are blown by the seven angels who stand before God in heaven (8:2, 6). Most elaborate is the way the seven last plagues are portrayed as issuing from the throne room (15:5–8). Of particular significance is the literary link between the statement in 4:5a ("coming from the throne are flashes of lightning, and rumblings and peals of thunder") and the seventh of each series of judgments (8:5; 11:19; 16:18–21). In 4:5 the statement indicates a manifestation of God's holiness in heaven. The expansion of the formula in the other instances indicates that God's holiness is manifested in judgment on evil.

In all these connections between the vision of God's throne in chapter 4 and the three series of judgments, it is notable that the transcendence of God is protected and the absence of anthropomorphic representation, so

---

3. Schüssler Fiorenza, *Revelation*, 58.

notable a feature of chapter 4, is preserved. God is not directly depicted as judge. The living creatures who belong to God's throne commission the judgments, and angels carry them out. God's glory, power, and holiness are manifested in smoke, thunderstorm, and earthquake, but God himself is not seen or heard. Through this kind of indirectness John creates the greatest possible distinction between the judgments of God and the image of a human despot wielding arbitrary power. No writer of scripture is more aware of this difference than John.

As in all four visions of Revelation, the vision of the throne room portrays the heavenly glory of God together with the Lamb. The scene is awesome and majestic. John sees a figure seated on the throne, but that figure is not described (cf. 20:11). By failing to specify the figure on the heavenly throne, John avoids having to distinguish between God and Christ; both dispense judgment for both are ruling.

The setting is described in detail. To understand this passage and John's perspective, we should note the close connection between the throne vision and the first chapter of Ezekiel. At least eight corresponding themes can be identified:

an open door	Rev. 4:1	Ezek. 1:1
a throne	Rev. 4:2	Ezek. 1:26
jasper and carnelian	Rev. 4:3	Ezek. 1:26 sapphire
rainbow	Rev. 4:3	Ezek. 1:28
lightning, thunder	Rev. 4:5	Ezek. 1:13–14, 24
torches of fire	Rev. 4:5	Ezek. 1:12–13, 20
sea of glass, like crystal	Rev. 4:6	Ezek. 1:22, 26
four creatures, full of eyes	Rev. 4:6–8	Ezek. 1:5–11

Despite their similarities, John's account is marked by greater reserve. He uses suggestion rather than description to convey the majesty and mystery of God. In telling us that God's presence has a radiant, gemlike splendor, John is using evocative language to hint at what defies description. With every sentence our sense of mystery deepens. Overarching the throne is a rainbow, resembling an emerald. The idea of a rainbow that is circular (completed) and only one color so teases the imagination that some translations substitute the word "halo" for rainbow. The parallel with the bow of Ezekiel 1:28 could suggest that the intent is to conceal the deity, but the more likely understanding of the rainbow is its appearance in Genesis 9:16, where it is a sign of God's covenant with humanity. The color green suggests "mercy" or "peace," underscoring God's providential care for nature and God's promise to make all things new.

The majesty and mystery of God are conveyed by other symbols taken from Ezekiel. The lightning and thunders that proceed from the throne are reminders of the great theophany of Sinai, when God descended in fire and smoke heralded by thunder and lightning (Exod. 19:16–19). Such imagery underscores the awesome power and majesty of God. Before the throne burn "seven flaming torches, which are the seven spirits of God" (4:5), an expression that reminds us of the sevenfold aspect of the Spirit of God in 1:4. John never uses the term "the Holy Spirit" in his book, for his understanding is clearly Jewish and still somewhat primitive by later Trinitarian standards. Nevertheless, the expression undoubtedly points to the Holy Spirit.

Between John and the throne is a flat pavement-like surface that looks like a crystal sea. This much-debated image, compared with references in Revelation 13:1–2, where the sea is viewed as evil, and in 21:1–4, where the sea is included with suffering and death among items that will cease to exist in the renewed creation, has been famously described by G. B. Caird as a "reservoir of evil" in heaven.[4] "Sea" in those passages clearly signifies suffering, distress, and the precariousness of human life on earth. Viewed from this perspective, John might have had in mind the Red Sea, from which Israel was saved during the exodus, an event interpreted by Israel's prophets against the background of ancient chaos myths (Isa. 51:9–10; cf. Rev. 15:1–4). Following Caird, N. T. Wright depicts the sea within the throne room as a symbolic representation of the fact that, within God's current world, evil is present and dangerous. Though contained within God's sovereign purposes, it will eventually be overthrown.[5]

John's imagery, however, is polyvalent, and should not be forced into a literalistic straightjacket or subjected to logical consistency. Instead of the Red Sea, John may have had in mind Israel's temple, in which there was a huge bowl called the Bronze Sea (1 Kgs. 7:23–26), although more likely he took the image from Ezekiel's vision (1:22), where it served as a visual phenomenon to heighten the awesome splendor of the throne room. The picture enhances the holiness of God, creating a scene of distance but also of immense serenity. The sea's crystal surface stretches out before the throne, reflecting the brightness of the throne and adding to the sense of God's transcendence.[6]

---

4. Caird, *Revelation*, 65.

5. Wright, *Revelation*, 45.

6. See the discussion on Revelation 15:2 for additional information on this image and its connection with the New Jerusalem in chapters 21 and 22.

A Vision of a Rightly Ordered Universe (Revelation 4–5)

Around the throne are other thrones on which are twenty-four white-robed elders (4:4), crowned with gold. It is difficult to know precisely what John had in mind here, particularly since this detail does not correspond to Ezekiel's vision. Some interpreters argue that the elders represent the church in its totality—a combination of the twelve patriarchs (tribes) of the Old Testament and the twelve apostles of the New, who are thus seen to form a unity. This solution correlates with John's closing vision of the New Jerusalem, where the names of the twelve tribes are on the gates and those of the apostles are on its foundations (21:12, 14). While attractive, this view seems unlikely here, primarily because the elders' song of praise in 5:8–10 definitely sets them apart from the angelic choir (5:11–12) as well as from the redeemed (most certainly the church in its entirety), who sing their song in 5:13.

It seems best to take the twenty-four elders as an exalted angelic order (like archangels), a specific group within the divine council. They may well be the angelic beings who compose the divine council (cf. Isa. 24:23; Dan. 7:9; 2 Enoch 4:1). Their white garments speak of holiness and their golden crowns of royalty (4:4). As their own thrones and crowns indicate, they are themselves rulers. They rule the heavenly world on God's behalf. Their function may be the divine counterpart of the twenty-four courses of Aaronic priests (1 Chron. 24:5), who on earth render to God imperfect worship of which the heavenly worship is the perfect model. In John's day the term "elder" was a title for those who led Jewish and early Christian congregations. They were to exhibit wisdom and pious behavior for others to emulate. In like manner, the heavenly elders model leadership to their earthly counterparts. By casting down their golden crowns before the throne, the elders acknowledge that, as created beings (4:11), their authority is wholly derivative from God's. He alone is to be worshipped as the source of all power and authority. Through their dramatic gesture, they provide an example of true worship to be followed by the communities of faith on earth.

John's description of the four living creatures on each side of the throne also derives from Ezekiel. Ezekiel numbers them among the cherubs (Ezek. 10:20), meaning that like the twenty-four elders, they too are angelic beings. In 1 Kings 6:23–28 we learn that Solomon had two such figures carved of olivewood and placed in the inner sanctuary of the temple in Jerusalem. Their height was fifteen feet and their outspread wings overarched the sacred ark within the sanctuary. Their presence in the temple symbolized God's eternal throne.

Their role in Revelation is important. Their closeness to God's throne (5:6; 14:3) means that they attend to God. They are associated with the praise of God (4:8; 5:8, 14; 7:11; 19:4) but also with the outpouring of the wrath of God (6:1–7; 15:7). Having many eyes, front and back, and six wings (as did the seraphs in Isa. 6:2), they are likened to a lion, an ox, a human, and an eagle. In Ezekiel's vision each creature has four faces, in the likeness of human, lion, ox, and eagle (1:10). These are believed to derive ultimately from the Babylonian pantheon, where they represent the four leading deities of Babylon: Nabu, the human-faced revealer; Nergal, the lion-faced god of the netherworld; Marduk, the winged bull patron deity of Babylon, and Ninib, the eagle-faced god of hunting and war. With other polytheists, Babylonians viewed their deities as personifications of the powers of nature. Ancient Jews sometimes found it expedient to borrow such imagery, though the borrowing required massive retranslation.

Commentators often depict Ezekiel's creatures as epitomizing what is noblest (lion), strongest (ox), wisest (human), and swiftest (eagle) in nature, but this approach seems erroneous. If these creatures represent beings in the natural order, John does not suggest it. When he wishes to refer to all creatures, as he does in Rev. 5:13, he does so clearly, distinguishing earthly creatures from heavenly ones. If John, following Ezekiel, views these creatures to be angelic, they should be defined by angelic roles. The four living creatures, like the twenty-four elders, have a unique role and place in the heavenly council, which is where they belong biblically. They should not be confused with creatures in the natural realm. We should also avoid associating them with the four evangelists (Gospel writers), as many have done, for such association is entirely fanciful.

The living ones—heaven's choirmasters—are said to praise God continually. Their song reminds us of the seraphs' chant in Isaiah 6:3: "Holy, holy, holy, is the Lord Almighty." The first hymn (4:8) praises God's holiness, the quality that distinguishes God from all finite beings. The threefold repetition of "holy" in that context is not a reference to the Trinity, as some suppose, but rather emphasizes God's superlative degree of holiness.

While "holy" means primarily "separate" or "distinct," it also implies purity, goodness, and power. Christian worship, based on a radical theology, has a revolutionary, even counter-cultural, quality. John's audience lived in a world where evil was rampant and seemed all-powerful. To say that God is Almighty in such a setting is to say that real power is not with temporal authorities but with God, who is righteous and good. This hymn offers encouragement to those on earth who are marginalized, victimized, or otherwise oppressed.

The second hymn (4:11) praises God as creator. The opening line, "You are worthy," reminds us that God alone is worthy to receive the glory and the honor and the power. Use of the definite article in the Greek for each noun indicates totality. Here the twenty-four elders ascribe to the Creator the name that Emperor Domitian was said to have usurped, "our Lord and God." Christian worship begins with the affirmation: "God reigns."

The Scroll and the Lamb (Chapter 5:1–14)

Whereas chapter 4 records a vision of God the Creator, chapter 5 provides a vision of God as Redeemer, the Lamb who has conquered through his death. Chapter 4 closes with the worship of the Creator and chapter 5 ends with the worship of the Redeemer. These two chapters are significant for an understanding of the message of the book. There are mysteries in life. At times, caught up in the world's evil and misery, we feel a sense of hopelessness. Evil is real; suffering is real. Chapter 5 points beyond human inability to divine ability.

In the midst of worship around the throne a setback threatens everything. God is holding a scroll that must be opened, but no human is worthy to break open its seals. The book was sealed at seven different points, so that as each seal is broken a new column or section would come to view.[7] The scroll contains humanity's destiny, and with it the destiny of the world, as decreed by God's redemptive plan to undo and overthrow the cancerous evil that has attained so much power and control. The divine decree awaits the emergence of a human agent, willing and worthy to put it into effect. To open that scroll by breaking the seals means not merely to reveal but to carry out God's plan. The opening of the scroll indicates the execution of God's plan. When the scroll is opened and the seals are broken, then God's redemptive purpose becomes realized in history.

Only a human, someone who has not contributed in some way to the problems of creation, can open the scroll and carry out God's plan for human history. John weeps, for no one is found worthy. The term John uses here signifies complete inability; no one is able or deserving to open the scroll. John's tears are not simply because his expectation of seeing the

---

7. Morris, *Revelation*, 92. The nature of the scroll, including its contents, remains controversial. Some scholars, noting the oddity of a scroll whose contents could be progressively revealed by the opening of a series of seals, suggest that the seven seals are merely preparatory for the revelation of the scroll's contents. Ladd, Mounce, and Schüssler Fiorenza maintain that the content of the scroll begins with chapter 8 and the sounding of the seven trumpets. Equating the sealed scroll with the "little scroll" of chapter 10, now opened (10:2, 8–10), Richard Bauckham locates the scroll's content in 11:1–13, arguing that the scroll reveals not God's redemptive plan—to defeat evil and deliver the saints—but rather the nature of Christian witness and sacrifice, *Revelation*, 80, 83. Such interpretations seem contrary to John's intention, which is to reveal recurrently and progressively the scroll's contents, beginning with the opening of the first seal in 6:1.

future is thwarted. His frustration is deeper than that, for until the scroll is opened, God's purposes remain not merely unknown but also unaccomplished. "Hence, if the scroll is not opened, then no protection for God's children in the hours of bitter trial; no judgments upon a persecuting world; no ultimate triumphs for believers; no new heaven and earth; no future inheritance!"[8]

In 5:1 the scroll is said to have writing on the inside and on the back. Once again the background is Ezekiel, where in chapter 2 a book of lamentations had writing "on the front and on the back" (2:10). From a practical view, this might mean that the scroll was fully inscribed, with no room for additional writing or for change of perspective. Like Ezekiel's scroll (2:10), also written on both sides, the decrees were finalized and the prophet was to speak only what the Lord had written. A deeper possibility, however, resides in the imagery of the double-sided scroll, an understanding that God's judgment has beneficial effect. As with the Egyptian plagues (envisioned in the trumpet and bowl plagues), in which God executed judgment through nature and society in order to liberate Israel from Egypt, so the cosmic plagues of the trumpet and bowl series execute the judgment of God over the cosmos, enabling the liberation of the Christian community from the oppression of Babylon/Rome.

Ezekiel is commanded to eat the scroll (3:3), a scenario duplicated in Revelation 10:8–11. The idea of a heavenly book containing the future course of history is a common feature of Jewish apocalyptic literature (1 Enoch 81:1–2) and is found reflected in the Hebrew Bible in Psalm 139:16, which alludes to a book of individual destiny, and in Daniel 8:26, where the seer is told to "seal up the vision, for it refers to many days from now." At the appointed time, the seals would be removed and history would move swiftly to its consummation. For John, that time had arrived.

At this point we come to one of the great surprises of Revelation. An elder informs John that one described as the Lion of Judah is worthy. Finally, a Messiah who could defeat Rome! That is what first century Jewish nationalists expected. Finally, a Messiah who can defeat jihadists and other global militants! This is what twenty-first century Jewish and Christian zealots expect, a lion-like Messiah who will judge evil and defeat it in all its manifestations. Two words—"lion" and "conquer"—lead us to expect a fierce animal here, one who conquers through ability and force of will. John *hears* the announcement of the Lion, but what he *sees* is a Lamb.

Seeing is central to Revelation. What John hears is a tease by comparison with what he sees. The Greek word John uses for "lamb" (*arnion*)

---

8. Hendriksen, *Conquerors*, 109.

actually is a diminutive form, something like "lambkin," suggesting great vulnerability. In addition to Revelation, two other passages in the New Testament use this Greek word: in John 21:15, when Jesus tells Peter to "feed my sheep," and in Luke 10:3, when Jesus says he is sending his disciples out into the world "like lambs into the midst of wolves."

In a sheep-oriented culture, John could choose many Greek words for "lamb" to use for his purpose, but the one he chooses is not used for Jesus elsewhere in the Bible. He most likely chooses this particular term because he plans to designate the false Christ (the antichrist) as *therion*, the "beast" in 13:11 that looks like a lamb but speaks like a dragon. Vernard Eller promotes the upcoming bout between the lamb and the beast as one might promote the main draw in a boxing match for the heavyweight championship of the entire universe: Arnion vs. Therion. It doesn't seem fair, a wee lambkin against a monster. The contest, in fact, is not fair, for the *arnion* is going to annihilate the no-good *therion*; the beast doesn't have a chance.[9]

The distance between what John hears and what he sees represents a monumental reversal, one of the most decisive in scripture, for it counters human expectation and takes us straight to the heart of the gospel. Two images of the Messiah, "Lion" and "Lamb," appear in this vision; their relationship is crucial to Revelation's theology. Lions were typical characters in an apocalypse, but no other apocalypse portrays its divine hero as a lamb. John depicts Jesus in the most vulnerable way possible, as a victim, a lamb who is slaughtered. He is slain, yet stands upright, showing that what was crucified is risen.

The first occurrence of "Lamb" is in Revelation 5:6. It is absent in the opening chapters because John has reserved it for its dramatic entrance at this point. Lamb is John's definitive title for Christ, occurring twenty-nine times in Revelation. There are important reasons for depicting Jesus as a lamb: first, this image underscores Jesus' vulnerability and innocent suffering—something to which many of John's ancient readers could relate, given the exclusion they experienced by rejecting Roman culture. The Lamb is a wondrously disarming image. In the face of Rome's ideology of victory through violent power, Revelation reveals the Lamb's nonviolent power. Instead of prevailing military strength, we are given the power of love. This reversal of images must have come as a great surprise to first-century Jews and Christians accustomed to Rome's brutality. Revelation reveals that true power and true victory at the heart of the universe lie with God's slain Lambkin. This imagery is reminiscent of the servant-lamb of Isaiah 53, the "lamb that is led to the slaughter." But this extraordinary Lamb has seven

---

9. Eller, *Revealing Book*, 79–80.

horns and seven eyes, symbolizing fullness of power and of insight, the fulfillment of Isaiah's hopes for the seed of David.

This Lamb may be weak, but its weakness is strength, a quality Paul commended to the Corinthian church: "whenever I am weak, then I am strong" (2 Cor. 12:10). From beginning to end, Revelation teaches us a way of life that theologian Ward Ewing calls "Lamb Power," a lifestyle oriented around Jesus' self-giving love. "Lamb power is the power of vulnerable but strong love to change the world," Ewing writes.[10] Much of Revelation can seem so violent, but "if we look at the subversive heart of the book that redefines victory and conquering, we can understand how Revelation actually subverts violence itself."[11] Lamb theology is true victory in the book of Revelation. This redefinition of power, the notion that a slain lamb has somehow conquered, is at the very heart of God's plan. It reveals greater hope than first-century Christians—and twenty-first century ones—could ever imagine, for in Revelation "conquering" never designates destructive judgment on the enemies of Christ or Christians. For Christians, winning is defined by the cross of Jesus.

In Revelation 5 "Lamb" is preceded by two other titles for Jesus: "the Lion of the tribe of Judah" (taken from the blessing of Jacob to Judah, recorded in Genesis 49:8–10) and the "Root of David" (drawn from a prophecy in Isaiah 11:1–4, which describes the rising of a shoot from the stump of Jesse, a branch endued with the sevenfold Spirit of God). These Christological titles resemble "the faithful witness, the firstborn of the dead, and the ruler of the kings of the earth" provided earlier in Revelation (1:5).

Singing breaks out in heaven when the Lamb is introduced. The four living creatures and the twenty-four elders who first praised the Creator now sing a new song to the Redeemer. Soon an infinite number of angels join in. Repeating three qualities of praise used by the elders—glory, honor, and power (4:11)—they add four qualities of their own—wealth, wisdom, might, and blessing (5:13), seven terms that symbolize the fullness of praise. Then, with thrilling crescendo, the climax is reached as all creation joins in adoration and praise to God and to the Lamb. Chapter 5 concludes with a great "Amen," as does Handel in the *Messiah*'s unforgettable finale, "Worthy is the Lamb that Was Slain."

Both halves of the breathtaking scene John calls to our imagination in chapters 4 and 5 end on a universal note. John's grand heavenly vision proceeds in concentric circles from God through Christ to the living creatures, to the twenty-four elders, to an innumerable host, to include everything

---

10. Ewing, *Power of the Lamb*, 98.
11. Rossing, "Journeys Through Revelation," 26.

that is. Absolutely nothing is excluded from this picture. This segment introduces a topic John addresses directly at the end of his book: that no part of the universe should be viewed as ultimately rebellious and lost. As every passage in Revelation points to the climax, we too must keep our eyes on the finale. Having joined in this grand chorus, the audience is now prepared to place in context the violent message of judgment presented in the opening of the seven seals and should not misunderstand these penultimate pictures of judgment as representing God's final word, the word of salvation we have witnessed in this scene.

The redemption of "saints from every tribe and language and people and nation" in 5:9, complemented in 5:13 by the voices of every living creature, should not be dismissed as mere hyperbole. John knows well that there is much on earth that has no inclination to join in the worship of Christ, but such is his confidence in the universality of Christ's accomplishment on the cross that his vision cannot stop short of universal response. In this respect John's vision agrees with the testimony of Colossians 1:20, the Christological passage which proclaims that in the cross God has already reconciled the whole universe to himself.

Essay 3: The Centrality of Worship and Doxology in Revelation

Twice in the letters to the churches Christ alludes to a "door" that enables communion between himself and his followers (3:8, 19). In 4:1 John crosses this threshold: "and there in heaven a door stood open!" As the church (*ekklesia*) is itself a site where the heavens are opened, worship enables John's hearer-readers to cross that threshold with him.

Worship makes each religion unique. It is also what marks humans as authentic. According to Genesis 1, joyous, heartfelt Sabbath "rest"—a euphemism for worship—represents not only the climax of God's creative work but also a pattern for human beings. When people worship, they are at their most human, because worship is the reason they were created. In Revelation 5:11–14, when all creation joins the elders and the four living creatures in praise to God, creation is simply praising its Maker. As the Israelite slaves celebrated the crossing of the Sea with praise, they found themselves to be alive as never before, for to praise was to participate in divine freedom. William Temple, Archbishop of Canterbury from 1942 to 1944, affirmed this exalted sense of freedom and fulfillment when he wrote: "To worship is to quicken the conscience by the holiness of God, to feed the mind with the truth of God, to purge the imagination by the beauty of God, to open the heart to the love of God, to devote the will to the purpose of God. All this is gathered up in that emotion which most cleanses us from selfishness because it is the most selfless of all emotions—adoration."[12] For Christians, worship is not optional; not because it is a requirement, but because it is a need and a delight. "We have a resilient hunger to move beyond self, to return our energy and worth to the One from whom it has been granted. In our return to that One, we find our deepest joy."[13]

Worship is always an act of response, for the initiative is with God. Worship is our response to the overture of God's love. It is where intimacy with God is gained. Through worship the Spirit of God touches our human spirit, kindling our deepest need for love, acceptance, affirmation, and truth. In his spiritual classic, *Celebration of Discipline*, Richard Foster notes that forms and rituals do not produce worship, but neither does their absence. We may have the best liturgy, but "we have not worshipped the Lord until Spirit touches spirit."[14]

A modern temptation is to substitute service for worship. Helping others in need, being compassionate, working for the betterment of others, all are commendable ideals, but the priority is worship first, service second. As we find in Revelation 4 and 5, our lives are to be punctuated with praise, thanksgiving, and adoration. Service flows out of worship, but when service becomes a substitute for worship, it is idolatry.

Worship, however, should not be equated with pietistic retreat from the public world. In Revelation, worship is the source of resistance to the idolatries of the public world. It points representatively to the acknowledgement of the true God by all the nations, in the universal worship for which the whole creation is destined (5:13; cf. 4:11; 15:4; 21:3, 24–26).

As all liturgical activity, praise is constitutive as well as responsive, creating reality by embracing a future that is full of promise and hope. For John, as for Christians ever since, worship (liturgy) reflects heaven and, mystically speaking, is heaven on earth. This understanding has been central to worship in Eastern Orthodoxy, as it is to Roman Catholics in the Mass and to Lutherans, Anglicans, and other Protestants with a high-church liturgy. It is also true for Pentecostal Christians, currently the fastest growing of all Christian communities globally, for whom the Holy Spirit is present in power and glory during charismatic worship. Ukrainian Christians tell the story of how their ancestors encountered the liturgy in the year 988 when Prince Vladimir of Kiev, upon converting to Christianity, sent emissaries to

---

12. Cited in Foster, *Celebration of Discipline*, 138.
13. Brueggemann, *Israel's Praise*, 1.
14. Foster, *Celebration of Discipline*, 138.

A Vision of a Rightly Ordered Universe (Revelation 4–5)   73

Constantinople, the capital of Eastern Christendom. There they witnessed the Byzantine liturgy in the cathedral of Hagia Sophia, the grandest church in the East. After experiencing the chant, the incense, the icons, but above all the Presence, the emissaries sent word to the prince: "We knew not whether we were in heaven or on earth."[15] The author of the letter to the Hebrews assumes, like John, that Christian worship has replaced the earthly Jerusalem and the site of the Jewish temple, for to worship Christ is to participate in the heavenly Jerusalem (Heb. 12:22–24).

Singing is a profound source of hope in Revelation. The author's primary purpose is not so much to describe the liturgy of heaven as to provide earth-bound victory to his people in the struggle that lies ahead. Songs are not intended to be understood factually or literally. Their symbolic dimension is precisely what gives them their power, connecting God's people to something deeper. Many spirituals are based on Revelation, for they evoke our capacity for solidarity and resistance, providing courage and hope. Worship and doxology are central to the book of Revelation, as the following points indicate.

1. The conflict of sovereignties is often portrayed in Revelation by references to worship. Rome's usurpation of divine rule is indicated by the universal worship of the beast (e.g. 13:4, 8, 12), whereas the coming of God's kingdom is indicated by universal worship of God (15:4; cf. 19:5–6). In the conflict of sovereignties the lines are drawn between those who worship the beast and those who worship God. Every stage of God's victory in chapters 7 through 19 is accompanied by worship in heaven. In the end, the book is about the incompatibility of the exclusive monotheistic worship portrayed in chapter 4 with every other kind of idolatry, including the political, social, and economic idolatries from which more narrowly religious idolatry is inseparable.[16]

2. Revelation contains at least fifteen hymns and songs of praise. The first five (4:8; 11; 5:9, 12, 13), constituting the heavenly anthem, form a group by themselves, as do the "four Hallelujahs" of chapter nineteen. Appearing at important junctures, the hymns help to explain the meaning of the action.

3. Like the entire book, the worship scene in the heavenly throne room (Rev. 4—5) has inspired many hymns. Framed in liturgy, from the opening setting "on the Lord's day" (1:10) to the eucharistic closing (22:17), Revelation overflows with songs and heavenly choruses praising God and exhorting worshippers to sing through their struggles. No other book of

---

15. Cited in Ware, "Eastern Christendom," 165–66.
16. Bauckham, *Theology of Revelation*, 34–35.

the Bible, except perhaps the Psalms, has shaped Christian music as much as has Revelation.

4. The rich musical legacy of Revelation ranges from classical music to popular to folk, from George Frederic Handel's "Hallelujah" chorus to the "Battle Hymn of the Republic" to "When the Saints Go Marching In." The list includes hymns widely used as calls to worship, including "When Morning Guilds the Skies" (Rev. 5:12); meditational songs of praise such as Don Wyrtzen's "Worthy is the Lamb," Jimmy Owens's "Holy, Holy," and Jerry Sinclair's "Alleluia"; and several by famed hymn writer Charles Wesley, including "Ye Servants of God" and "Love Divine, All Loves Excelling." In this hymn's final stanza, anticipation of eternity includes praise of the redeemed, who join the elders of heaven: "Till we cast our crowns before Thee, lost in wonder, love and praise." According to N. T. Wright, Revelation 4 "remains the foundation for everything that follows in the rest of this powerful and disturbing book. All that is to come flows from the fact that the whole creation is called to worship the one true God as its creator."[17]

Questions to Ponder

1. What verse, passage, or theme stands out for you as the key to chapters 4 and 5 of Revelation? Support your answer.
2. When the author notes that "heaven" is about perspective rather than about place, what, in your estimation, is gained and what is lost by such emphasis?
3. If "heaven" is realizable on earth, how would you acknowledge and celebrate its presence?
4. Using Archbishop William Temple's definition as a template, construct your own definition of worship in a way that reflects your experience and understanding.
5. What message of hope do you find in chapters 4 and 5 of Revelation?

---

17. Wright, *Revelation*, 49.

PART II

God's Message of Warning
Critiquing the Prevailing Order

Chapter 4

First Vision of Judgment: Seven Seals (Revelation 6:1—8:5)

Summary: In Revelation 6:1 through 8:5 we encounter the seven seals, a terrifying glimpse into the threats to the prevailing order of things and a reminder of the limits to which society can guarantee the wellbeing of its people. Like an urgent wake-up call, the opening of the seals renders God's diagnosis of the evils of Rome and of all unjust systems. They also provide assurance that injustice and violence will come to an end. In order to reach the hope at the end of the journey of life, we must experience great conflict. But God interrupts the opening of the seals to safeguard the church and secure Christians for greater faithfulness.

Assignment: Read chapters 6:1—8:5 of Revelation

Key Passage: Revelation 7:15–17

Central Theme: God provides hope even in the midst of judgment

Learning Objectives

Participants will examine:
1. The symbolic nature of Revelation's imagery of judgment
2. The inability of secular society to safeguard its citizens
3. How the message of the seven seals is consistent with the message of the Hebrew scriptures

4. How the message of the seven seals is consistent with the teaching of Jesus
5. The meaning of "sealing" and how God safeguards followers of the Lamb
6. Various descriptions of followers of the Lamb

OUTLINE TO REVELATION 6:1—8:5

I. The Six Seals 6:1–17
   A. First Four Seals: The Four Horsemen 6:1–8
      1. The First Seal: The White Horse 6:1–2
      2. Second Seal: The Red Horse 6:3–4
      3. The Third Seal: The Black Horse 6:5–6
      4. The Fourth Seal: The Pale Green Horse 6:7–8
   B. The Fifth Seal: The Cry of the Martyrs 6:9–11
   C. The Sixth Seal: The Great Earthquake 6:12–17
II. An Interlude: Visions of Security and Salvation 7:1–17
   A. The Church on Earth 7:1–8
   B. The Church in Heaven 7:9–17
III. The Seventh Seal: Silence and Prayer 8:1–5

THE SEVENFOLD PATTERN

With the sixth chapter, the main action of the narrative begins. The portrayal of woes that now begins depicts the struggle of the church amid conflict but also the judgments of God upon the church's enemies. The pattern John follows is loosely structured into three series of sevens: seals (6:1—8:5), trumpets (8:6—11:19), and bowls (15:5—16:21), with various interludes and digressions. The sevenfold sequence is not chronological. In other words, we should not suppose that the seven seals take place prior to the sequence of the trumpets and the bowls of wrath. Rather, each sequence, like facets of a diamond, represent a second and third angle of vision on the same complex reality. Whereas humans long for simple solutions, decisive breakthroughs, and climactic finales, God's healing of the world, like all therapy, entails a process: complex, comprehensive, and protracted.

First Vision of Judgment: Seven Seals (Revelation 6:1—8:5)

The seals and trumpets form one interrelated unit, not separate sequences, and follow an identical pattern (a group of four, then two, then one). The first four elements of each series present a concise description of four interrelated catastrophes. The fifth and sixth sections provide a more elaborate description, as the woes intensify. Some intermediate material leads finally to the seventh element, which brings judgment to a close, provides vindication to faithful believers, and brings history to an end. The third series, the visions of the bowls of God's wrath, also repeats the pattern of four, two, and one. They are separated from the series of seven trumpets by a block of material that does not neatly fit the pattern of sevens (12:1—14:20), though some recognize here another series which they designate "seven actors" or "seven significant signs." John's sevenfold sequence, wherever it appears, is not chronological (four down, three to go) but an exposition of a sevenfold reality. And when we get to the seventh seal, we are at the End; likewise, the seventh trumpet and the seventh bowl of wrath represent the End. Nothing can happen after the seventh seal, the seventh trumpet, or the seventh bowl. Each brings us to the same place in time, but with progressive intensity and greater depth of insight.

From very early in the history of the church, Christians have disagreed about how to interpret the highly symbolic visions in the middle chapters of Revelation. Some believe the series of numbered sevens represent literal predictions of a series of calamities that will happen in the future, at the end of the world. This is misleading, for John's purpose is not to predict but to imagine, not to foretell but to envision. Any attempt to make sense of these visions in a strictly linear chronology is faulty. For example, the stars fall from the sky after the sixth seal is opened (6:13), yet later, during the trumpet visions, the stars are back in the sky again (8:12). Similarly, after the third trumpet, the earth's green grass is destroyed (8:7), yet later, after the fifth trumpet, the green grass is present (9:4). John's use of images here is repetitive rather than sequential, kaleidoscopic rather than logical, surrealistic rather than realistic. His images cannot simply be reduced to one level of meaning. Their nature is tensive, meaning that they provoke tension rather than eliminate it, evoking overtones of meaning that cannot be reduced to the level of clarity. The goal is not to figure out what each image represents, as though Revelation were a secret code, but to allow John's message to grip us through its rich imagery.

As we proceed, we need to recall what we learned earlier about the type of literature we are reading. This is an apocalypse, and we are on an apocalyptic journey. The key will be to explore how the seals—as well as the trumpets and bowls—unveil increasingly urgent aspects of the reality that

John wants the churches of his day to see. Since God promises blessing to those who read and hear this message, we are led by hope and not by fear.

ANALYSIS OF REVELATION 6:1—8:5

The Six Seals (Chapter 6:1–17)

Thus far John has been calling his readers to a vision of life that is centered on loyalty to the reign of God the Creator. As a contrast to this majestic heavenly picture, John now presents a portrait of the world in which they live, though still from a heavenly perspective. The change comes when the Lamb starts opening the seals on God's scroll, and John's focus shifts to earth. The first four seals unleash the infamous four horsemen, perhaps the best known of the images in Revelation. They do not portray a sequence of events but instead reveal and highlight the true nature of Roman power and rule. Each rider depicts a threat to the prevailing order of things; together they critique imperial rule, questioning society's ability to guarantee the wellbeing of its people.

While the four horsemen represent man-made calamities, in Revelation they also appear as "judgments" of God, being worked out on the same plane of history. On the surface, these approaches seem contradictory, but they need not be. Although the seal plagues are authorized by God, they are not willed by God. Part of John's intent is to show how human power fits into the divine scheme of things. John begins with the belief that all power comes from God, the absolute ruler of the world. But because God gives humans free will, there is always the possibility that humans might misuse the portion of power entrusted to them. The way that God's power is manifested in the world is that the misuse of power brings consequences such as suffering and disaster. Wars, hunger, devastation—these disasters are the means by which it becomes clear that power abused is still under God's control. God does not approve of famine, bloodshed, disease, and death, but they are what follow if people persist in opposing God's rule. God does not will the woes, but as long as humans are free agents God allows them. So the four horsemen are "brilliant little vignettes of God's judgments working out in history. *This* is what happens in the sphere of politics whenever men and women oppose the will of God; and *this* in the military sphere; and *this* in the sphere of economics."[1]

The first four seals (6:1–8) are unified by their common image; their unity is essential to John's message. To overlook this feature is to introduce

---

1. Metzger, *Breaking the Code*, 58–59.

First Vision of Judgment: Seven Seals (Revelation 6:1—8:5)

confusion at a key point in the text. The description of this vision has features borrowed from Zechariah 6:1–5, where four horses of various colors—red, black, white, and dappled gray—are sent by God to patrol the earth. In Zechariah they are identified as the four winds/spirits of heaven. John, however, borrows only the symbol of the horses and their colors, and instead of yoking the horses to chariots he sets on each of them a rider. The riders are more important than the horses.

The vision begins when the Lamb opens the seven seals one at a time. The four living creatures reappear, each one introducing a different horse and rider. In John's mind the four living creatures are angels, but they represent the cosmos—the four directions, the four winds, and so the entire world. Like Zechariah's four winds, each quadrant of the earth has something it wants to reveal about the self-defeating power of evil that grips the earth. The destruction unleashed by these riders is not directly attributable to God, nor is it independent of God's will. The actual actors in this drama, the perpetrators of the eschatological woes, "are the forces of evil in the world, demonic anti-God forces permitted and used by God as agents of divine judgment. These forces which seem to be powerful are actually mere parodies of the ultimate power of God represented in the Lamb."[2] Each rider unveils a different aspect of the Roman imperial system. Together they portray the judgment of God on human arrogance and rebellion. The four agents of death are like those sent by God in Ezekiel 14:21.

When the first living creature calls, a white horse bolts forth, its rider holding a bow. Because John later sees a rider on a white horse who is called "The Word of God" (19:11–13), many interpreters conclude that the first horseman is Christ. The first rider "came out conquering and to conquer" (6:2). Here we have the same Greek word for "conquer" used to describe Jesus in 5:5 (cf. 3:23). But this horseman is not Jesus. His bow is meant for killing, the very opposite of Jesus' way of conquering. Everything in this chapter unfolds a series of disasters. Albrecht Dürer, in a series of woodcuts carved in 1498, correctly connected the first horseman with the other three, turning the tide of interpretation of the first horseman from Christ to an agent of eschatological judgment. This rider, unlike Jesus, not only goes forth to conquer but also is bent on conquest, his entire aim. Some see in this horseman a symbol of the victorious progress of the gospel, although there is nothing to indicate this. The four horsemen must be taken together, and they all represent destruction, horror, and terror. The white horse surely stands for the terrifying reality of war. "White," the color of victory, and

---

2. Boring, *Revelation*, 124.

"crown," the symbol for victory, can be used in a variety of settings. Once again we note the polyvalency of John's imagery.

The second rider, on a bright red horse, holds a great sword and is permitted to take peace from the earth. Like modern weapons of destruction, dubbed "peacekeeper," "peacemaker," and other euphemistic titles, the Roman Empire actually had a name for the peace it claimed to have established—the *Pax Romana*. Yet this peace was false, a peace instigated by Rome in its desire to expand the empire and gain more control. Rome achieved this peace through violent conquest and subjugation, a far cry from the peace God brings.

The third rider, on a black horse, symbolizes inflation and famine, which always accompany war. This horseman holds a pair of scales, representing the weighing of grain. John hears a voice saying, "A quart of wheat for a day's pay, and three quarts of barley for a day's pay, but do not damage the olive oil and the wine!" (6:6). The underlying message is one of economic hardship, depicting the struggle of people who cannot afford to buy food because of inflation and rising prices. A whole day's wage cannot buy enough simple grain for people to eat, while luxury items such as wine and oil are protected for the rich. This third seal offers a picture of an economy that serves only the elite of society, the very opposite of God's economy in which everyone has enough. It is striking to note the way Revelation singles out economic issues. In chapter 18, John narrates the fall of Rome in pointedly economic terms.

The fourth horseman represents death, riding a horse the color of decaying flesh. The rider has two ghostly companions, Death, which in the Greek can mean "pestilence" or "plague," and Hades, the ruler of the dead. We have here the appalling aftermath of war—famine and pestilence affecting humans and even the wild animals; in other words, ecological disaster.

To reiterate, John is not asking us to believe that war, rebellion, famine, and disaster are the deliberate creation of God, or that they represent God's will for the humans and animals he has made. They are the result of human sin. It is significant that out of all the apocalyptic disasters he could have chosen, John has at this point omitted the natural ones, like earthquakes, and included only those in which human agency has a part. The heavenly voice that says "Come!" is not calling disasters into existence. Rather the voice is declaring that nothing can occur that cannot be woven into God's gracious pattern of cosmic renewal. Because Christ reigns, even when the horsemen ride forth on their destructive mission, they do so as emissaries of Christ's redemptive love. "For the moment all we are told is that the content of the scroll is God's redemptive plan, by which he brings good out of evil and makes everything on earth subservient to his sovereignty."[3]

The four horsemen invite reinterpretation in our time, as in every age. While the seals do not "predict" anything in the twenty-first century, we may draw helpful analogies. When stock markets plunge, when wars rage or plagues or disasters kill, interpreters invariably bring up the four horsemen. We can learn important insights from John's apocalyptic visions of the Roman Empire as it gallops toward destruction, lessons about social and economic injustice and what we can do in our own time to lessen prejudice and inequality, as well as the endless violence, oppression, exploitation, and despair world-wide.

With the opening of the fifth seal, the focus narrows and intensifies, characteristic of John's telescoping pattern. The scene appears to shift back to heaven, but in fact does not, for all seven seals portray the events of earth from the heavenly perspective. As we noted earlier, the visions beginning in Revelation 4 assume a three-layered universe (heaven, earth, and under the earth; see 5:3 and 13), a perspective we must view figuratively rather than literally. Going to "heaven," in John's vision, is not about cosmic geography but about divine perspective, for "heaven" is the place where heavenly realities are made plain. "Heaven" represents discernment, a way of seeing that is beyond the control of earthly rulers. Heaven is the deeper dimension that offers God's perspective on what happens on earth.

John's understanding of heaven as a place of perspective, closely connected to events on earth and contiguous with earth, is influenced by Zechariah's vision in chapter 6, where the prophet sees the gates of heaven—two mountains of bronze. These mountains represent the place where heaven and earth meet, to which the messengers of God return at evening and from whence they come in the morning to accomplish the restoration God has planned. In Genesis 28:12, Bethel's "ladder" is such a place, where Jacob saw angels ascending and descending, encountered God, and received a blessing. When Jacob awoke he proclaimed: "How awesome is this place! This is none other than the house of God, and this is the gate of heaven" (Gen. 28:17). In Revelation John experienced what Jacob, Ezekiel, Zechariah, and other Old Testament figures witnessed: "I looked, and there in heaven a door stood open!" (4:1). In John's Gospel we find a commentary on Genesis 28:12, for Jesus becomes Bethel, the gate to heaven (cf. 3:13, 31; Acts 7:56). The coming of Jesus opens what was previously concealed in heaven, as the baptism of Jesus makes clear (Matt. 3:16; Mark 1:10; Luke 3:21).[4]

---

3. Caird, *Revelation*, 83.

4. Like Paul in Philippians 3:20, the author of Hebrews encourages Christians to

In 6:9 John looks into heaven and sees an altar, and under the heavenly altar he sees martyrs. This is a fascinating passage, in part because it is the only place in the New Testament where anything definite is said about the present state and location of the Christian dead. They are under an "altar"— John hasn't previously mentioned an "altar," but we gradually discover that the throne room where he is receiving his vision is also the heavenly temple. The martyrs long for justice, not simply in the sense of retribution, but in their heart-wrenching desire to see the world made right at last. They represent all believers, past and present, who have died or are being killed for their faithful witness, but more importantly for John, they represent those who are going to die in the great persecution he sees as already beginning. While Jews and Christians consider martyrdom from their vantage on earth, John wants us to see martyrdom from the point of view of the heavenly altar. In his understanding, their death is not meaningless tragedy but sacrifice on an altar. In the sacrificial worship with which John is acquainted from the Bible and from his earlier Jewish experience prior to the destruction of the temple, when the worshiper presented on the altar the sacrificial animal to be killed, its blood was poured out at the base of the altar (Lev. 4:7). Since life for animals and humans was considered to be in their blood, and since "life," "soul," and "self" were interchangeable concepts, the lives of sacrificial victims could be thought of as being at the base of (or "under") the altar. John is not here thinking of individual "souls" of Christians as something separate from their bodies, for that would be foreign to Jewish-Christians, nor is he thinking of martyrs as already present in heaven. It is far more accurate to view this as John intended it: "The chopping-block of the Roman executioner has become a cosmic altar. Christians who refused to sacrifice to the image of the emperor are nonetheless Christian priests who sacrifice themselves on the true altar of God. The image used metaphorically by Paul (Rom. 12:1) is filled with stark literalism in John's situation."[5]

Here, it seems, three things go together. First, the evil represented by the four horsemen must reach its height with the martyrdom of yet more believers. Second, and more important, that martyrdom will itself be part of the means of God's just judgment. This is how the Lamb's victory is worked

---

consider their citizenship to be "heavenly" rather than earthly (11:13–16), but as John makes clear, in the new world heaven and earth are joined at last, for what God is currently preparing in "heaven" will be brought to birth in a world that we will recognize as physical (Rev. 21:1–3). All this depends, however, on a particular meaning of "heaven." In biblical language, heaven is usually neither a location within our cosmos nor a destination within our time sequence; rather, it is God's dimension of day-to-day reality (cf. Ps. 115:16).

5. Boring, *Revelation*, 125.

First Vision of Judgment: Seven Seals (Revelation 6:1—8:5)

out in practice (Rev. 11:7-13; 12:11; 14:14-20).[6] John knows nothing of a "rapture" of the church to heaven to escape earthly tribulation. Christians ascend to "heaven" through suffering and death, as Jesus did; they are not taken to heaven to escape the sufferings of earth. Third, in speaking of martyrs, John speaks of the whole church. In 20:4-6, the martyrs are to be resurrected to reign with Christ for "a thousand years." Likewise it is said that the inhabitants of the New Jerusalem are to reign forever (22:5). Surely these are overlapping concepts.

Because of their courageous witness, the victims cry out for an end to injustice, "How long?" Their cry continues by victims of violence throughout the world, across time and space, who long for God to intervene. This was the cry of ancient Israel in Psalm 35:17, followed by a call for "vindication" (Ps. 35:24), a better translation than "vengeance" in Revelation 6:10. Those who are killed are triumphant from God's perspective, but those who remain are told more would follow (6:11), until evil ran its course. Then all who have suffered unjustly would be vindicated together. The first Christians found a problem in the fact that God does not punish sin here and now. They saw part of the answer in the cross, in the sacrificial love of God. But the cross also points to the final destruction of evil and to God's determination to renew the cosmos and make everything right.

To press the issue further, the Lamb opens the sixth seal, in which John presents the most ominous picture thus far: the terror of an impenitent world. As if in response to the victims' cry for justice, John pictures the cosmos itself giving signs of God's final retribution. The sun becomes black as sackcloth, the stars fall to the earth, and the moon turns red as blood. The ground shakes and people of every social class (note that John lists seven classes in verse 15) make a futile attempt to escape the justice of God. The vision warns that there is a higher authority to which even those at the pinnacle of society will be held accountable. (See essay 7 for Old Testament background to John's imagery in 6:12-17.)

Verse 16 introduces a most unusual expression, found only here in the Bible: "the wrath of the Lamb." Is it possible for a gentle lamb to be angry? The book of Revelation has a good deal to say about wrath, even about divine wrath, and so we must take it seriously. In speaking of wrath, John is speaking of the wrath of God, who "so loved the world that he gave his only Son" (John 3:16). He is speaking of the wrath of love, a love that is tenacious in its desire to make all things new, but equally tenacious to abolish evil. Every event of apocalyptic violence in chapter 6 must be seen as derived from chapters 4 and 5. In understanding this passage, as other apocalyptic

---

6. Wright, *Revelation*, 66.

passages in chapters 6 through 19, we should heed Jacques Ellul's advice that "all is situated in the cross of Jesus Christ . . . [T]hese texts must not be read in themselves but only in relation to that love which sacrifices itself for those who hate it."[7] This means that everything transpires from the hand of the Lamb. These scenes are scenes of "wrath," but it is the "wrath of the Lamb." Death and Hades still rampage (6:8), but the Messiah who holds the keys to Death and Hades (1:18) will finally cast them—not their victims—into the lake of fire (20:14).

Interlude: A Vision of the Servant Church (Chapter 7:1–17)

As we await the opening of the final seal, John delivers an amazing surprise. The apocalyptic pattern has run its expected cycle through the messianic woes and dissolution of the cosmos; all that remains with the seventh seal is the appearance of God and the final events themselves: resurrection, judgment, salvation in the heavenly realm for the redeemed, and damnation for the unfaithful. But John is more creative with his interpretation of apocalyptic traditions. Instead of the anticipated breaking of the seventh seal, John introduces another type of seal, the sealing of God's servants—another motif taken from tradition. Instead of seeing the expected End, what we see is two visions of the church. What initially seems to be a digression from the narrative, a postponement of dramatic flow, turns out to be a dual vision of the historical nature and significance of the church—a skillfully constructed interlude that builds suspense before the final seal is broken. The Christians of Asia needed a vision of the church to which they belonged; John's dual vision addresses this need.[8] (For additional information see essay 5, "John's Strategic Use of Interludes in Revelation.")

In the first vision (7:1–8) four angels appear, interrupting the process of judgment to deliver a message of hope; no more shaking of the earth; no more devastating winds. In Zechariah's vision, the four horsemen were explicitly identified with the four winds of heaven (Zech. 6:5). Here, the angels hold back the four winds of earth, keeping in check their destructiveness.

Another angel appears, bearing God's protective seal. Unlike the seals that guarded the heavenly scroll of destiny, this seal is a mark of ownership, reminding the early churches they belong to God. The seal is also protective, safeguarding them spiritually rather than physically (the two witnesses in chapter 11 are physically killed by the beast) from specific dangers. Two Old Testament passages contribute to John's understanding, even though

7. Ellul, *Apocalypse*, 123.
8. Boring, *Revelation*, 127–28.

they do not entirely determine its meaning. The first is Ezekiel's vision of seven angels, one who, with a writing case, marks the foreheads of all loyal servants of God and six with swords to kill all the citizens of Jerusalem who do not bear the protective mark (Ezek. 9:1-11). Ezekiel may well have had in mind the second passage, the story of the Israelites in Egypt who "sealed" their doorposts with the blood of the Passover lamb to spare their families (Exod. 12:21-27).

For early Christians, the imagery of sealing is probably baptismal imagery, even though there is no actual mention of baptism in Revelation. As in the baptismal homily found in 1 Peter, where the writer has in mind Noah and the flood, baptism serves as a reminder that God previously safeguarded his people through trials and tribulations, and will do so again. In this chapter, and in many others, John wants readers to make the connection back to the exodus and the flood, both representing new beginnings for God's people. John believes that God is calling the churches of his day to undertake a dramatic new journey of faith. Just as Noah led eight people through the waters into a new world of promise, and as Moses led the people through the sea toward the promised land, now Jesus the Lamb will lead his people on a journey into God's New Jerusalem. But first, the people of God must be sealed. The sealing interlude provides ancient and modern readers the assurance that God's people are being prepared and protected, even in the midst of judgment. It does not guarantee escape from suffering, but promises that God will bring us through the suffering. The sealing is always *from* judgment and *for* "salvation." The language is theological, not sociological.

Throughout history there has been great speculation about the identity of those who are sealed. Premillennial dispensationalists take the first group ("the 144,000") to be the remnant of Israel (or Jews who convert to Christianity) in the end times and the second ("the great multitude") to be the generation of end-time Christians who are either "raptured" to heaven and spared the horrors of the great tribulation awaiting humanity at the close of history or Gentile saints who are martyred during that tribulation on account of their loyalty to Christ.[9] Others, arguing from references to the martyred witnesses described in chapter 6:9-11, in 11:3-12 and to the group of 144,000 in Revelation 14:1-5, find a common identity for both groups. They represent a segment of the church, those martyrs of God in all times and places who have served God faithfully to the point of death,

---

9. One cannot resist noting the misguided sectarianism of the Jehovah's Witnesses in their claim that the number 144,000 refers to the first generation of their followers exclusively and has no pertinence to Jews or Christians.

without distinction of race.[10] While both views are defensible, depending on mindset and theological perspective, each is guided by its understanding of the book of Revelation as a whole. As we have already noted, Revelation is an apocalyptic book and should not be read as presenting a timetable of end-time events. Those who argue that this vision represents the eschatological bliss of the elect or, more narrowly, the martyrs in heaven, must explain the references to earth in 7:1 and 3. The context indicates that the author is alluding to people on earth.

The dispensational view, which interprets Revelation literalistically, views the 144,000 as Jews or Jewish Christians, but this cannot be the case, since the same number in 14:1–5 cannot be limited in this way. Furthermore, taking the word "Israel" literally in 7:4 presents more problems than it solves. For example, the list of the twelve tribes is peculiar, when we compare it with the great biblical lists in Genesis 49 or Deuteronomy 33. The list omits the tribe of Dan, includes the priestly tribe of Levi (which was never among the territorial tribes), and also adds a tribe of Joseph (instead of the usual Ephraim) while including the tribe of Manasseh, one of Joseph's children. The dispensational approach, a fairly recent approach to eschatology and the book of Revelation, constructs futuristic scenarios that are speculative, sectarian, and contentious. They are contrary to anything John might have had in mind and are simply not helpful for the modern church. In the past, the predictive approach to Revelation has proven to be false and has distracted adherents from the church's mission on earth.

The second outlook affirms a common identity for both groups but misidentifies these believers. It seems clear that both visions refer to the same group, but John has in mind the entire church and not just a portion of believers. While John does use the word "Israel" in 7:4, his usage should be applied to all Christians, regardless of their nationality. He would certainly have described himself as a Jewish Christian, as evidenced in Revelation 2:9 and 3:9, where believers are the true Jews. Paul clearly understood all Christians to constitute "the Israel of God" (Gal. 6:16). For Paul, Abraham is "the ancestor of all who believe" (Rom. 4:11) and believers are thus his descendants (Gal. 3:7). Elsewhere in the Pauline corpus believers are the true Jews (Rom. 2:28–29), God's own people (Titus 2:14), and "the circumcision" (Phil. 3:3).

We need to recall that John often uses multiple images to describe the same thing, only from different perspectives. As with the Lion and the Lamb in 5:5–6, we notice that John *hears* (7:4) the number—144,000, 12,000 from each tribe—but then, when he looks, he *sees* (7:9) a great multitude that no

---

10. Caird, *Revelation*, 94–96.

one can count. This strongly suggests the same people, symbolically represented as the complete people of God (12,000 times 12). And the people in this great crowd have not escaped suffering, but have survived safely, as Jesus passed through death to eternal life. Moreover, John speaks of the New Jerusalem as the spiritual home of all believers, having on its gates the names of the twelve tribes (21:23). There is thus good reason for seeing all the 144,000 as believers.

In Revelation 14:1–5, the number 144,000 describes those who "follow the Lamb wherever he goes" (14:4). The language there is clearly metaphorical, since the followers of the Lamb are described as those "who have not defiled themselves with women, for they are virgins" (14:4). Taken literally, that would mean that only an exclusive group of celibate men could be followers of Jesus—not women or married men. Such interpretation is inconsistent with the universal redeeming love of God we find in Jesus Christ. In both scenes, if we can resist fixating on the number 144,000, we find splendid pictures of the Christian community. *We* are the saints of God who have been sealed. *We* are to "follow the Lamb wherever he goes" (14:4). And wherever *we* go, Jesus is with us, leading us on a journey into a new way of life. This is the picture John wants us to carry into our daily lives.

In the second vision (7:9–17), John returns to where the vision began, the heavenly throne room, where he "sees" many of the same people, only pictured in a new way. In 5:13 he heard all earthly and heavenly creatures praising "the one seated on the throne and . . . the Lamb." This time John sees a multicultural multitude "from every nation, from all tribes and peoples and languages, standing before the throne and before the Lamb" (7:9). Variations of this phrase occur seven times in Revelation. It is a wondrously inclusive image for first-century churches, as for us today. The churches of Asia comprised people from various ethnicities and social groups—Jewish and Gentile Christians that included immigrants, slaves, freed slaves, and others—from many parts of the Roman Empire. As stated earlier, we do not know the details of John's own cultural identity. John wrote in Greek, but his Greek is full of grammatical peculiarities, which leads many scholars to conclude that Greek was neither his first language nor the first language of many of his readers. John may have been a refugee from Palestine, following the Jewish war against Rome in AD 70.

Revelation 7:9–12 describes this multitude waving palm branches and singing hymns. This liturgical activity represents thanksgiving and praise of Christians for the salvation procured by God and the Lamb. The word "salvation" in 7:10 translates more effectively as "victory," for it is not salvation from sin that John has in mind but the Hebrew cognate "victory." Revelation

7:9–17 presents the church from the point of view of heaven, triumphant.[11] As in 6:9–11, those who have "conquered" are dressed in the white robes of victors, holding palm branches, also emblems of triumph. They have "won" only from the heavenly perspective of the Lamb's definition of winning, for on earth they have died.[12] They join the heavenly host of angels, elders, and living creatures in a hymn of praise practically identical to the sevenfold praise of 5:12. This multitude consists of those who have come "out of the great ordeal" (7:14), an ordeal, sometimes translated as "the great tribulation," great because all-inclusive. It represents all the persecutions and trials of God's people, not simply a futuristic seven-year period of persecution led by an antichrist, as commonly depicted by dispensationalist authors, preachers, and evangelists.

The final vision in this interlude introduces various paradoxical images. In an incongruous combination of colors and imagery, those who have successfully endured the spiritual struggles of life on earth have washed their robes and made them white "in the blood of the Lamb." Those words, taken literally, are paradoxical, but they do convey the symbolism consistent throughout the New Testament, that their present blessedness and fitness to appear in the presence of God have been won for them by the sacrificial death of Christ. What John conveys here with startling symbolism is expressed more prosaically by Paul: "Work out your own salvation with fear and trembling; for it is God who is at work in you, enabling you both to will and to work for his good pleasure" (Phil. 2:12–13).

The chapter ends with an even more paradoxical image: Christ is both Lamb and shepherd, guiding the multitude to springs of living water (7:17; cf. 21:6; 22:1). God's people will not hunger or thirst on their new journey, nor will any scorching wind or sun touch them (7:16). This verse is drawn from Isaiah 49:10. John's chapter ends with words of comfort and consolation that point us to John's grand finale, when the new heaven and the new earth become one: "And God will wipe away every tear from their eyes" (see Rev. 21:4).

The Seventh Seal: Silence and Prayer (Chapter 8:1–5)

As the salvation interlude concludes, the Lamb opens the seventh seal. The result is mysterious, almost ominous—there is silence for half an hour. Is it the awe-inspiring silence of being in the presence of God, or is it a foreboding stillness, like that in the eye of a hurricane? However we view it, we need

---

11. Ibid., 100.
12. Boring, *Revelation*, 131.

to recall that this is the *seventh* seal, and that the seventh day for Jews and early Christians was the Sabbath, a cessation of the mundane and a time for peace, quietness, prayer, worship, and rest.

From a literary perspective, the vision of the seven trumpets is introduced in 8:2–5, where an angel offers up the victims' prayers for justice. This passage brings to mind the heavenly throne room in 5:8, where the four living creatures and the twenty-four elders fall before the Lamb, "each holding a harp and golden bowls full of incense, which are the prayers of the saints." Once again we learn that heaven and earth are umbilically connected, with ordinary, faithful prayers on earth appearing in heaven as sweet-smelling incense. The same is likely true of all human worship, with the heavenly harps corresponding to the hymns sung by humans to God's praise. Worshippers on earth are no longer spectators but actors on a cosmic stage (5:10). In Revelation 8:3 an angel appears at the altar in heaven, and this time given a large quantity of incense. The incense and the prayers, it seems, are not exactly the same. Perhaps the prayers are the coals on which the incense burns. Either way, the prayers of God's people are offered before God's throne.

The sequence of divine judgments, necessary for evil to be conquered and God's glorious new world to emerge, is not a mechanical plan that will march forward inexorably, irrespective of human agency, for God is committed to working in the world through human beings. Prayer is a vital element in this endeavor (cf. Rom. 8:26–27). The angel, having offered the incense, fills the censer with fire from the altar and throws it on the earth (in Revelation 15 and 16 John explores this idea under the imagery of "the seven golden bowls full of the wrath of God," 15:7). Until evil has been judged, condemned, and uprooted from the earth, the only word that earth can hear is judgment. The phrase "thunder, rumblings, lightning, and earthquake" of 8:5 appears at critical junctures throughout the book, beginning with its initial appearance at God's throne in 4:5. The expression brings to completion the vision of the seven seals, as it does the vision of the trumpets (11:19) and the bowls of wrath (16:18).

Essay 4: The Old Testament Background of Revelation

Readers of Revelation soon realize that much of its language is filled with references to events and characters of the Old Testament. Despite this dependence, including a great deal of phraseology taken directly from Old Testament books, there is not one direct quotation from the Old Testament.

Of the 404 verses that comprise Revelation, 70 percent (278) contain one or more allusions to an Old Testament passage.[13] In addition, scholars have found in Revelation allusion to some 250 different passages from the Old Testament.[14] Apparently John had so thoroughly pondered the Hebrew scriptures that when recording his visions, he expressed himself by using phrases borrowed from across the spectrum of that literature, including not only the prophets of Israel but also the Pentateuch (Torah), the Psalms, and the Wisdom tradition as well. The most influential of these were Psalms, Isaiah, Daniel, Ezekiel, Jeremiah, and Zechariah. In attempting to understand John's message and symbolism, it is instructive to consider not only John's book itself but his use of the Old Testament. The following examples serve as a sampler.

1. John uses the Hebrew scriptures as *a tool to look more deeply into his present situation*, a kind of X-ray vision not everyone has. His familiarity with biblical tradition allows him to make connections to the history of ancient Israel as he interprets the present for the churches he is addressing. When John describes the heavenly Christ in Revelation 1, he finds adequate vocabulary in the books of Daniel and Ezekiel. In his vision of heaven (4:3–8), his language and imagery are influenced by Ezekiel's daring vision of the throne-chariot of God. John's vision is thus not a reporter's account of something actually seen. It is "the literary expression in traditional terms of his prophetic experience, carefully composed to communicate his theological meaning."[15]

2. In *portraying deity*, John fully relies on the Old Testament, conveying his sense of the reality of God with a remarkable economy that takes nothing away from the divine mystery. The following titles are instructive in this regard: (a) *Creator of heaven, earth, and sea* (10:5; 14:7) draws from Exodus 20:11; (b) *He who is and who was and who is to come* (1:4, 8; 11:17; 16:5) draws from Exodus 3:14; (c) *The Almighty* (1:8; 4:8; 11:17; 15:3; 16:7, 14; 19:6, 15; 21:22) draws from Amos 3: 13 and 4:13, where it is the Septuagint translation of *Yahweh Sebaoth* (Lord of hosts);[16] (d) *The God of heaven* (11:13; 16:11) draws from Daniel 2:19; (e) *The Alpha and Omega* (1:8, 17; 22:13), draws from Isaiah 44:6 and 48:12; in Revelation the title is applied both to God and to Christ; (f) *Lord of lords* (17:14; 19:16) draws from Deuteronomy 10:17, where the title is ascribed to God by Moses in one of his

---

13. Swete, *Apocalypse*, cxxxv.

14. Tenney, *Interpreting Revelation*, 101.

15. Boring, *Revelation*, 102.

16. This title, which features the matchless power of God that none can resist, is peculiarly applicable to the political context of Revelation. The title is used nine times in Revelation but only once in the rest of the New Testament (2 Cor. 6:18).

First Vision of Judgment: Seven Seals (Revelation 6:1—8:5)

final orations prior to the conquest of Canaan by Israel; in Revelation the title is coupled with "King of kings" and is applied to Christ as he ventures to seize his kingdom from his enemies.

3. In Revelation 5:5-6 John addresses the *messianic hope* of the Old Testament, which promised that one day God would reign openly on earth, punishing the wicked and justifying the oppressed, bringing an end to their sufferings and vindicating their faith. It is unfortunate that most translations insert a paragraph break between what John hears and what he sees, for what John sees is connected to what he hears but clearly supersedes it. What John hears is couched in the traditional messianic imagery of the Old Testament: "The Lion of the tribe of Judah, the Root of David, has conquered" (5:5). What he sees "constitutes the most impressive rebirth of images he anywhere achieves":[17] the Lion is a Lamb! By a stroke of brilliant artistry John gives us the key to his use of the Old Testament. The Old Testament was indispensable to his understanding of the character and purpose of God, but for John it must now be read in the light of the fuller illumination of Christ. In much of Revelation the only title for Christ is "the Lamb," and this title is meant to control and interpret all the symbolism. It is almost as if John were repeatedly saying that "[w]herever the Old Testament speaks of the victory of the Messiah or the overthrow of the enemies of God, we are to remember that the gospel recognizes no other way of achieving these ends than the way of the Cross."[18]

4. In some instances *two or more Old Testament passages are combined by John* into one continuous thought. The following examples make this clear: (1) In Revelation 1:7, the first phrase: "Look! He is coming with the clouds," is influenced by Daniel 7:13, while the remaining material, "every eye will see him, even those who pierced him, and on his account all the tribes of the earth will wail," is influenced by Zechariah 12:10–12. (2) The picture of the conquering Christ in Revelation 19:15 is a composite of three Old Testament passages: (a) the first image, the sharp sword emerging from Christ's mouth, is taken from Isaiah 11:4; (b) the second notion, ruling the nations "with a rod of iron," is taken from Psalm 2:9; and (c) the third concept, "he will tread the wine press of the fury of the wrath of God," is probably a reference to Joel 3:13. All three passages refer to God's terminal judgment upon the earth.

5. Many *additional images of Revelation* also have roots in the Hebrew scriptures. John's memory of ancient Israel's history helps him see the similarities between Rome and other ancient empires such as Babylon. He

---

17. Caird, *Revelation*, 73.
18. Ibid., 75.

knows the way oppressors have tried to intimidate God's people in the past, and he knows how the Hebrew prophets responded. He also knows that apocalyptic hope can sustain people through difficult times, just as it had for the ancient Israelites. His use of references to the Hebrew scriptures would have been familiar to his first-century audience as well, reminding them of God's grace, mercy, and love throughout history.

6. In judgment passages, John often utilizes *theophanic language*, traditional poetic language associated with the coming or presence of God on earth (theophany). Literary theophanies describe God's presence in language descriptive of earthquakes, thunderstorms, and other natural phenomena. In the Old Testament, theophanic language is used particularly to picture the day of wrath associated with God's final appearance. The description follows a fixed pattern: the first part refers to the "going forth" or descent of Yahweh; the second refers to the resultant effect on nature (mountains quake; heaven and earth fall into confusion). This pattern is documented in the oldest poetry of Israel (Judges 5:4–5) and was in use throughout the entire biblical period. Examples of eschatological theophanies may be found in the prophetic literature of the Old Testament (Isa. 30:27; 63:1–6; Zeph. 1:14–18; Hab. 3:3–16). The sixth seal of the book of Revelation (6:12–17) introduces the typical apocalyptic pattern for the end of history, much of it drawn from Old Testament symbolism. The language is highly colorful and need not, indeed cannot, be taken literally.[19]

Questions to Ponder

1. What verse, passage, or theme stands out for you as the key to chapters 6:1—8:5 of Revelation? Support your answer.

2. After reading this segment of Revelation, how would you reconcile the phrases "the wrath of the Lamb" and "the great day of their wrath" in 6:16–17 with the love of God and the compassion of Jesus?

3. If the language of sealing (7:3) can refer to the ritual of baptism, how do you understand your baptism in light of this imagery of being sealed? (cf. 7:14)

4. After reading this segment of Revelation, how would you reconcile the prayers of God's people in 6:10 and in 8:3–4 with God's mercy and the teaching of Jesus that we should love our enemies (Matt. 5:43–48)? Should Christians be vindictive toward their adversaries and pray for

---

19. This topic is explored more fully in essay 7: "Interpreting Revelation's Violent Imagery."

retribution? How does Paul's advice in Romans 12:9–21 influence your reading of Revelation?

5. What message of hope do you find in chapters 6:1—8:5 of Revelation?

Chapter 5

Second Vision of Judgment: Seven Trumpets (Revelation 8:6—11:19)

Summary: In Revelation 8:6—11:19 we encounter John's vision of the seven trumpets. John uses conventional apocalyptic imagery in this section to emphasize that God is sovereign and in control of all things. Like the seals, God interrupts the blowing of the seventh trumpet to offer a twofold perspective on the church, promising victory for those who remain faithful in witness. The final trumpet offers divine perspective on the church's task and on God's redemptive plan (see 10:7).

Assignment: Read chapter 8:6—11:19 of Revelation

Key Passage: Revelation 11:15

Central Theme: God always has the final word; in the interim, God enables believers to witness faithfully despite the circumstances.

Learning Objectives

Participants will examine:
1. Two ways of reading the trumpet visions (from a futuristic and a literary perspective), and the effect such readings can have in shaping Christian life in the present
2. The relationship between the seals and the trumpets in Revelation's imagery of judgment

Second Vision of Judgment: Seven Trumpets (Revelation 8:6—11:19) 97

3. How the message of the seven trumpets correlates with the plagues in the book of Exodus
4. The meaning of "the abyss" in chapter 9 and of the "locusts" that emerge from its shaft
5. The meaning of the "little scroll" in chapter 10 and how it differs from the scroll with the seven seals
6. The meaning of John's symbolic imagery in chapter 11
7. John's strategic use of interludes in passages of judgment

OUTLINE TO REVELATION 8:6—11:19

I. The Six Trumpets 8:6—9:20
   A. First Four Trumpets: The Natural Plagues 8:6-12
      1. The First Trumpet: Effects upon the Earth 8:7
      2. The Second Trumpet: Effects upon the Sea 8:8-9
      3. The Third Seal: Effects upon the Fresh Water 8:10-11
      4. The Fourth Seal: Effects upon the Heavens 8:12
   B. The Eagle 8:13
   C. The Fifth Trumpet: The First Woe (Release of Demonic Forces 9:1-12
   D. The Sixth Trumpet: Release of the Four Angels 9:13-21
II. An Interlude: 10:1—11:14
   A. The Angel with the Little Scroll 10:1-11
   B. The Two Witnesses 11:1-14
III. The Seventh Trumpet: Accessibility to God 11:15-19

THE MEANING OF THE SEVEN TRUMPETS

As with the seals, there is a distinction between the first four and the last three trumpets. The first group of trumpets is largely concerned with nature and the last three with humans. More exactly the division is four, two, and one, in which case the first four deal with physical anguish and the next two with spiritual anguish. The last trumpet is singled out for emphasis by an interlude after the sixth. While the seals drew attention to threats caused by the misuse of human power, the trumpets serve as a warning of God's action in judging evil. Like the seal visions, the seven trumpets are not a prediction of future events but describe the apocalyptic pattern of woes that must precede God's victory at the End, which John saw as rapidly approaching in his own day. This second cycle is not a chronological continuation of the seals but a retelling of the first cycle at a more intense level. In the first cycle one-fourth of the earth's inhabitants were affected (6:8); in this cycle the scale grows to one-third (8:7, 9, 11, 12). The trumpets do not follow one another in a sequential pattern but function to communicate a surrealistic impression of the terror of the final judgments on evil. John sees the impending terrors as analogous to the plagues with which God struck Egypt in the exodus. There the plagues not only confronted the Egyptian misuse of power, but they served also to liberate those who were in bondage to the Pharaoh's imperialistic regime. For John, previous autocratic states, whether Egyptian, Babylonian, or others who oppressed the Israelites, were clearly comparable to the current Roman regime. From his perspective, the trumpet plagues could become good news and could be endured because the ultimate exodus was about to occur.

In this segment we will examine the visions of the seven trumpets from two contrasting perspectives: the futurist and the literary perspectives. The futuristic perspective approaches chapters 8 and 9 of Revelation as a series of predictions about future events, for this is how many traditionalists (including most dispensationalists) read Revelation today. The literary perspective views Revelation as apocalyptic literature that uses vivid imagery to indicate God's way of dealing with the world.[1]

A Futurist Approach

According to the futurist perspective John is a prophet, and like all biblical prophets, his primary task is to predict the future. In chapters 8 and 9 of Revelation John is predicting a series of coming disasters. And since he is predicting through divine inspiration, these disasters are inevitable. Some futurists conceive these disastrous events as still in our future, while recognizing that such events could start happening at any time. Other futurists think that some of these events are already taking place, a sign that we are currently in the end times.[2]

---

1. The material in this segment is adapted from Koester, *Apocalypse*, lecture 7, "Seven Trumpets, Temple, and Celebration."

2. Polls indicate that one-third of all Americans believe they are living in the final generation of history, meaning that Christ will return and the "rapture" of believers

Second Vision of Judgment: Seven Trumpets (Revelation 8:6—11:19)

In Revelation 8:3 an angel stands beside the heavenly altar. The angel offers the prayers of all Christians before God and then hurls fire down to the earth, signaling the onset of a devastating series of plagues that will destroy large sections of the earth. Seven angels appear, each holding a trumpet. As each trumpet is blown, the horrors multiply. The futuristic approach assumes that each trumpet can be equated with a particular event in human history. Some argue that the trumpet visions predict events that began to unfold in the middle of the twentieth century. The following examples illustrate how this approach works:

1. The fiery vision introduced by the first angel (8:7) is associated with World War II. The hail and fire that fall from the sky are identified with aerial bombings that occurred during the war, wreaking unprecedented devastation;

2. The second vision (8:8–9) is associated with the mushroom clouds that followed the nuclear blasts at Hiroshima and Nagasaki to end World War II. This is the said to be the meaning of "something like a great mountain, burning with fire," that is thrown into the sea, turning a third of the sea to blood and bringing destruction to ships and death to many sea creatures;

3. The third vision (8:10–11) is associated with the 1986 meltdown of the nuclear reactor at Chernobyl in the former Soviet Union. This is the meaning of the star called Wormwood that falls from heaven, embittering the waters of the earth and causing those who drink these waters to die;

4. The fourth vision (8:12) is associated with the Gulf War of 1991, which ended when Saddam Hussein set hundreds of oil wells on fire, darkening the sky with smoke. This is the meaning of the sky becoming dark and the light of the sun, moon, and stars being dimmed;

5. The fifth vision (9:1–11) is associated with modern attack helicopters, which have human pilots, yet fly like insects and can shoot fire in combat. For some people, this is the meaning of the locusts that fly out of the underworld, having faces like human beings, teeth like lions, scales like iron breastplates, noisy wings, and the mysterious power to inflict pain using their tails;

6. The sixth vision (9:13–19) is associated with the war in Iraq, which lies along the Euphrates. This is the meaning of the enormous army

---

will occur in their lifetime; for them, the events of Revelation are beginning to unfold.

of demonic horses and riders gathered at the river Euphrates; the fire-breathing horses are said to be prophecies about modern tanks.

Those who follow this script find the pattern unfolding with a kind of mechanical precision, bringing humanity to the moment when the seventh trumpet is blown, the signal that the end has come. They find comfort and assurance that God has a plan and that events are occurring as they should. This understanding of Revelation, while imaginative, is fanciful and misguided, for Revelation is not prophetic in that way. The book is apocalyptic in nature and its imagery is symbolic; the intention is to warn and reassure believers living under an oppressive Roman regime during the late first century. To interpret the imagery as predictive of events in the future is to distort the author's intention; such interpretation would have been meaningless and totally incomprehensible to the original audience.

A Literary Approach

Those who take a literary approach to Revelation interpret this sequence quite differently. They note that in the prologue to the trumpet vision (8:2–5), John speaks of a temple in heaven, with a golden altar before the throne. They are aware that earlier, in chapters 4 and 5, readers are introduced to God's heavenly throne room, where God is praised as the Creator of all things. When God is joined by Jesus the Lamb, all living things gather to give praise. If God is Creator and life-giver, it is unimaginable that God would want to devastate the world he has made. A literary perspective views God to be on the side of life, not death.

The vision of the seven seals provides additional context. The fifth seal (6:9–11) introduced the martyrs, the victims who had suffered unjustly on account of their faith. They long for justice, while it seems that the perpetrators of injustice are being allowed to continue their work unchecked. The innocent suffer, and their cry for justice informs the vision of the seven trumpets. The saints under the altar ask how long before God brings justice against a wicked world (6:10); the trumpet visions provide a surprising answer. Not told when God will bring a final judgment against the world, the saints are given a rationale for God's delay. One might speculate that the reason for the delay is to lead people to repentance, but the trumpet visions indicate that sending plagues of wrath against the world does not produce repentance. God could hurl punishment from heaven repeatedly and it would not change a thing. As 9:20–21 indicates, the reason for the delay in bringing final judgment is not to allow for repentance but rather to provide believers with additional time to bear witness, to call for change in the world. That is John's reason for introducing the two witnesses in chapter 11, because change is what God desires.

What the trumpet visions reveal is not that plagues of wrath are inevitable, but that plagues of wrath are ineffectual. In Revelation 8 John seems to be saying, "Let me show you what an outpouring of divine wrath would look like." The author then provides an unimaginable nightmare as plague after plague affect the wicked on earth from every side. We see flames falling from the sky, scorching the earth with fire and turning the sea into blood. In chapter 9, demonic beings rise from the abyss below. These monsters are as hideous as anything the Jews, Greeks, or Romans had ever imagined. John then portrays the horrors of warfare coming from the east, with supernatural armies numbering in the hundreds of millions bringing death and carnage to the world. But as the nightmare reaches the climax, after six of the trumpets have blown, nothing changes in humanity's relationship to God or to each other. John indicates that humans do not repent of their idolatry and false worship (9:20–21). God could send plagues of wrath against a sinful world but nothing would change. People would simply continue on the paths of unfaithfulness and injustice. Punishment does not seem to be effective.

A remarkable thing now happens in Revelation, when we take its literary context seriously. After six trumpets have blown their warning and nothing changes, we expect the last trumpet to sound and bring final devastation upon the world. It seems that this is to happen in chapter 10, when John sees a mighty angel descending from heaven, "wrapped in a cloud, with a rainbow over his head; his face was like the sun, and his legs like pillars of fire" (10:1). The angel plants his feet on the sea and the land and then seven thunders begin to roar. It would seem that the end has come. But then a voice from heaven interrupts the movement toward judgment, telling John not to write down what the thunders are saying. That message is not the one God intends. God interrupts the movement toward final judgment in order to do something different.

ANALYSIS OF REVELATION 8:6—11:19

Having examined the flow of the argument in chapters 8 and 9 and having assessed its literary meaning, we need to address some of the remaining details, not to solve a mystery or decipher a timetable but to explore John's peculiar imagery contextually in order to understand his intended message more clearly.

PART II: God's Message of Warning

The First Four Trumpets (Chapter 8:6–13)

Like the first four seals, the first four trumpets belong together. John seems to have in mind here the ten plagues with which God struck Egypt at the time of the exodus. The plagues mentioned in the first, second, and fourth trumpet visions are allusions to the seventh plague (Exod. 9:23–26), the first plague (Exod. 7:20–21), and the ninth plague (Exod. 10:21) respectively. The third vision, like the second, contains an allusion to the first plague; the locusts in the fifth trumpet vision also have a connection with the plagues, in this case the eighth (Exod. 10:12). Just as Egypt was smitten with plagues as both a warning and a means of liberation, so the whole world is to experience similar plagues as warnings to its inhabitants and for the deliverance of God's people.

The image of the burning mountain in 8:8 might have been inspired by the eruption of Mount Vesuvius in AD 79, although John was probably recalling Old Testament imagery, where mountains symbolize nations (Isa. 13:4; Jer. 51:25; Isa. 10:32) or obstacles to faith (Zech. 4:7). For example, in Jeremiah 51 the burning of a mountain indicates that Babylon is subject to God's judgment. The idea of a huge mountain being thrown into the sea was familiar from other Jewish writings of the time, and it was an image used by Jesus (Mark 11:23).

The picture of a giant star falling from the sky in 8:10 alludes to the old story of a fallen angel being cast out of heaven; in Isaiah 14:12 the ancient legend is applied to the king of Babylon. The star is named Wormwood (bitter herb), and it embitters a third of the waters. The background of Wormwood is difficult to determine. While the name appears twice in the Old Testament (Jer. 9:15; Prov. 5:4; cf. Deut. 29:18), there is no clear explanation as to why John gives the star a name. In the Bible, rivers and fountains, when pure, are sources of life and serve as symbols of spiritual nourishment (Deut. 8:7; Ps. 1:3). Impure fountains, on the other hand, have the opposite spiritual effect (Prov. 25:26), for bitter water is unable to sustain life and growth.

A brief interlude marks the transition between the fourth and fifth trumpet visions. A solitary eagle (the Greek word *aetos* can also mean "vulture") flies high in the sky, proclaiming a threefold warning to the earth's inhabitants. The triple woe is related to the three trumpet blasts which are yet to sound. The first is said to have occurred already in 9:12 and the second in 11:14. The third woe, however, is not specifically mentioned, though some interpreters locate it in the descent of Satan to the earth in 12:12. The solemn words of the eagle indicate either that the plagues to come are worse than those already experienced or a change in focus. If the image represents a vulture, that presents an ominous picture, for a vulture hovering over something indicates death. But if John is thinking of an eagle, particularly one flying "in midheaven" (cf. 14:6), the verdict could be auspicious, for such an image is reminiscent of Isaiah 40:31, where the suffering exiles are told they will fly like eagles, a metaphor for renewal and newness of life. In this case John's trumpet plagues could be promissory, the birth-pangs of God's new age.

Furthermore, the Greek word *ouai*, translated as "woe" in verse 13, can express deep lamentation or mourning, as in the laments over Rome in chapter 18, where the same Greek word is translated "alas" (18:10, 16, and 19). It is as if God is lamenting the suffering of the world instead of cursing it: "Alas for the inhabitants of the earth." In the Bible, lament conveys God's sympathy in a way that "woe" does not.

The Fifth and Sixth Trumpets (Chapter 9:1-21)

The image of a star falling from heaven to earth reappears in 9:1. In the Bible, particularly in apocalyptic contexts, angels are often associated with stars. Like the third trumpet, the vision of the fifth trumpet (9:1-12) seems to have been influenced by the ancient myth of the fallen angels, which appears frequently in traditional apocalyptic literature. One version of this account tells how Athtar the "Day Star" (Venus) unsuccessfully attempted to replace the Canaanite deity Baal but was cast to the earth instead. In Isaiah 14:4-20 this mythical pattern is applied to the king of Babylon, who aspired to attain the divine throne but instead was cast down to the pit of Sheol, the abode of the dead. Isaiah 14:12 is a taunt against that king: "How you are fallen from heaven, O Day Star [translated "Lucifer" in the King James Bible], son of Dawn [Shahar, the name of a Canaanite deity]!" Although the myth originally had nothing to do with the idea of Satan or the origin of evil, this connection was later made in Jewish and Christian tradition. In other adaptations of the myth, an entire order of angels came down from heaven and corrupted earth (cf. Gen. 6:1-4), but the good angels defeated and imprisoned them in the Abyss (1Enoch 6-10; 54; 2 Baruch 56). In various versions of the myth, evil angels were placed in the pit for future judgment (2 Pet. 2:4). An additional apocalyptic element included the notion that evil would be restrained for a time, only to reemerge at the end, when it would be defeated forever. John uses this general pattern in in his understanding of history as a whole, particularly in his description of the final events in 19:11—20:15.

Interpreters disagree on the identity of the "star" in 9:1. While some connect it with a Lucifer, an evil spirit, or even with Satan, others see it as a representative of God (cf. 20:1). According to Revelation 1:20, where John spoke of the seven stars as "angels of the seven churches," the image of a "star" can have a positive as well as a negative connotation. In the context of Revelation 20:1–3 the angel cannot be Satan, for this angel holds the key to the bottomless pit (the Abyss), where Satan is eventually bound.

Taken literally, the notion of a "bottomless pit" contradicts reason, for a pit by definition has a bottom. The image is clearly symbolic of the underworld, which in John's cosmology lies under the world and like the entire cosmos must one day be redeemed. To understand this imagery we must revisit the ancient Near-Eastern creation myth, in which God subdued the ocean monster of chaos (named Tiamat, Leviathan, or Rahab) and out of the two halves of its body made heaven and earth. In Genesis 1 this myth survives in the division of the waters above the firmament from the waters under the earth (Gen. 1:6–8) and in the word *tehom* in verse 2 (the Deep), which in the Septuagint is translated by the Greek word Abyss. While John and his contemporaries believed in a three-story universe, they did so for theological rather than geographical reasons. They recognized that within God's created order there were elements resistant to God's will. This pit, like a black hole in modern astrophysics, is "a place of anti-creation, anti-matter, of destruction and chaos."[3] Spiritually, it represents the black hole inside us all. Like Pandora's Box, it must be kept under restraint, for it represents the virulence of evil, to which all humans contribute and by which all are affected.[4] The bottomless pit, though inhabited by malevolent forces, is subject to God's control.

When the star-angel opened the shaft, smoke arose like that of a great furnace, darkening the sun and polluting the air. From the smoke came a swarm of demonic locusts, a further reminder of the plagues of Egypt (Exod. 10:4–6). John's description owes a great deal to the first two chapters of Joel, in which the prophet depicts a plague of locusts as an invading army of the Lord, sent to punish God's people and to summon them to repentance. Locusts were familiar in biblical times, representing an unstoppable force that devoured everything in its path. But these are not ordinary locusts. Instead of injuring grass and plants they injure humans, doing so with a scorpion's sting. In the Middle East, scorpions do not kill humans, but their poison attacks the nervous system, unleashing an excruciating pain that lasts for hours (9:6). Unlike natural locusts, these locusts have a king named

---

3. Wright, *Revelation*, 86.
4. Caird, *Revelation*, 118–19.

Second Vision of Judgment: Seven Trumpets (Revelation 8:6—11:19)

Abaddon, the destroyer. Lest readers fail to grasp the significance of this Hebrew name, John adds the Greek equivalent, Apollyon, a pun for Apollo, the divine name the emperor Domitian used for himself. Furthermore, the locust was the symbol for the god Apollo.

John's power of description is amazing, for these locusts have human faces, they wear gold crowns, their hair is like women's hair, and their teeth are like lions' teeth. Their mission is to attack the oppressors of the Christians for a period of five months (9:5)—the usual lifecycle of certain species of natural locusts. Just as the Israelites were exempt from the plagues of Egypt, so now Christians who have God's seal upon their foreheads will be completely unharmed by these terrible creatures.

When the sixth angel blows his trumpet (9:13), he summons a vast cavalry, two hundred million in number (two-thirds of the current population of the United States), to cross the Euphrates River and to kill a third of humanity. This passage alludes to the first seal (6:1-2), where the bow carried by rider signified the Parthian threat lying on the eastern border of the Roman Empire. The four angels who are bound at the Euphrates are not those mentioned in 7:1 but are likely evil angels, another allusion to the mythical pattern of fallen angels discussed in the fifth trumpet vision. By picturing such a vast demonic army intruding into the civilized world, John again heightens anxiety to an apocalyptic level. The bizarre description of the horses and the plagues they unleash is reminiscent of the Parthian barbarians, elevated to demonic proportion.

The first six trumpets represent warnings of evil's appearance at its worst; it will eventually self-destruct! Despite the dire imagery, the overall intention of the seven trumpets is not to inflict vengeance but to bring people to repentance. Though we need not take these visions literally, we should take them seriously. The key lies in verses 20 and 21. Like devout Jews of his day, John believed that human evil emerged from idolatry: one becomes like what one worships. Those who worship that which is not God become something other than the image-bearing human beings they were meant to be. Those who worship idols that are blind, deaf, and lifeless become blind, deaf, and lifeless.

Six trumpets later, the world has not repented. We expect the seventh trumpet, but as with the seventh seal, John makes us wait.

Interlude: A Vision of the Faithful Church (Chapter 10:1—11:19)

In this interlude, as in John's parenthesis in chapter 7, two interrelated visions are presented. The first concerns a "little scroll" and the second presents a composite picture of authentic witness spanning biblical history. Both describe the worshipping community, whether the duties it performs or the troubles it undergoes.

In chapter 10 John sees descending from heaven a mighty angel, whose description combines elements elsewhere used of God and Christ. Like God in the Old Testament, this angel is clothed in a cloud (Exod. 19:9; Ps. 104:3; cf. Ps. 18:9–12) and speaks like a roaring lion (Amos 3:8). Like God enthroned as the sovereign of the universe in 4:1–3, he is surrounded by a rainbow (4:3), holding a scroll in his right hand (5:1). Like the description of Christ in chapter 1, his legs are like pillars of fire (cf. 1:15) and his face shines like the sun (cf. 1:16). But this angel is neither God nor Christ, for nowhere in Revelation are God or Christ identified as angels. While in the Bible the word "cloud" is often a metaphor for God's glory and holiness (Jesus is said to ascend in a cloud and will return on a cloud), such references are not limited to divine presence but can depict the mediated authority and power of God. John seems to be indicating that because he holds in his hand God's scroll, this angel represents God's authority and will.

Unlike the scroll with the seven seals, which God held in his hand in 5:1, this scroll is said to be small. It is not size that matters, however, for the contrast is not between "large" and "small" but between "sealed" and "open." The scroll, which is not the sealed scroll of chapter 5, is a special message from God to John. The connection of this scene with Daniel 12:1–10 is important. Although John changes many of the details, the great angel standing above the waters and commanding the sealing of a message is taken from Daniel 12:6–7. Unlike Daniel, who is commanded to "keep the words secret and the book sealed until the time of the end" (Dan. 12:4), John's scroll is open, meaning that its message pertains to the near future, for the time of its fulfillment is near (Rev. 10:6).

At this moment another cycle of seven is introduced briefly, only to be removed again (10:3–4). The effect is tantalizing. This cycle, which involves seven thunders, was witnessed by John. He was about to put its content into writing, but was forbidden to do so. While the purpose may be mainly dramatic, the message indicates that some things must be kept secret (cf. 2 Cor. 12:4). The figure of the thunders and the prohibition to write are best understood as a literary means to stress that no one can know the day and hour of the end. This message warns against the kind of date-setting that characterizes innumerable schemes of prophecy based on this book. What we *need* to know is accessible; the remainder is not.

The "mystery of God" in 10:7 refers to the plan of God to bless all humanity through Abraham (Gen. 12:3) and his progeny, meaning ethnic Jews (cf. Isa. 49:6) but culminating for Christians in Jesus (cf. Eph. 3:3–6;

Col. 1:27). Christians in New Testament times understood God's "mystery" as a reference to something hidden in the Old Testament but now made clear through apostles and prophets such as Paul and John. The angel is said to have one foot on the sea and the other on the land (10:2, 5) simply to indicate that his message is inclusive and universal.

At this point John is told to take the scroll and eat it, meaning he is to read it eagerly and to internalize its message. In his mouth the scroll is sweet as honey, but in his stomach it is bitter (10:10), signifying that while receiving God's message is sweet, its contents makes John sorrowful. The subject matter of the scroll is likely that of chapter 11:1–13, where John divulges the message he has digested concerning how the followers of Christ are to conquer the idolatrous and destructive powers of the beast, imitating the Lamb in witness, sacrifice, and victory.

The reference in John's vision to a scroll is based on Ezekiel 3:1–3, though in Ezekiel's case the message remains sweet because it stays in his mouth. For John, who fully assimilates the message, it becomes like Jeremiah's "burning fire shut up in [his] bones" (20:9), an unpleasant communication that must be proclaimed because he carries it in his bloodstream and it dwells in his bones. Contemporary Christians, like John, need such passion for God and for scripture. What good is pedantic, careful scrutiny of a biblical text if the fire does not burn within? Having assimilated the contents of the scroll, John is commanded to proclaim it "to many peoples and nations and languages and kings" (10:11), meaning everyone. This is a favorite expression of John's, one he uses seven times, though only here does it include "kings" (cf. 5:9; 7:9; 11:9; 13:7; 14:6; 17:15).

What follows in chapter 11 is acknowledged to be one of the most perplexing sections of the entire book. A bewildering collection of symbols interwoven from Old Testament literature provide reference to the temple and the altar, to Moses and Elijah, to the wild olive trees and the lampstand seen by Zechariah, to the plagues sent upon Pharaoh, to the tyrant predicted by Daniel, and to Sodom, Egypt, and Jerusalem. The first three verses alone are said to be so enigmatic that to understand them is to comprehend Revelation. The key lies in discriminating between what is to be understood literally and what is to be understood symbolically. We can state with confidence that "the author views the people of God as bearing faithful testimony but also as suffering pain and persecution and indignity. They are delivered not *from* martyrdom and death, but *through* martyrdom and death to a glorious resurrection."[5]

---

5. Metzger, *Breaking the Code*, 68.

When John says that he was given a measuring rod and told to "measure the temple of God and the altar and those who worship there" (11:1), this cannot refer to the Jewish temple in Jerusalem, for when John is writing, the temple had been lying in ruins for some twenty years after the city was sacked by Roman armies in AD 70. And the reference cannot be to a temple yet to be built on the spot of the old, unless one misses the apocalyptic nature of Revelation and is content simply to speculate about the unknown future. As elsewhere, John here seems to have been inspired by Ezekiel, who envisioned the new temple and God's future kingdom (chapters 40–48) and who measures the temple's precincts in chapters 40–43. The purpose of the new temple, which foreshadows John's New Jerusalem in Revelation 21–22, is made clear to Ezekiel by a message from within the temple: "Mortal, this is the place of my throne . . . where I will reside among the people of Israel forever" (Ezek. 43:7).

The connection of this scene with the visions of Daniel is also important, particularly the references to forty-two months (again in 13:5) and one thousand two hundred and sixty days (again in 12:6) in Revelation 11:2–3. The meaning of these mysterious references is associated with the phrase "three and a half days" in 11:9, an expression that holds the key to a series of temporal concepts in Revelation, including the enigmatic "time, and times, and half a time" (12:14). These expressions are co-terminus, so if we decipher one, we can understand all. The key to their meaning is found in Daniel 7:25 and 12:7, where "a time" equals one year, "times" equals two years, and "half a time" equals six months. This is the traditional apocalyptic term of Gentile domination, the length of time that the Syrian ruler Antiochus IV Epiphanes tyrannized the Jews in Jerusalem (from 167 to 164 BC). This period of time (forty-two months) is one thousand two hundred and sixty days, which defines the period during which the two witnesses in Revelation exercise their ministry (11:3), the woman stays in the wilderness (12:6, 14), and the beast exercises authority (13:5).

In the Old Testament scene, Daniel asks the poignant question of suffering apocalyptic communities, "How long?" (12:6). The angelic figure replies, "three and a half years." John receives and passes on this picture to his audience. He believes he is living in the eschatological end-time, for unlike Daniel, he sees an angel with an unsealed book swearing that there will be no more delay (10:6–7). The time of waiting and hoping is over; the time of fulfillment dawns. But before it arrives, there is the pre-dawn darkness of the final tribulation announced by Daniel, "a time of anguish, such as has never occurred" (Dan. 12:1). John believes he and his churches are already entering this final terrible period. The one thousand two hundred and sixty days is not for him speculative but promissory: the tribulation will not last long!

In 11:1-3 we avoid many problems if we keep in mind that John refers to the Christian church when he speaks of "the temple of God." Earlier, in the messages to the churches at the beginning of the book, John used the concept of the temple as a metaphor for the worshipping community. There he referred to a temple with human beings as its pillars and columns (3:12). John's description of the Holy City in chapters 21 and 22 does not include a physical temple building, for there God dwells in the community of believers. This idea was already present in the Pauline tradition, where God's people are said to be "God's temple" (1 Cor. 3:16; cf. 2 Cor. 6:16). In a later epistle, Christians are called living stones, built into a spiritual house (1 Pet. 2:5). Thus the whole church is growing "into a holy temple in the Lord" (Eph. 2:21). For John, the temple is not an actual building but the Christian community that worships God. The "measuring" of the temple, like the earlier "sealing" of God's people (7:3-4), is to mark it out for protection. This does not mean that Christians will be exempt *from* suffering and death but that they are protected *through* these tribulations. In addition, measuring is done to build and repair, and John is therefore given a measuring rod so that he can restore and revive the church.[6]

To call the two witnesses "prophets" in 11:10 is not to say that they spend three and a half years making predictions. Those who "prophesy" speak and act for God. In that sense they may be designated "martyrs" (cf. 6:8-11; 7:14-17), for the Greek word translated "martyr" can be translated "witness," and the ministry of martyrs is summed up in 11:7 in the word "testimony" (*martyria*). For John, "prophet" and "martyr" were not two words but one; the prophetic ministry is "martyrdom." The two martyr-prophets of 11:1-13 represent in John's imagery the entire church in its faithful witness to the world. Their story must be taken neither literally nor even as an allegory, as though the sequence of events in this story was supposed to correspond to a sequence of events in the church's history. The story is more like a parable, which dramatizes the nature and the result of the church's witness.

Their ministry takes place during the age of the church, which John characterizes as forty-two months (or one thousand two hundred and sixty days; three and a half years; and three and a half "days"). Their ministry takes place in "Jerusalem," for they are God's holy temple in God's "holy city" (11:2). The "two witnesses" are the "two olive trees" and "the two lampstands" of Zechariah's vision (Zech. 4:1-14), reflections of Joshua the priest

---

6. Ibid., 69.

and Zerubbabel the king. They represent the channels through which God's power flows and are thus appropriate symbols for the church.

That the church is a community of royal priests is one of Revelation's themes throughout (1:6; 5:10; cf. 20:6). The witnesses are called "lampstands" in 11:4, explained as "churches" in 1:20. When they are killed, people throughout the world gaze on the dead bodies of the witnesses (11:9), a reference to the small vulnerable Christian community scattered across the Roman Empire without legal status or protection and therefore indiscriminately subject to persecution, locally or empire-wide.

The two witnesses are pictured as representing the prophets Moses (11:6; cf. Exod. 7:17–19) and Elijah (11:5–6; cf. 1 Kgs. 17:1; 2 Kgs. 1:10–12; Jas. 5:17–18), two biblical figures who were believed not to have died but to have been taken bodily to heaven. According to apocalyptic tradition, two such figures would return to prepare the way before the coming of God or the Messiah at the End (2 Esdras 6:26; cf. Mal. 3:1–4; 4:4–6; for an expansion of this tradition, see Matt. 11:7–15 and 17:1–13). But they are not Elijah and Moses in the flesh, since the powers of both Elijah and Moses are attributed to both witnesses (11:6). Nor do Moses and Elijah here stand for the law and the prophets. Both figures are prophets, setting the precedent for the church's prophetic witness to the world.

The suffering of the oppressed Christian community is not here understood as mere passivity, suffering until the End comes. Rather the prophetic ministry of the church, that is, its testimony by its own suffering, is, like their prayers (5:8; 8:3–4; cf. 6:9–11), interpreted as an active agent in bringing about the final victory of God. This faithful community is thus acting powerfully (with the power of God) through its word of testimony. These two things—their willingness to give their lives and their redefinition of power in light of the crucified Lamb—represent John's Christological redefinition of power.[7] Their "power" over their enemies is not vindictive or arrogant but humble and repentant, for their ministry is conducted in "sackcloth" (11:3).

To ordinary observation (from a temporal or earthly perspective), the witnesses are powerless. In 11:7 they are attacked and killed by the beast from the bottomless pit. This demonic monster, which here appears for the first time in Revelation, is described more fully in chapters 13 and 17. John holds up an utterly realistic picture here of faithful Christian witness in response to Roman pressure. Unless they had Roman citizenship (and few Christians did), Christians possessed no legal rights in the empire, and they could easily be dispatched by the Roman courts or discriminated against by

---

7. Boring, *Revelation*, 147.

the Roman populace. Faithfulness would not deliver them from persecution but could actually precipitate it. Yet their conquest and death at the hands of the beast in 11:7 is used as a parody, for the beast's ability to "conquer" is only a weak imitation of the Lamb's power.

Amidst the gloating of their enemies the church has the last word, for God intervenes to provide his servants resurrection-life, calling them into "heaven," where they are vindicated for their faithfulness (11:12). The church's experience of being called into God's heavenly realm is no escapist "rapture" from this earth. Christians are not spared trials and tribulations but rather experience God's presence and care *through* life's struggles. The city in verse 13 is any and every city in which the church bears its prophetic witness to the nations. The visionary narrative elaborating the task and witness of the Christian community concludes with a cosmic earthquake, which causes the partial destruction of the great city and its inhabitants.

Elsewhere, where the cosmic plagues did not bring about repentance (6:12–17; 9:20–21; 16:18–21), here the prophetic witness of Christians does. Nine-tenths of the nations and citizens of the world repent and give "glory" (Gk. *doxa*, praise, honor) to God. The expression "give [God] glory" is repeated in 14:7 and announced as the content of the gospel that is proclaimed to all peoples of the earth. Thus, 11:13 seems to anticipate the pronouncement of 15:3–4 that all the nations will come and worship God. In the judgments announced by Old Testament prophets a tenth part (Isa. 6:13; Amos 5:3) or seven thousand people (1 Kgs. 19:18) are the faithful remnant who are spared when the judgment wipes out the majority. In a characteristically subtle use of allusion, John reverses this. Only a tenth suffers the judgment, and the "remnant" spared is the nine-tenths. Not the faithful minority, but the faithless majority, is spared, so that they may come to repentance and faith.[8] Thanks to the witness of the witnesses, the judgment is actually salvific. "It is crucial to recognize that Revelation's rhetoric of judgment expresses hope for the conversion of nine-tenths of the nations in response to Christian witness and preaching. Otherwise, one will not understand that the author advocates a theology of justice rather than a theology of hate and resentment."[9]

The coming of the final kingdom is also the coming of the last "woe" (cf. 8:13; 9:12; 11:14), which is not identified. While judgment is an inseparable part of John's depiction of the End, he does not have a dualistic view in which God's punishment and justice are co-equal or co-eternal with his mercy and grace. Nevertheless, because evil is real and must be punished,

---

8. Bauckham, *Theology of Revelation*, 87.
9. Schüssler Fiorenza, *Revelation*, 79.

we cannot have good news without announcing the destruction of the destroyers of the earth (11:18).

What John is emphasizing in this section is that the church, whose lot is to suffer the persecution of this world ("If they persecuted me, they will persecute you" John 15:20), will nevertheless continue to give faithful witness to the truth. By means of symbolism he focuses on the security of the church's true life and identity, which cannot be touched. The violent death of the two witnesses, their resurrection after three and a half days, and their ascension into heaven are not historical events, but are symbolic of the ultimate triumph of God's people.[10]

The Seventh Trumpet (Chapter 11:15-19)

After a lengthy but important interlude, we come finally to the sounding of the seventh trumpet. Instead of judgment on earth, John hears rejoicing in heaven, a note of finality, for the heavenly chorus is celebrating victory. The long-awaited rule of God on earth, what Christians have longed for, indeed prayed for fervently—"Your kingdom come. Your will be done, on earth as it is in heaven" (Matt. 6:10)—has become a reality: the earthly city has become the City of God, a city whose co-regent is the Messiah (11:15).

The outburst of praise is followed by a response from the twenty-four elders. They celebrate God's assumption of power, his overthrow of evil powers, his judgment of the dead, and his rewarding of the faithful (11:16-18). Suddenly God's temple is opened, revealing the Ark of the Covenant. What was previously hidden and mysterious is now open and disclosed. Central to the message of Revelation—the result of all the judgments and the essence of all the rewards—is greater access to God and a clearer vision of God's splendor. John has brought us to that point. What else remains?

If John had finished his book here, we would have considered this a proper ending, for the judgment of the dead and the rewarding of the saints is now accomplished. But John is not done. He wishes to revisit the matter and repeat his message anew, with greater detail, clarity, and finality. In particular, John needs to identify and destroy the destroyers of the earth.

---

10. Metzger, *Breaking the Code*, 70–71.

Essay 5: John's Strategic Use of Interludes in Revelation

One aspect of the structure of Revelation that many find difficult to explain is the parenthetical material that interrupts the flow of the narrative. The more important of these interludes are (1) the sealing of the 144,000 and the great multitude (7:1-17), which intervene between the sixth and seventh seals; (2) the angel with the little scroll and the two witnesses (10:1—11:14), which intervenes between the sixth and seventh trumpets, and (3) the counterfeit trinity and the angels (12:1-14:20), which intervenes between the trumpets and the bowls.

The last mentioned section may not be an actual interlude, since it is introduced by the phrase "A great portent appeared in heaven" (12:1), which parallels the phrase that introduces the seven plagues (bowls of wrath) in 15:1, "Then I saw another portent in heaven." This similarity has led numerous commentators to propose a group of seven in chapters 12-14, in part because this helps them arrive at a sevenfold pattern for Revelation, which denotes completeness or finality in the Semitic world, something they assume John intended. If chapters 12-14 are understood as a sequence of seven, then the message of the three angels and of the voice from heaven (14:6-12) may be regarded as an interlude between the sixth and seventh signs, similar to the interludes between the sixth and seventh seals and between the sixth and seventh trumpets.

The bowls parallel the seals and trumpets in message and setting. While the series of signs is not numbered, they too conform to the others in this regard. The fact that all four series come to the same general conclusion—climactic judgment and the establishment of God's rule on the earth (8:3-5; 11:15-19; 14:14-20; 16:18-20)—suggests that the series are parallel and that they present differing aspects of the same process rather than its successive historic stages. The interludes in Revelation, having been inserted intentionally, offer visions of protection and salvation. These compositions temper the horrific plagues of the book's middle chapters while providing valuable information, as the following examples demonstrate.

1. Most important about the interludes is their content, for they affirm faithful witness—not judgment or vindication—to be paramount to Revelation. In each case the movement toward final judgment is interrupted in order that the church might offer prophetic witness. This phenomenon of interrupted judgment tends to be ignored in futuristic interpretations of Revelation, but is indispensable to a literary reading of the book. Interludes are vital to John's message and are indispensable to his methodology. Those

who emphasize patterns of judgment in Revelation violate John's intention, for he regularly interrupts those visions to provide an alternative perspective. He does so because he understands God's goal to be life rather than death, renewal rather than damnation, continuity rather than discontinuity.

2. When John interrupts his patterns he seems to be reminding his readers not to get caught up in chronology or to take his imagery literally. Revelation belongs to a particular literary genre, one that uses imagery symbolically. John's intention is to provide assurance and hope, not pat answers or neat timetables. Revelation calls readers to discernment, beckoning them to ask where they too might be witnesses to God's truth in the contexts of their lives.

3. When John interrupts a cycle, the interruption is central, not the cycle. The interruption points to celebration, not destruction, to grace and not to evil. Early in the cycle of sevens John introduces minor changes in scenario, initially appearing intrusive, even bizarre, but eventually revealing their value. For example, the fifth seal shifts from the threats represented by the horsemen to the threat of injustice, a central concern for John but one that is veiled in the sequence of threats. When the Lamb opens the fifth seal, John sees martyrs, victims of violence and injustice. Like other visions, this one raises questions about the readers' most basic commitments. John pictures the victims crying out to God, yet their voices are also heard by the audience. Having heard the call for justice, will readers identify with the victims, or will they simply turn away?

4. Eschatological delay is as much a feature of Revelation as eschatological imminence. While John often indicates that his prophecy is a revelation of "what must soon take place" (1:1; cf. 1:3; 22:10), he also introduces delay into the structure of the book, as in 6:10–11, when the martyrs cry, "How long?" and are told to wait a little while longer. Interludes, such as those between the sixth and seventh seals and between the sixth and seventh trumpets, both symbolize and explain the delay. In chapter 10:6 we read that there is to be no more delay for the sake of further warning judgments, but in 11:3 we learn that there is to be a delay, lasting the symbolic period of three and a half years, for the sake of the church's prophetic witness to the world. Delay is also characterized as "a little while" (cf. 6:11; 12:12; 17:10), a phrase which assures the church that her time of trial is not indefinite. John creates his own version of the tension between imminence and delay that runs through the whole apocalyptic tradition. The logic of imminence is that God's kingdom must come, but the logic of delay is that God is patient and gracious. The tension is theological rather than merely chronological.

5. Interludes also produce suspense, using drama to greater effect. When the fourth trumpet sounds, John introduces an eagle in the heavens,

Second Vision of Judgment: Seven Trumpets (Revelation 8:6—11:19)

interrupting the sequence. The eagle announces three woes, but then only two are mentioned. When the seventh trumpet sounds, hearers expect climactic judgment, but instead find hope. Interludes of salvation and heavenly worship are one way that Revelation tempers the horrific plagues of Revelation's middle chapters.

Questions to Ponder

1. What verse, passage, or theme stands out for you as the key to chapters 8:5—11:19 of Revelation? Support your answer.
2. What assumptions do people make when reading the trumpet visions futuristically? What kind of effect might the futuristic reading of the trumpet plagues have on Christian life in the present? Conversely, what assumptions do people make when reading the trumpet visions from a literary perspective? What kind of effect might a literary reading of the trumpet plagues have on readers?
3. Should Christians expect to experience hardship for their faith? Have you ever experienced hardship on account of your faith?
4. What message of hope do you find in chapters 8:5—11:19 of Revelation?

PART III

God's Message of Judgment
Destroying the Destroyers of the Earth

Chapter 6

A Vision of Evil: Seven Significant Signs (Revelation 12–14)

Summary: At the center of Revelation (chapter 12) readers encounter two of the most dramatic stories at the heart of the book. These stories—mythological in nature—utilize flashback, for they are about Jesus' victory on the cross, an event that has already happened and in which Satan and evil are defeated. To communicate key spiritual truths, they relate the story of the birth of Apollo and the story of Satan's defeat in an epic heavenly battle. In chapter 13 we encounter two beasts—one arising from the sea and the other arising from the earth; they portray Rome's violent, conquering power over the whole world. The original readers of Revelation were victims of Roman imperial power. As in the ancient story of the exodus, salvation comes through God's action, the blood of the Lamb, and faithful witness (chapter 14).

Assignment: Read chapter 12:1—14:20 of Revelation

Key Passage: Revelation 12:11; cf. 13:10; 14:12

Central Theme: With Christ's victory on the cross, Christians are given power to defeat the forces of evil through faithful witness.

Learning Objectives

Participants will examine:
 1. The usefulness of myth to provide Christian perspective

2. The wilderness as a refuge where God's love can be found
3. The meaning of the two beasts in chapters 13
4. Living between "promise" and "fulfillment"
5. The power of Christian witness
6. The meaning of the "wine press of God's wrath" in chapter 14
7. The blessing of hope, not the distraction of fear

OUTLINE TO REVELATION 12:1—14:20

I. The Six Signs 12:1—14:20
   A. The Woman, the Dragon, and the Child 12:1-6
   B. Satan Cast from Heaven 12:7-12
   C. War Between Satan and the Woman 12:13-17
   D. The Beast from the Sea 13:1-10
   E. The Beast from the Earth 13:11-18
   F. The Lamb and the 144,000 on Mount Zion 14:1-5
II. An Interlude 14:6-13
   A. Three Angels Proclaim Judgment 14:6-12
   B. The Voice from Heaven 14:13
III. The Seventh Sign: The Harvest of the Earth 14:14-20

THE AGENTS OF EVIL

The first half of Revelation introduced readers to a series of judgments called the seven seals and the seven trumpets. One would expect that the seventh trumpet would lead into the seven last plagues (chapters 15 and 16) but that is not the case. In between comes another series of visions—the seven signs—unnumbered by John but so organized that it seems he intended them as a series. This group of visions concerns the troubles of the church in the face of evil.

The series of visions in 12:1—14:20 form the central axis of the book and the core of its argument. This section constitutes one unit, a drama of operatic proportions in which "the characters and actions are exaggerated, larger than life. Chapters 12–13 pull away the curtain that hides the

A Vision of Evil: Seven Significant Signs (Revelation 12–14)

transcendent world from ordinary sight and offers a behind-the-scenes view of the powers of evil at work in the present, while chapter 14 proleptically presents a behind-the-scenes view of the victory of God in salvation and judgment."[1] This unit introduces some of the most dramatic images in the entire book. The four depictions of evil include Satan—the great dragon hurled from the sky to prowl the earth—and Satan's cronies, consisting of a seven-headed beast from the sea, a cunning beast from the land, and Babylon the harlot. A key to this segment is the announcement of the heavenly chorus in 11:18 that the time has come to destroy the destroyers of the earth. If God is the Creator and God's will for the world is life, then he must defeat those forces that threaten life.

An analogy to help us understand John's view of evil is to consider evil as a cancer that invades a person's body. As malignant cancer cells grow, they destroy the healthy tissues around them, and if the cancer becomes aggressive, these life-destroying cells spread and damage an entire organ. From there they can spread to other parts of the body, where they do more and more damage until eventually the person dies. If life is to be preserved, the cancer must be stopped. Cancer treatment aims to restore life-giving power so that life can thrive again. Revelation views evil and its defeat in like manner. God the Creator desires a healthy organism. God's battle is with the cancer, not with the organism. Some people presume that God is out to destroy the world, but the heavenly chorus affirms that God is out to destroy evil so that life will triumph. And at the end of Revelation, that occurs. Death is abolished, and with its destruction sorrow and grief are gone as well. When death is annihilated, God's victory is complete.

When we read Revelation as a literary work, we find that the second half of the book is dominated by the struggle against these agents of evil. In following the plot, one discovers that John systematically introduces four depictions of evil, only to defeat them—in reverse order. The harlot is first to be destroyed, when the seven-headed beast turns against her (17:16). Then the two beasts are defeated, when Christ overpowers them with the sword (the word) that comes from his mouth (19:19–20). Only Satan is left, temporarily banished from earth to the abyss below only to be hurled into the lake of fire (20:10). The second half of Revelation is the story of the defeat of these agents of evil.

---

1. Boring, *Revelation*, 150.

ANALYSIS OF REVELATION 12:1—14:20

Chapter 12 represents a flashback, because chapter 11 closes with a vision of the end, including references to judging the dead, rewarding the servants of God, and opening the inner sanctum of God's temple in heaven, where the Ark of the Covenant is visible to all. In 11:17 God is described in present and past tenses ("who are and who were") but not in the future tense, as in 1:4, because the future is now present. The seventh trumpet presents the kingdom of God as having come with finality. The second half of the book takes us back to the beginning of God's cosmic conflict with evil. Two stories are told, the first about a pregnant woman in the throes of labor chased by a dragon (12:1–6 and 12:13–17) and the second the account of a cosmic battle in which Satan is thrown out of heaven, down to earth, along with his angels (12:7–12). Allusions to Satan and the fallen angels appeared previously in Revelation (see comments on 8:10 and 9:1–19). In its entirety, the vision intends "a multivalent mythological symbolization of transpersonal divine realities."[2]

The First Signs (Chapter 12:1-17)

The first story begins with two characters—a woman and a dragon—who play the role of good and evil. The dragon is undoubtedly Satan, the embodiment of evil and the antagonist of God and God's people. Ezekiel had called Pharaoh a dragon (Ezek. 29:3; 32:2), and there is no question that much of the imagery in Revelation is associated with Egypt and the exodus. John calls the great city in league with the dragon Sodom and Egypt (11:8) as well as Babylon (17:5). Egypt stands for all that is evil, and specifically for the oppression and persecution of the people of God. It is not clear why the dragon's color is red, but it is no coincidence that the beast on whom the great whore sits is scarlet, as is her clothing (17:3–4). This red dragon is a monster with seven heads and ten horns. The horn is a symbol of strength, so that ten horns depict the mighty power of the dragon (this image is also an allusion to the beast with ten horns in Daniel 7:7, 24). The point of the seven heads is not immediately clear, but the reference is repeated in chapter 13, this time as a description of the beast from the sea (13:1), and again in 17:3 and 17:9–10, where it indicates the seven hills of Rome as well as the totality of Roman imperial rule.

The identity of the pregnant woman "clothed with the sun, with the moon under her feet, and on her head a crown of twelve stars" (12:1) is

---

2. Schüssler Fiorenza, *Revelation*, 81.

A Vision of Evil: Seven Significant Signs (Revelation 12–14)

much debated. Christians acquainted with the Gospels often think of Mary, the mother of the Messiah, who is saved from wicked Herod by divine intervention (Matt. 2:1–15). This interpretation, favored by many Roman Catholic exegetes today, has a long-standing history going back to the early patristic period. This view was reiterated by Pope Pius X in his 1904 encyclical letter *Ad Diem Illum Laetissimum*: "Everyone knows that this woman signified the Virgin Mary."

In *The Lamb's Supper* (1999), Scott Hahn, a student of mine during the late 1970s and now a well-known Roman Catholic scholar who writes apologetically on behalf of Catholicism, provides commentary on Revelation, correlating its imagery with the Catholic Mass. Hahn proposes that "the key to understanding the Mass is the biblical Book of Revelation—and further, that the Mass is the only way a Christian can truly make sense of the Book of Revelation."[3] He further states that the vision of the woman in Revelation 12 represents "the essence of the Book of Revelation."[4] And who is this woman? She is Mary, the mother of Jesus. To Hahn's credit, he indicates that the image of "the woman" is polyvalent, for in addition to representing Mary she is also Israel as well as the church. Most scholars favor one or both of these latter interpretations: "In the context of Revelation, the woman clothed with the sun who is in labor is best understood as the messianic community."[5]

Dr. Hahn's method reflects a pragmatic approach generally supported by apologists, preachers, and religious communicators, who view scriptural exegesis not as an end in itself but as a means to a hermeneutical end. Every author and communicator has in mind a specific audience and targets that audience with a particular message. Because Hahn writes for devout Catholics, he communicates Catholic dogma (with an occasional evangelical twist) to that audience effectively. It is easy for Protestants to be critical of Catholic application, and vice versa. Each of us, however, when exposed to religious, political, economic, social, or cultural perspectives, should be aware that communicators write and speak autobiographically. While we need to be judicious in evaluating the perspectives of others, we should avoid regarding alternative perspectives and explanations as invalid simply because they differ from our own. Those who remain open to new ideas or possibilities may find themselves joining forces with adversaries or conceiving new dimensions for their spiritual journey. As history indicates, innovation is born from conversation. Diverse perspectives offer avenues for growth because they bear transformative potential. While rational and mature individuals

---

3. Hahn, *Lamb's Supper*, 4.
4. Ibid., 77.
5. Schüssler Fiorenza, *Revelation*, 81.

can and should disagree, they should avoid hastily judging something right or wrong, true or false, orthodox or heretical. At some contextual level most views have merit, and thus I value Dr. Hahn's interpretation, despite fundamental differences.

Eugene Boring's explanation of the pregnant woman in chapter 12 is prudent: "The woman is not Mary, nor Israel, nor the church but less and more than all of these. John's imagery pulls together elements from the pagan myth of the queen of heaven; from the Genesis story of Eve, mother of all living, whose 'seed' shall bruise the head of the primeval serpent (Gen. 3:1–16); from Israel who escapes from the dragon/Pharaoh into the wilderness on wings of an eagle (Exod. 19:4; cf. Ps 74:12–15); and Zion, 'mother' of the People of God from whom the Messiah comes forth (Isa. 66:7–9; 2 Esdras 13:32–38). She reflects the historical experience of the People of God through the ages, Israel and the church, and yet she is the cosmic woman . . ."[6]

The heavenly woman likely does not represent the Virgin Mary (since John does not appeal to other stories of Jesus' mother or family) but is a symbolic depiction of Israel, the whole people of God, imaged in cosmic terms, as evidenced by the twelve stars in her crown. This understanding would certainly have made sense to John, himself a Jewish Christian. In this story, Jesus is born of the people of God. The woman's labor pangs also draw on imagery from the Hebrew scriptures (Isa. 26:17–18; 66:7–8; Mic. 4:10; 5:3). The woman flees for protection to the wilderness, a familiar biblical place of refuge. To the wilderness Hagar fled for safety when Sarah tried to kill her and her son Ishmael (Gen. 21:14–21). In the wilderness the Israelites found refuge after the exodus. It is understood that God sustains and cares for people when they are in the wilderness. The dragon's pursuit of the woman represents persecution of God's people throughout time, whether past, present, or future. John's purpose throughout Revelation is to remind the churches that God is the only one who deserves their worship, even if they suffer for their witness.

In 12:17 we read that the woman actually has many children, namely all who keep the commandments of God and hold the witness of Jesus. This detail invites the readers to see themselves in the story of the woman. At this point John's reader can say, "That's us!" We are the ones who keep the commandments of God and the witness of Jesus. We are living the experience of the woman and her child. Ours is the world where evil is real, where the faithful are threatened and the innocent suffer.

---

6. Boring, *Revelation*, 152.

In Revelation 12:1-6 and 13-17 the pregnant woman gives birth to a son, who is clearly Jesus. We should not, however, see the birth of the child as a reference to the Nativity but rather as a reference to the Cross. Otherwise the passage would have us jump directly from the Nativity to the Ascension (12:5) without any mention of the intervening life of Jesus. In 12:5 John continues his exposition of Psalm 2, begun in the vision of the seventh trumpet. In that psalm it is not at his birth but at his enthronement that the anointed king is addressed as the son of God (Ps. 2: 7) and given authority to smash the nations with a rod of iron (2:9). A king's birthday is the day of his ascension. John is following here a well-known Christian exegesis of this psalm that declared Jesus "to be the Son of God with power" at the time of his resurrection (Rom. 1:4). "Sonship and enthronement belong inseparably together, and therefore the male child is no sooner born than he is snatched away to God and to his throne. For John [of Patmos] as for the fourth evangelist, the Cross is the point at which Jesus entered upon his kingly glory" (John 3:21).[7]

For further support that this is not the Christmas story we know from the Gospels, in Revelation 12 we see instead of shepherds, sheep, and angels a great red dragon who wants to devour the woman's child. Instead of the star that leads the wise men to Bethlehem, the stars are the crown that the woman wears on her head, with the moon under her feet. Instead of fleeing with his parents to Egypt, the boy child is snatched to heaven for safekeeping. When the dragon chases the woman, the woman acquires two wings of a great eagle and flies away. What are we to make of this cosmic story of the woman and her child, and their daring rescue?

The ancient Romans frequently related their own history in terms of mythological battle stories, sometimes recycling Greek myths to legitimize Rome's claims. At a huge altar to Zeus in the city of Pergamum (recall Rev. 2:12-17) a frieze covered with sculptures depicted battle scenes of epic proportions. Lining the main streets in many cities were arches and monuments filled with sculptures of battles and other famous scenes. Everyone living in the Roman Empire, including those to whom John was writing, would have known the epic stories of the battles and victories of these gods and goddesses.

In Revelation 12 John uses the popular story of the birth of the god Apollo to captivate the imagination of his Christian audience and to provide his followers encouragement and hope. The original myth John uses to relay his message was said to have taken place on the island of Delos, the birthplace of Apollo. His mother Leto had fled there to escape the dragon

---

7. Caird, *Revelation*, 149-50.

Python, who wanted to kill the newborn son of Zeus. At the end of the story, the child grew up and defeated the dragon. This story, found in the folklore of many peoples, is a variation of the story of how the forces of darkness, chaos, and sterility/death rebelled against the divine forces of light, order, and fertility/life, attempting to overthrow the divine order, kill the newborn king, or seize the kingdom to establish the rule of darkness. This story, like all such myths, interprets the human story as part of the cosmic conflict between good and evil while also expressing the common human experience that the darkness of night is followed by the dawning of a new day. A grateful citizen of the Roman world could readily think of the story as a reflection of his or her own experience, the woman representing the goddess Roma, the queen of heaven; the son representing the emperor, who kills the dragon and establishes the Golden Age; and the dragon representing the power of darkness that opposes the goodness of life.[8]

The sun god Apollo was a favorite of Roman emperors, including Domitian, who used Apollo to legitimize their lordship over the empire. John uses the story differently, to assert the lordship of Jesus and to help his Christian audience affirm its own identity in light of God's larger story. John wants them to comprehend their present situation as part of a larger conflict, a once-for-all victory that has already been won in Jesus' death and resurrection.[9]

If the notion of using mythology as a vehicle for talking about God makes us uncomfortable, we need to remember that such a connection would have made great sense to the original readers of Revelation. Even in our contemporary society, pastors and educators often use modern stories or movie scenes to help convey the love of Christ and the power of God. John's use of the story of Apollo's birth is not much different than using a scene from *Harry Potter* or *Star Wars* to convey Christian themes. While John incorporates references to a number of pagan myths in chapters 12 through 14, his purpose is to demonstrate that the true answer to people's problems is in Christ, not in paganism. As often happens in Revelation, what John sees he describes largely in traditional imagery, to which he gives Christian interpretation. Ultimately, his imagery is to be understood from its use in Revelation, not from its use in pagan myths. The "woman clothed with the sun," for example, is to be understood in contrast to the harlot (17:1), whereas the dragon and beasts of chapter 13 are parodies of the Trinity.

---

8. Ibid., 151.
9. Rossing, "Journeys Through Revelation," 48.

A Vision of Evil: Seven Significant Signs (Revelation 12–14)

Into this spectacular cosmic story of the woman's childbirth and rescue in the wilderness John inserts a second dramatic story, the defeat of Satan and his fall from heaven, along with his angels (Rev. 12:7–12). Since Revelation is an apocalypse, its imagery does not generally depict actual events. As modern Christians do not accept the biblical cosmology as factual, they need not view the world as a battle between angels, dragons, and a personified Satan. Furthermore, in apocalyptic literature events that take place in heaven often are reflective of events on earth. That is certainly true for John; in Revelation, everything he sees in heaven is the counterpart of some earthly reality. John tells this story to affirm that God and his Messiah are enthroned in heaven, meaning there is no sign of evil and rebellion there. This affirmation provides perspective and offers hope to those who live in a social wilderness and are threatened by local dragons. The cosmic war in heaven, with the defeat of the dragon and his angels by Michael and his angels, also depicts the heavenly, spiritual dimension of Jesus' victory on the cross, a victory Christians conceived of as a great spiritual battle in which Jesus attained cosmic victory over satanic evil. To see Satan as thrown down to the earth is to affirm that he no longer has access to God's throne.

To digress for a moment, we note that Revelation 12 is not the first time Satan comes to earth. John assumes that Satan has been active in both heaven and earth since the beginning of time. So what happens is that when Satan is thrown down from heaven, his range of operation is severely limited (see Luke 10:18; cf. Rom. 16:19–20). He is limited to working on the earth, where Christians can resist his influence (Jas. 4:7; cf. 1 Pet. 5:8–9). This concept differs from the traditional idea that Satan was expelled from heaven at the dawn of time. That notion—which appears in some ancient Jewish sources—was derived in part from Isaiah 14:12, where a tyrant is associated with the fallen angel (Lucifer) and then thrown into Sheol (the Abyss; note the comments on Revelation 9:1). That passage was then connected to the story of creation from Genesis 3, where the serpent lures Adam and Eve into sin. By combining these texts, people concluded that when Satan was expelled from heaven he must have survived in the Garden of Eden, where he could tempt the first humans. This tradition, which achieved classic form in John Milton's epic work *Paradise Lost*, is mythical and not biblical.

Revelation's perspective is different, for John's viewpoint is based on passages from Job and Zechariah, where Satan surveys the earth, checking up on people. He can also enter God's presence to accuse people of wrongdoing. The Hebrew word "satan" actually means "accuser," since Satan is so depicted in the book of Job, as a fault-finding prosecuting attorney in the heavenly court (Job 1:6–12). Revelation 12:9 provides a long list of other names for Satan or the dragon, culminating in "deceiver of the whole world."

According to Revelation, God no longer tolerates Satan's accusations, so Michael acts as the bouncer, confining him to the world below. In Jewish tradition Michael, one of the leading angels in heaven, is familiar from the book of Daniel, where he is called a "prince" and "protector" (Dan. 10:21; 12:1).

As we celebrate this victory and find great hope in it, a major question yet remains: if the power of evil has been defeated, then why do God's people continue to suffer on earth? The answer John gives is symbolic and temporal, having to do with Satan's past and present locations. In the universe John portrays, with heaven, earth, and the underworld as distinct realms, the satanic dragon has been expelled from heaven (12:12a). At this point, though, the dragon has not yet been thrown into the Abyss (the underworld). Satan will ultimately be thrown into that pit, but the climax is not recorded until Revelation 20.

For the time being Satan still prowls the earth, the middle level of John's symbolic universe (12:12b), trying to inflict as much damage as possible in his current confinement. And that is the key to the story. According to 12:12, the devil does not ravage the earth because he is powerful but because he is desperate. His options are severely limited, and he knows his time is running out. And if the readers know this, they can see that the best response to evil is not to capitulate but to resist, knowing that ultimate power belongs to God. That, we recall, is the meaning of the enigmatic temporal expressions here and elsewhere in Revelation; the references to the woman nourished in the wilderness for one thousand two hundred and sixty days (12:6) and for "a time, and times, and half a time" (12:15) indicate duress as temporary and limited in severity, with ultimate victory assured.

The middle scene in Revelation 12 shows that as soon as the devil and his allies are cast out of heaven, the heavenly voices explain that this victory is actually won through the blood of the Lamb and the word of those who bear witness (12:11). These voices relate a strange sort of victory, encountered before in the vision of the slain, yet living Lamb (5:6). John has already declared that the Lamb won a victory by suffering death faithfully, which from an ordinary perspective seems nonsensical. If you die, you lose and your opponents win. But that is not the way John sees it. According to Revelation, the blood of the Lamb brings victory over evil. The Lamb conveys the sacrificial power of love, which triumphs over hatred and despair. And where this love prevails, there is victory. From John's perspective, the real defeat would be to capitulate to the forces of hatred, deception, and death that diminish life on earth. So he calls his readers to join in the struggle by bearing witness with their words and their lives to the redemptive power of God.

The call to Revelation's audience to "conquer" is fundamental to the structure and theme of the book. It demands the readers' active participation

A Vision of Evil: Seven Significant Signs (Revelation 12–14) 129

in the divine war against evil. Everything that is said in the seven messages to the churches has this aim, expressed in the promise to the conquerors that concludes each (2:7, 11, 17, 28; 3:5, 12, 21). As 21:7 shows, it is only by conquering that the members of the churches may enter the New Jerusalem (cf. 22:14). The visions that intervene between the seven messages to the churches and the final vision of the New Jerusalem help the readers to understand what conquering involves. The verb "to conquer" is left intriguingly without an object until chapter 12. This is because it is only in chapters 12–13 that the false trinity, the principal enemy of God that must be defeated to make way for God's rule, is introduced. Babylon, the great harlot, who represents the corrupt and exploitative Roman civilization, is not properly introduced until chapter 17, but she has a rather different status. Christians are not called to conquer her but to "come out of her" (18:4), that is, to dissociate themselves from her evil.

The use of the verb "to conquer" in Revelation, anticipated in 11:7, is complex. In 12:11 we learn that the Lamb's followers have already defeated the dragon, whereas according to 13:7, the beast is "allowed to make war on the saints and to conquer them." The point is not that the beast and the Christians each win some victories; rather, the same event—the faithful witness (martyrdom) of Christians—is described both as the beast's victory over them and as their victory over the beast. In this way John poses the question: who are the real victors? The answer depends on whether one sees things from the earthly perspective of those who worship the beast or from the heavenly perspective that John's visions open up for his readers. To the inhabitants of the earth (13:8) it is obvious that the beast has defeated the martyrs. But John's message is that from the heavenly perspective things look quite different. The martyr-witnesses are the real victors. To be faithful in witness to the true God even to the point of death is not to become a victim of the beast, but to take the field against him and win. John's message in Revelation is not, "Do not resist!" Rather it is "Resist!"—but by witness and martyrdom, not by violence. Conquering is not represented as something to which only some are called, but as the only way for Christians to reach their eschatological destiny. According to 21:7–8, there are only two options: to conquer and inherit the promises or to suffer the second death in the lake of fire.[10]

This scene in 12:7–12 is a pictorial way of depicting the "already-but-not-yet" tension of the Christian life described by other New Testament writers in various ways: Jesus has died, yet he is with us now; deception, brutality, arrogance, and injustice are present all around us, yet evil has been

---

10. Bauckham, *Theology of Revelation*, 90–92.

defeated; when we are weak, then we are strong. For people of faith, paradox elicits vision and fervor, not cynicism or skepticism. Even though earth cannot yet rejoice, in 12:10 a voice calls out in heaven, celebrating Satan's defeat and his expulsion from heaven: "Now have come the salvation and the power and the kingdom of our God . . ." The song in 12:11 informs us that the people of God are not just passive spectators in the heavenly drama but actual participants in the defeat of Satan. This verse gives Christians a starring role in the theme of "conquering," first introduced in the seven letters but central to the entire book. While the seven letters do not indicate how believers become conquerors, this passage provides an answer.

The first way that God's people conquer Satan (evil) is by the blood of the Lamb, through Christ's vicarious life and death. The second way is by the power of our witness or "testimony" (Greek *martyria*). The story of the two witnesses in chapter 11 shows the power of testimony, as does Jesus' own testimony (1:2), a term from a courtroom context. John is showing that those who witness faithfully are in line with the prophets of old—those who spoke God's truth boldly and courageously. Those who conquer confront the powers and principalities of this world, telling the truth about corruption and the misuse of power in all places and at all social levels. This passage brings to mind those throughout history who have risked harassment, torture, even death to proclaim God's truth concerning equality, justice, freedom, and peace, including individuals still alive or in recent memory such as Nelson Mandela, Martin Luther King, Mahatma Gandhi, Archbishop Oscar Romero, and the American nuns in El Salvador who were murdered in 1980 for working with the poor in that country. Among those who have been imprisoned, tortured, intimidated, killed, or placed under house arrest unjustly is Malala Yousufzai, the fifteen-year-old Pakistani student who on October 9, 2012 was shot in the head at pointblank range by a Taliban gunman for taking a bold and public stance in support of girls' education. All Malalas belong to that group, young or old, female or male, Christian, Buddhist, Muslim, Hindu, of whatever race, creed, color, and nationality who have been martyred, literally or figuratively, for speaking truth to power. Their witness, like the public witness of the seven churches, makes a difference, John says. Our witness makes a difference too—it conquers evil.

Christians live in the in-between time, pictured in Revelation as the time between Satan's expulsion from heaven and the time when he will be thrown into the abyss. The symbolic picture of Satan stalking the earth serves to warn Christians that things will worsen under Rome's rule before they improve. During the sequence of the seven bowls (Rev. 16), the suffering will be twice as intense as during the seven trumpets. This is a call for perseverance.

The final character in the dramatic stories of Revelation 12 is the earth, personified as a woman (12:16). In this chapter the earth comes to the rescue of the woman being pursued by the dragon. Earth's heroic swallowing of the river which poured from the dragon's mouth saves the woman from Satan. Earth's action is reminiscent of the Israelites' victory song after crossing the Red Sea in the story of the exodus. There the Israelites give thanks that the earth "swallowed" up their Egyptian pursuers (Exod. 15:12). This verse serves as a reminder of the many positive references in Revelation to the earth and to the goodness of creation. Gruesome depictions of natural calamities in the warning and judgment scenes sometimes give the impression that Revelation is anti-earth. However, the starring role given to the earth in chapter 12, in chapters 21–22, and in God's judgment against "those who destroy the earth" in 11:18, reminds us of God's great love for the earth, which God does not intend to destroy. Earth plays a heroic role in Revelation, as it does throughout scripture.[11]

Following these flashbacks, the final verse in chapter 12 sounds an ominous note for believers in the present. The woman and child have been rescued, but Satan is angry because he has been cast out of heaven. Since he cannot devour Jesus, he goes off to make war against God's people. But their faithfulness will sustain them, no matter what evil they face. Hope is central to John's apocalyptic imagination.

The Middle Signs (Chapter 13:1–18)

In chapters 12 and 13 John presents a cast of characters polarized into antithetical groups, with no middle ground. On one side are the forces of good: the woman, the male child, Michael, the angels, the woman's seed (Christians), earth, and God (the hidden actor; see 12:5–6). Opposite this group are the forces of evil: the dragon, the beast from the sea (often called the antichrist), and the beast from the land (called the false prophet in 16:13; 19:20; and 20:10). The beast from the sea and the beast rising out of the earth likely are allusions to a Jewish tradition that on the fifth day God had created two mythical creatures, Leviathan and Behemoth, one to inhabit the sea and the other the land.[12]

Revelation 16:13 depicts the forces of evil as a unit, so they are often characterized as a counterfeit "trinity." While John does not display a developed doctrine of the Trinity, his depiction of divine activity does anticipate later conceptions. The dragon is portrayed as a parody of God the Father,

11. Ibid., 52.
12. Caird, *Revelation*, 161.

the beast of Jesus Christ, and the false prophet of the Holy Spirit. The latter correspondence, while useful, is not altogether accurate, since the false prophet corresponds more closely to the two witnesses of chapter 11, who represent the church's prophetic witness inspired by the Holy Spirit. The false prophet's activity relates to the whole world (13:12–17), as does that of the two witnesses; he performs signs (13:13–14), as they do (11:6); he makes the world worship the beast (13:12), just as the career of the two witnesses brings the world to worship God (11:13).[13]

What does this imagery mean, and how can we make sense of it today? A helpful way to understand John's literary strategy is to compare his use of images to their use in popular culture. On the editorial page in current newspapers we often see political cartoons depicting an elephant or a donkey, which are known to represent the Republican and Democratic parties. And alongside these animals cartoonists sometimes include images of people in the news. If the subject is the economy, the cartoon might feature a bull as a symbol for a prosperous economy; in bad times the cartoonist may depict a bear, which symbolizes bleak economic prospects. The imagery might be bizarre or humorous, but its use enables the artist to render a perspective on current events, utilizing conventional imagery. This is similar to what John does with the images of the two beasts, which represent conventional apocalyptic imagery well-known to first-century Jews and Christians.

In 13:1 John sees rising from the sea a seven-headed monster, having ten horns and seven heads, on which are blasphemous names. With qualities of a leopard, a bear, and a lion, its power and authority come from the dragon. This is the same monster rising from the Abyss in Revelation 11:7. While the description of this monster is intriguing, the details are ultimately unimportant. Some scholars—particularly those with axes to grind or perspectives to substantiate—find significance in the details (whether the seven heads represent emperors of Rome or nations in the European Common Market or characteristics of the antichrist; or whether the ten horns and the blasphemous names written on the heads of the beast symbolize sacrilegious titles assumed by these emperors or by the coming antichrist), but the overall message is important. Broadly speaking, the monster represents Roman imperialism.

The references to the leopard, bear, and lion come from the vision of four beasts in Daniel 7:1–14 (where they depict successive empires that conquered or persecuted the Israelites/Jews in pre-Christian times). John, using artistic freedom, depicts a monster with characteristics of all four of Daniel's beasts, listed in reverse order. In John's time the fourth beast of

---

13. Ibid., 114–15.

A Vision of Evil: Seven Significant Signs (Revelation 12-14) 133

Daniel was often interpreted by Jews as signifying the Roman Empire. John clearly wants his readers to interpret his beast from the sea as Rome and her emperors (particularly Nero, the first emperor to persecute Christians; cf. 17:9-10). John may also have had in mind here the ancient Middle Eastern mythological sea monster Leviathan, representative of the evil or chaos restrained at the creation and repeatedly subdued through annual dramatic reenactments at imperial cultic centers during religious festivals in antiquity. Leviathan, a hydra-like creature, was believed to reside in "the deep" or "the Abyss," as the Septuagint translates *tehom* in Genesis 1:2.

Revelation 13:3-4 depicts this beast as a parody, which imitates Christ's crucifixion and resurrection. The death and resurrection of this beast may have included a reference to the rumor spreading during this time concerning Nero, the late emperor who committed suicide in AD 68 but was said to be alive, taking revenge on Rome at the head of the Parthian army. While this side note has historical value, it was of little concern to John and his followers. John's message was clear: persecution of Christians is coming or is already present, and instead of cowering in fear, Christians need to endure persecution faithfully (13:10). The reference to the beast's ability to utter blasphemy for "forty-two months" is a parody of Christians in 11:3, who witness ("prophesy") faithfully for one thousand two hundred and sixty days (the identical period of time; see 11:2).

John saw in his vision that "all the inhabitants of the world" worshipped the beast. However, this authority came from God, and was limited to forty-two months. The repetition of "given" and "allowed" in verses 5 and 7 emphasizes that God is in control and that evil is powerless without divine permission. Evil's time is limited (cf. 12:12) and is under God's plan to restore earth to its original pristine condition. Furthermore, the beast is restricted to his sphere of influence, for his worship is limited to those whose names are not written in the Lamb's book of life. The book of life in 13:8, reminiscent of the sealing of the 144,000 in chapter 7, represents a "register" of those who acknowledge the redemptive power of Jesus' life and death. The reference to their names having been written in the book of life before creation has nothing to do with the controversy between predestination and free will. John's concern is to provide those who are suffering for their faith assurance and hope that God's providential care is everlasting. Readers who get caught up in theological details, wondering whether salvation is guaranteed or can be lost, seem to miss the main point entirely. The passage calls believers to loyalty and faithfulness. For John, hope is central; compromise and condemnation are not options. Persecution may come, indeed will come, and Christians must follow the example of Jesus, allowing themselves to be conquered as he was on earth. This is an important point for John and should be for us as well. Believers must submit without resistance to the attack of the beast because this is the only way the beast can be stopped. (Christian resistance as nonresistance figures prominently in the discussion of Revelation 14:12–20.) Conquering evil may be compared to the multiplying heads of a hydra monster. Retaliation is like chopping off one head, which a hydra can regrow. If the hydra head is not removed, it is easier to defeat.

In verse 11, John sees another beast come forth, rising out of the earth. This beast had "two horns like a lamb and it spoke like a dragon." Some scholars think this is a parody of Jesus, but since this beast promotes the worship of the first beast, John depicts him as a false prophet (see 16:13). Like Elijah, this false prophet could "perform great signs, even making fire come down from heaven" (1 Kgs. 18:20–39). If the first beast is an image of Roman imperialism, the beast from the land represents the imperial cult. Verses 11–15 may depict the priests of the Caesar cult, who not only promoted the worship of the emperor but were also known for deceiving people with magic tricks and ventriloquism as the beast of the earth did with its false miracles. John may also have in mind leading citizens of the province of Asia, who actively supported the imperial cult, using their own wealth to build temples and statues to the emperors. Many of these people held both civic office and served on city councils. They understood that good relationships with Rome would benefit their local communities. Therefore they staged public festivals, parades, and athletic events, as well as sacrifices and banquets that many attended, keeping the cult of the emperor a regular part of social life in the province of Asia. In this context, Christians who remained loyal to Christ were exposed to ridicule, economic hardship, political injustice, and on occasion even death. Another theory is that this beast represents opponents within the church, false teachers and charismatic prophets who allowed Christians to mingle with the Roman culture (note earlier references to Balaam, Jezebel, and the Nicolaitans in 2:6; 2:14–15; and 2:20–25).

To complete the "counterfeit trinity," scholars find here a parody of the Holy Spirit. The false prophet promoted false worship, whereas the Holy Spirit leads people to worship God and the Lamb. The false prophet advocates culture religion, embodied in predominant political and economic values (13:16–17), whereas the Holy Spirit espouses counter-cultural values and norms (see Gal. 5:19–24). The "mark of the beast" (13:16–17) might refer to the image of the emperor on Roman coins or to some other economic or cultural aspect of the empire that John wants his audience to avoid. Christians must not commit to the values of the violent and unjust Roman culture.

A Vision of Evil: Seven Significant Signs (Revelation 12–14)

Of the two beasts in chapter 13, the first has generated the most interest over the years. He is the figure traditionally called the antichrist, that sinister figure whose name equals the number 666. For centuries people have been fascinated by this image, applying it to a world leader they detest. In John's time the beast might have been Nero. During the Middle Ages, some thought it was the Pope. During the Reformation, when Martin Luther applied it to the Pope, Catholics retaliated by saying Luther was the antichrist. Later, when Tolstoy wrote his novel *War and Peace*, one of the characters made the letters in Napoleon's name equal the number 666. In the twentieth century the antichrist was said to be Hitler, then Stalin. The speculation continues to the present, where one finds it in popular literature and in debates on the Internet. Most people today have heard of the number 666, which they view as a bar code, a global computing and credit-card system, but mostly as an unlucky number, much like the number 13.

The most common explanation for the number 666 comes from a Jewish system known as gematria, whereby every letter in an alphabet represents a number and every word creates a numerical sum. Using the Hebrew language, Nero's name and title (Neron Caesar) add up to 666; Nero Caesar adds up to 616, a number we find in some manuscripts instead of 666. Gematria is highly speculative and can be used to substantiate most hypotheses.

A better explanation comes from Revelation 13 itself, where evil masquerades as good. According to this interpretation, Satan attempts to imitate what God does or represents. In Revelation 7:1–8, for example, the Lamb seals his followers on the forehead as a sign of ownership and protection. In chapter 13 Satan's prophet parodies this seal, marking his followers on the forehead and right hand. But evil falls short of good, for the mark of the beast signifies the brand of ownership (slavery), whereas the Lamb's seal symbolizes protection and security in addition to ownership (love). Since the number seven, which signifies totality or perfection, is central to John's thinking and is said to represent God, the number six can represent a parody of seven. Because the number represents deception, it is said to represent judgment. In the book of Revelation, the judgment of God comes during the sixth seal, trumpet, and bowl, whereas in the seventh seal, trumpet, and bowl, the number seven represents completion in the kingdom of God. John saw himself and his churches to be living in the time of the sixth king/emperor (see 17:10), which he deemed the time of idolatry and judgment.[14]

Since the number seven is considered the number of perfection, it is likely that 666 symbolizes incompleteness, falling short of seven. As God is

---

14. Boring, *Revelation*, 162.

777, "holy, holy, holy," it is as if John is calling Rome "imperfect, imperfect, imperfect." As 777 represents perfection and holiness, so too it represents the Sabbath, the day declared holy and set apart for rest and worship. In the Bible, work done in six days is sanctified by the seventh day. Using this analogy, the number 666 represents people stalled in the sixth day, concerned with buying and selling (13:17), committed to Roman economic and religious values and practices, without resting for worship. Though all work (service to God, *latreia*) is holy and therefore an aspect of worship, it becomes evil when it remains secular. The beast, the enemy of the church, consecrates nothing. His followers work tirelessly, but their labor is sterile. The beast is 666, "the creature stalled in the sixth day . . . never reaching the seventh day of Sabbath rest and worship."[15]

Those who focus on a future historical figure as the antichrist ignore additional insights on this topic from the Johannine school, passages such as 1 John 2:18–22 and 4:1–6, which identify numerous antichrists as already present in the late first century, in this case believers who had lapsed under persecution or who had apostatized; they were false believers. There "Christ" represents truth and "antichrist" represents deception or denial. According to 1 John, those who deny Christ are "antichrist," for to deny the Son is to be anti-God. Just as there were false prophets and false teachers throughout the biblical period, so the Bible warns that in the future there would be an increase of this phenomenon (2 Thess. 2:1–10; 2 Pet. 3:3; Jude 18–19). Once readers figure out that the number 666 is connected to John's overall perspective, it sharpens the essential question he is asking: Where does your loyalty lie, with God or the Empire? Who gives you your identity, the Lamb or the Beast? Whose mark do you bear, that of the faithful witness or that of the Imposter?

In chapter 13 John portrays the Roman Empire as a tool of Satan—a bold and shocking portrayal, since Rome was still very powerful. Specifically, John links the leaders of the empire with the images of two beasts. As Satan embodies total evil, the beast from the sea is said to represent the realm of politics. The government of Rome is imaged as a hideous beast from the sea that is "allowed to make war on the saints and to conquer them" (13:7). Local leaders in Asia, through religious and economic practices that serve the interests of the empire, are imaged as the beast from the land that "deceives the inhabitants of earth" (13:14). The beast of Rome intimidates and seduces people, forcing them to worship or give allegiance to the empire. This was a daring caricature of the empire while it was still in power. In John's view, government is evil and it should not be honored or obeyed.

---

15. Hahn, *Lamb's Supper*, 138.

This is a different view of government from Paul's counsel in Romans 13 that government is "God's servant for your good" (Rom. 13:4) or from 1 Peter 2:13-17 and other passages that exhort Christians to honor government. In John's view Rome itself is the primary perpetrator of violence in the world—and the reason that the Roman Empire must come to an end. We too live in a world in which terror and uncertainty make us feel powerless and vulnerable. We wonder how God can be victorious over evil. The "beasts" of the Roman Empire are long gone, but today's "beasts"—violence, economic vulnerability, terrorism, environmental degradation, and other global threats—still stalk our world, causing fear. Revelation provides the final word of hope, not the beasts and their degrading violence.

Here as elsewhere John resorts to satire to depict the enemies of God. The point of the satire, of course, is that no amount of deception (13:3-4, 14-15) can change what the monster really is. Those who worship the beast are giving loyalty to leaders known for brutality and deception. The true violence that Revelation depicts is the violence of empire, absolute, self-serving power. God and the Lamb represent polar opposite values.

The Final Signs (Chapter 14:1-20)

Following his account of the evil trinity, John seemingly provides an interlude in 14:1-5, intending to reassure the church amid its trials and persecutions. We have noticed elsewhere how John alternates scenes of terror with scenes of security. The first part of chapter 14 is a scene of tranquility and rejoicing but is not an interlude; rather it is the sixth sign. As is regularly the case in Revelation, the interlude appears between the sixth and the seventh in a series, as it does here as well (14:6-12).

In chapters 12 and 13 John shows how things *presently* are, whereas in chapter 14 John shows how things *finally* are.[16] In a scene that recalls 7:1-8 and anticipates 21:1—22:6, John provides an advance picture of the redeemed church, the 144,000 in the holy city on Mount Zion (the heavenly Jerusalem), in the presence of God and the Lamb. The reference here is to the final triumph of believers and not to an intermediate victory. Unlike the beast, which stands on sand (13:1), the Lamb stands on God's mountain. This group, the same 144,000 mentioned in chapter 7:1-8, is the ideal representation of the people of God. This is the group later identified by John as "the bride" (21:9), though the marriage is in the future. Like the 144,000 in 7:4, this group is sealed, here with the name of God and the Lamb on their foreheads (see Ezek. 9:4), in contrast to those branded with the mark of the

16. Boring, *Revelation*, 168.

beast (13:7). The former are described as "virgins," meaning they have remained pure in their loyalty to the Lamb. This imagery comes from the Old Testament, where virginity is ascribed to the people of God (2 Kgs. 19:21; Jer. 18:13) and where unfaithfulness to God is likened to improper sexual relations (Ezek. 16; Hos. 5:4). In the New Testament Paul likens the church to the bride of Christ, presented to him as a chaste virgin (2 Cor. 11:2). The 144,000 are also called "the first fruits" (14:4), meaning that they represent the first of the harvest presented to God in gratitude for the pledge of the full harvest to come. The thought of belonging to God and the Lamb is foremost in John's mind at this point. Paul uses similar imagery to describe Christ in his resurrection in 1 Corinthians 15:20–23. The word translated "blameless" (*amomoi*) in 14:5 is cultic terminology for the physical perfection required in an animal acceptable for sacrifice (Exod. 29:38; Lev. 1:3; 3:1). The expression "and in their mouth no lie was found" relates to the theme of truth and falsehood, which is so important in Revelation, and evokes the third of the motifs which dominate Revelation's account of the work of Christ, that of faithful witness to the truth (1:5).

The message of the three angels and of the voice from heaven in Revelation 14:6–13 represents an interlude between the sixth and seventh signs. The message of the angels is threefold: (a) "Fear God" (14:7); (b) Babylon is fallen (14:8); and (c) those who worship the beast will "drink the wine of God's wrath" and will be "tormented with fire and sulfur" (14:10). As 14:1–5 anticipates the eschatological salvation of the New Jerusalem, 14:6–11 anticipates the coming fall of Babylon and God's judgment on those who bear the mark of the beast. The message appears judgmental and vindictive, but if we see only that, we miss John's perspective, found at the end of the interlude (14:12–13) and disclosed imaginatively in 14:14–20.

The terminology here must be taken biblically but not literally. To "fear God" is not to be afraid of God but to worship and love God, to be struck by God's awesome power and creative love. The message of the first angel, like that of the remaining angels, is essentially a message of hope, indicated by the phrase "eternal gospel" in verse 6. There is only one gospel in the Bible, one "good news," which is that the blood of Jesus has ransomed "saints from every tribe and language and people and nation" (5:9). This is the new song of the four living creatures and the twenty-four elders in heaven (5:9–10), and it is the new song of the 144,000 as well in 14:3. The distinctive thing about the "eternal gospel" in 14:6 is not that it is a different gospel, but that witness means "martyrdom." The gospel was first proclaimed by Christ himself, "the faithful witness" (1:5), and the meaning of discipleship is to preserve and repeat the testimony of Jesus (Mark 8:34–38). In John's Gospel Jesus states: "unless a grain of wheat falls into the earth and dies, it remains just a single grain; but if it dies, it bears much fruit. Those who love their life lose it, and those who hate their life in this world will keep it for eternal life. Whoever serves me must follow me" (John 12:24–26). Chapter 14, as we shall see, is not primarily about the punishment of unbelievers but about the vicarious suffering of God's people on behalf of the world. The images in chapter 14 are of salvation, not of condemnation.[17]

When we read that "the hour of [God's] judgment has come" (14:7) we often think of condemnation, but in this context we need to recall John 12:31–32, where Jesus announces another judgment of the world, which is to liberate all people from Satan's accusations and draw them to himself. If we allow this common ground between Revelation and the Gospel of John, then the angel's meaning must be that "the judgment is present in the death of the martyrs in the same way as it was present in the Cross."[18] And that is certainly Good News for the world.

The message of the second angel follows suit. In passages like these John is thinking symbolically, and it is important not only to feel the force of his images but also to probe the reality to which they point. The fall of Babylon is certainly central to Revelation, for this is a theme John revisits in 16:19, 17:5, and in great detail in chapter 18. This is the first mention of Babylon in Revelation, and here as elsewhere Babylon is called "great." John might have had the ancient city of Babylon in the back of his mind, for that city had conquered and exiled the nation of Judah in the sixth century BC. But "Babylon" metaphorically stands for arrogant pride and secular power, the symbol of human community opposed to the things of God, and to first century Christians and Jews there was no better illustration of such arrogance than contemporary Rome. In Revelation John anticipates the overthrow of all that Babylon represents. As elsewhere, the details of this angel's message—wine, woman, and fornication—are not meant literally. The author is appealing to his audience's understanding of Hebrew scriptures associated with Babylon's fall and Judah's redemption from captivity. For example, in the Old Testament Isaiah saw himself as a sentry on a watchtower, awaiting the couriers who would bring the news of Babylon's fall and Israel's release (21:8–9). Jeremiah depicted Babylon as "a golden cup in the Lord's hand, making all the earth drunken; the nations drank of her wine, and so the nations went mad" (Jer. 51:7). John weaves his own pattern from these Old Testament themes, "but there is no reason to suppose that he has departed from the original intention of his scriptural texts, in which the fall of Babylon brought the salvation, not the doom, of those who had been

---

17. Wright, *Revelation*, 133.
18. Caird, *Revelation*, 183–84.

made drunk with her wine."[19] God would certainly judge Babylon's idolatry and pride, but that judgment would work itself out primarily in history, for evil brings its own reward. Bearing within themselves the cancer of their own self-destruction, oppressors fall victim to the wicked systems they have devised. Evil cannot win, for at the end it will implode, collapsing into itself like into a black hole.

To readers who wonder about the impenitent, their hearts untouched by the redemptive love of Christ and the faithful witness of his followers, the third angel provides an answer. As with the imagery associated with previous angels, these metaphors are not to be taken literally. The prediction of "fire and sulfur" in verse 10 is associated with the fate of Sodom and Gomorrah (Gen. 19:24; Luke 17:29); metaphorically this notion represents a suitable scriptural fate for the great city figuratively called "Sodom and Egypt" (11:8). Though the angel purports to be speaking of individual destiny, he does so in terms proper to the destruction of a city. And it is this symbolic city (called Sodom, Egypt, Babylon, and even Jerusalem in biblical passages of judgment but symbolic of Rome in Revelation) and not individuals that John has in mind in chapter 14 (note the reference to "the city" in 14:20). It is only those who through their worship of the monster have fully identified themselves with the great city, because she was all they loved and lived for, that will experience eternal torment (14:11). The idea of individuals suffering eternal torment was repugnant to John. Objectifying language about what shall happen to one's enemies is not what John had in mind and is ultimately unchristian. Biblical language is confessional language, intended not to describe the fate of outsiders but to encourage insiders to remain faithful; it functions precisely like the language of Jesus in the Gospels (Matt. 10:28; 25:30, 46).[20] John believed that if at the end there should be any who remain resistant to the grace and love of God, they would be thrown, with Death and Hades, into the lake of fire, which is the second death (i.e. extinction and total oblivion; see 20:14–15; 21:8).[21] Yet even this is not the angel's final word, which is a call for endurance, a key theme in this unit (12:11; 13:10) and elsewhere in Revelation.

John's solemn message is followed by words of comfort, which comprise the second of the seven beatitudes contained in Revelation: "Blessed are the dead who from now on die in the Lord . . . they will rest from their labors, for their deeds follow them" (14:13). God's people may be persecuted and treated unfairly, even up to and including martyrdom, but they, not

---

19. Ibid., 184.
20. Boring, *Revelation*, 170–71.
21. Caird, *Revelation*, 186–87.

their tormentors, remain blessed; their deeds matter (20:12-13; cf. Rom. 2:6). The juxtaposition of Christian endurance with a sentence of doom on an unrepentant world is intentional and the two should not be separated. For a doomed world Jesus went to the cross to bear his witness to the redeeming love of God (Rom. 5:8; 1 Tim. 1:15), and for a doomed world the martyrs must bear their witness. John was writing a pastoral book for friends, not a manifesto against the pagan world. The speech of the third angel is addressed to the seven churches, not in order that they might long for retribution but in order to prevent it from happening. Thus they receive this benediction, not that their witness benefits them as merit, but that it results in the blessing and redemption of the nations.

John's seventh sign (14:14-20), like the message of the three angels, provides continuity to John's thought. It continues some of the violent imagery of Revelation, imagery inspired by Old Testament texts such as Joel 3:13, which John may have in mind here. At this point Eugene Boring addresses one of the fundamental issues readers of Revelation ultimately face, whether these visions represent condemnation or redemption. He provides three possibilities:[22]

1. the images refer to judgment, so that both the grain harvest and the winepress symbolize the destiny of the wicked;

2. some images of salvation are mixed with images of judgments, so that the grain harvest is the ingathering of the saved, as in the parables of Jesus, while the winepress is a picture of God's wrath upon the condemned;

3. the images refer to ultimate salvation, so that the blood of the winepress is the blood of the martyrs.

Boring takes a cautious approach at this point, concerned about placing limits on John's multivalent imagery. Nevertheless he settles on the second option, finding it least problematic. This passage is central to John's overall message, and I find a fence-sitting solution on this issue counterproductive to the message Jesus would have us proclaim today. While divine judgment is appealing here, literarily and intellectually, it is not morally appropriate. John seems to have something more subtle in mind, something more powerful and ultimately more deeply congruous with the message of the gospel. For that reason I maintain the third alternative, upholding it consistently throughout this commentary.

Evil is clearly real and Christians are enjoined to defeat it, but never on evil's own terms, utilizing its tactics and weapons. Violence and injustice

---

22. Boring, *Revelation*, 171.

cannot be countered with the rhetoric of retaliation. John knew that, and so do we. The world cannot improve unless modern Christians reject tactics of the past such as crusades and inquisitions and attitudes such as ecclesiastical triumphalism. They need instead to imitate the witness of Jesus, as John emphasizes. The Sermon on the Mount, found in Matthew 5–7, is a good place to begin, particularly the Beatitudes in 5:3–12 and the antithetical sayings in 5:38–48.

John's seventh sign depicts a figure like "the Son of Man" putting the sickle to the grain harvest of the earth (14:14–16). The figure of the "son of man," used earlier of Jesus (1:13), is taken from Daniel 7:13–14, where an apocalyptic figure receives from God "dominion and glory and kingship, that all peoples, nations, and languages should serve him." As in Daniel's vision, John depicts this figure as seated on the clouds of heaven. In the apocalyptic tradition of the Gospels the coming of the Son of Man with the clouds of heaven is the occasion when "he will send out the angels, and gather his elect from the four winds, from the ends of the earth to the ends of heaven" (Mark 13:27; cf. Matt. 24:31). In the Septuagint, the noun and verb for "harvest" (*therismos/therizo*) are never used for the judgment of enemies, even in passages where judgment is likened to reaping, and in the New Testament these terms are used of the ingathering of humans into the kingdom of God (Matt. 9:37–38; Mark. 4:29; Luke 10:2; John 4:35–38). John's use of harvest imagery in Revelation 14:14–16 is reminiscent of his earlier use of the word "first fruits" in 14:4. When the first fruits have been offered to God, the full ingathering will follow. In Jewish liturgical practice, the offering of the first sheaf of grain by the priest in the temple freed the rest of the crop for general use and was the signal for reaping to begin.

The grain harvest is followed by the grape harvest, executed not by Jesus but by other angels. Many scholars see the grain harvest positively, as a reference to salvation, but take the grape harvest negatively, as a reference to terrifying judgment, basing their interpretation on the notion of the "grapes of wrath," viewed as the wicked nations who are about to suffer God's eternal anger (cf. the reference to the "wrath of God" in 14:19).[23] But the harvest imagery and its natural implications suggest otherwise. The previous chapter warned believers against worshipping the beast; the following chapter presents those same people singing the new song by the sea of glass. Chapter 14 indicates how God's people go from the one to the other.

---

23. During the Civil, War Julia Ward Howe applied the violent imagery of the trampling of the grapes of wrath to what she viewed as God's judgment on citizens of the United States for their tolerance of slavery. In her famous abolitionist hymn "The Battle Hymn of the Republic," she saw the bloody Civil War as a loosing of God's "terrible swift sword" against a violent and unjust institution of her day—slavery.

A Vision of Evil: Seven Significant Signs (Revelation 12–14)

Harvest and vintage are not antithetical but variations on the same theme. Israel was required to offer first fruits of wine as well as of grain (Exod. 22:29), emblematic of the entire harvest season, which opened with the offering of the sheaf of wheat and ended with the grape harvest at the festival of Booths, in the fall of the year. Taken in their normal setting—pastoral, agrarian, rural—harvests and vintage are occasions of celebration and great joy. In a liturgical setting, they also represent the promise of harvest and thanksgiving for the fulfillment of promise. In a Christian setting, references to harvest (wheat) and vintage (grapes) suggest the bread and wine of the Eucharist. These are images of joy and salvation, not of sorrow and condemnation.

If that is so, what is the meaning of the reference to the "wine press of the wrath of God"? We must keep in mind that this phrase is followed immediately by a reference to the wine press that "was trodden outside the city" in verse 20. In a later chapter, those who stubbornly remain within the city share its sins and its doom (18:4; cf. 12:6). The judgment of the impenitent takes place within the city, for the great city ("Babylon"; cf. 17:18; 18:2) and her citizens will fall. It makes little sense to say that the inhabitants of this city would be judged outside the city. If judgment of the wicked is intended here, one would expect the winepress to be at the heart of the city, or perhaps even that the entire city would become a great winepress of the avenging angel. To be "outside the city" is to be crucified with Jesus and thus the proper place for the "martyrdom" of those who hold to the testimony of Jesus (cf. Heb. 13:12–13). So deeply was this notion ingrained in the minds of first century Christians that Matthew and Luke, editing Mark's parable of the wicked tenants (Mark 12:8), have the landowner's son killed outside the vineyard (Matt. 21:39; Luke 20:15), an obvious reference here to Jerusalem.

A winepress is a place where the juice is separated from the pulp. Thus it can be a symbol for punishment but also the place where grapes are made into wine. In Revelation the winepress is not itself the place of punishment but the place where the wine of God's wrath is prepared. From an earthly point of view it is "Babylon" that sheds the great river of blood across her territory. Two hundred miles (lit. sixteen hundred stadia/furlongs in Greek) is said to be the length of Palestine, but it could also represent the earth, the square of four (earth) times the square of ten (completeness). From a heavenly perspective the reference to the vintage is the testimony of believers, who like their Lord suffer vicariously as witness to the unbelieving world. The only other square numbers in Revelation are the 144,000, the faithful people of God (basically 12 x 12), and the dimensions of the New Jerusalem in 22:16–17 (12,000 stadia; the walls are 144 cubits). John is not here speaking of Babylon ("the city"), but of the New Jerusalem, the people of God "outside the city."

The imagery in this section is reminiscent of a royal figure in Isaiah 63:1–6 (an image drawn from references to the Messiah of Isaiah 9:5 and 11:4 and of the Servant of Isaiah in 42:1–4 and 52:13—53:12), who is trampling the grapes by himself, getting his clothes stained with juice in the process. There he is bent on vengeance, crushing the enemies of God's people. But when John appeals to Isaiah 63 later in the book, the staining on the clothes of the Messiah is from his own blood (19:13–16). In Revelation we hear repeatedly that the Lamb has conquered through his blood—his sacrificial death—and that his followers are to conquer in the same manner. This helps us interpret the oxymoron "the wrath of the Lamb" (6:16). It becomes apparent that "the way in which God works salvation, and the way he works wrath, are intimately connected—because they meet on the cross; and because they meet, too, in the martyrdom of Jesus' followers. The winepress is where God's wrath is being prepared, for Babylon and all monster-worshippers to drink. But the wine itself is the lifeblood of the martyrs who are being harvested."[24] By juxtaposing harvest and vintage, John has found a way of telling his audience that Jesus, "who turned the cross to victory and the four horsemen into angels of grace, can transform even the shambles of martyrdom into a glorious harvest-home."[25]

Like God's *opus alienum* ("strange deed") in Isaiah 28:21, where God judges by fire his own people as a means to judge their enemies, the redemptive work of God in this section is alien, more like the work of a surgeon—who uses a scalpel to cut living tissue, even stuffing gauze into the wound to keep the incision open until the blood flows red and the poison is gone—than like a parent, who uses "tough love" to discipline a child. The analogy applies to John 3:16, which can be revised to read: For God so loved the world that he bled—until his blood flowed red—that whosoever accepts this love may live in God's presence eternally.

When we connect this insight with the winepress "trodden outside the city" in 14:20, recalling the idea of something flowing away from a city and being measured for depth, we are reminded of the water of life that at the end of Ezekiel's prophecy flows from the New Jerusalem (Ezek. 47:1–12). Perhaps in John's imagination the swelling river of blood plays a similar role, promoting a further work of grace. The passage conveys a powerful message, needed as much today as ever: God's time will come; God will bring his people safely home; God will defeat evil in the world and turn it to

---

24. Wright, *Revelation*, 134.
25. Caird, *Revelation*, 194.

praise. In the meantime, God's people are to be encouraged in their suffering, for part of God's purpose is to bring healing upon the world. Like the plagues of Egypt—central to the next unit of Revelation—judgment serves to heighten the redemptive splendor of God's grand finale. John's perspective here is analogous to the story of the church's witness in 11:13, which ends with the conversion of all who survive the warning judgments.

Essay 6: Permeable Boundaries in Revelation

The first three chapters of Revelation take place on earth. Chapter four begins a new section, a vision of John's heavenly journey that extends through chapter 18. He remains in heaven through the sea and trumpet vision of chapters 6 through 9. From chapter 10 on, John's standpoint sometimes appears to be back on earth, yet all is still seen from the transcendent perspective.

Beginning in Revelation 4, the visions assume a three-layered universe (heaven, earth, and under the earth; see 5:3 and 13), a model central to the second half of the book. Divine beings such as God and heavenly creatures have a unique place within the three-story universe, and demonic forces are distinct and separate: the divine forces belong in heaven; evil forces belong below the earth; and earth becomes a place of conflict between the two. John's boundaries—spatial, temporal, and moral—while understandable to a first-century audience, are not as distinct as they seem. Heaven and earth, for example, are not separated by a great gulf, as they are in popular conception. Heaven, God's sphere of reality, is close beside us, intersecting with our ordinary reality.[26]

Since the term "boundary" applies to different contexts in what follows, I should comment on the word itself. Boundary is often associated with space; in common usage it refers to the outside perimeter of a space. My property, for example, is bounded by a road at the front and a row of trees behind; they mark the limits of my land. This common usage of boundary depends on the perspective of the one who is inside the boundaries. If, however, I fly over my land in an airplane, the boundaries will be seen quite differently. From that lofty perspective those boundaries are not so much limits as a way to distinguish between things. In other words, a boundary not only marks differences, it creates them. A boundary separates and delineates, thereby making a difference where otherwise there would be no difference. In considering the boundaries that delineate the contours

---

26. Wright, *Revelation*, 42.

of John's visionary world, what would that world look like if viewed from above, as from an airplane? From that viewpoint his boundaries are not outer limits to reality but simply dividers that create differences and distinctions among the objects in his world. Just as we learn about how land is controlled by noting where boundaries are placed, so we can learn about John's world by noting where he places boundaries and thereby creates differences. When we do this, we notice that the sharp distinctions we make between spatial boundaries and boundaries in other sets of relations are different from John's boundaries.

Although for John humans belong to the earthly plane, the divine belongs to heaven above, and the demonic to the plane below, those three levels are blurred. In Revelation soft boundaries exist between spatial and temporal planes and even between good and evil. Evil contrasts with good, but evil is not of a fundamentally different order from good. Creatures descend or ascend through the universe, and as they pass through the different levels, they are transformed in numerous ways. Thus movement through spatial planes functions as a transformational experience.

Time takes a curious turn as well, for past, present, and future are not separated by fixed, absolute boundaries. Once translated into heaven, John is able to see visions such as the throne of God; the series of seals, trumpets, and bowls; the fall of Satan and various demonic forces; conflict between divine and demonic armies; and finally, the New Jerusalem. John, rising above time as in an airplane, takes a transcendent view and traces the past, the present, and the future on his temporal map. Boundaries in the future are as penetrable to him as boundaries of the past. John sees both "what is and what is to take place after this" (1:19). His temporal map is analogous to a conductor's score: the conductor "sees" all parts of the score, that which has been played, that which is being played, and that which will be played.[27]

Permeable boundaries also mark the categories of good and evil. The fluidity between these is demonstrated through parodies between good and evil characters. Even God and Satan, the epitome of good and evil respectively, are not separated by hard, impervious boundaries. The demonic plane can claim no independent reality, for it derives from the heavenly, divine plane above. Demonic power becomes operative on earth when a "star" fallen from heaven is given a key to open the shaft to the abyss below (9:1). This "star" is later identified as the angel Abaddon or Apollyon, who rules over the bottomless pit (9:11)—and still later as the scarlet beast (17:8). In chapter 12 a similar transformation occurs when Satan "falls" from heaven. Through transformational symbols of descent and conflict, Satan—whose

---

27. Thompson, *Revelation*, 84.

authority and power lie behind all other evil forces in Revelation—is seen to metamorphose from the divine.

While boundaries do exist between heaven and earth, future and present, deity and humanity, and good and evil, there is dynamism to boundaries in Revelation. Boundaries do not fix limits beyond which it is impossible to pass. Rather "they locate the place where transformations occur, allowing a flow across planes, eras, social categories, or moral values. At the most fundamental level, the seer envisions reality as a world in process, a flow of becoming, a sequence of transformations that unfolds into various planes, eras, qualities, and objects."[28]

In the book of Revelation, "heaven" is the starting point for all revelation. John is taken into God's throne room so that he can see "behind the scenes" and understand how things fit together. "[A]nd there in heaven a door stood open" (4:1); this perspective is vital to the message of Revelation. John's cosmological perspective should be interpreted spiritually, not spatially. Going to "heaven," in John's vision, is less about cosmic geography and more about the place where God chooses to reveal himself, the place where heavenly realities are made plain. Heaven offers a divine perspective concerning events on earth, a new way of seeing that is beyond the control of earthly rulers. Heaven is the deeper dimension that offers God's perspective on what happens on earth.

We should not, however, restrict "heaven" to the spiritual dimension of reality, for it represents more than that. What John sees in heaven is not simply divine perspective. Heaven represents what is right and good and proper. When Jesus tells his followers to pray, "Your kingdom come . . . on earth as it is in heaven" (Matt. 6:10), he understands "heaven" not as a future destination for humans but as God's dimension of everyday reality. Heaven is in charge; heaven takes the lead; heaven represents what ought to be happening on earth.

Questions to Ponder

1. What verse, passage, or theme stands out for you as the key to chapters 12 through 14 of Revelation? Support your answer.
2. How do you picture evil in the world? Is personifying Satan as a hideous beast helpful or evasive? Explain your answer.

---

28. Ibid., 87.

3. Compare the view of government in Revelation 13 with Romans 13:1–7. How do we discern when a government is so violent and oppressive that it must not be obeyed?

4. How do you interpret the images about judgment, harvesting, and the winepress of God's wrath in chapter 14? Are they primarily images of condemnation or of salvation?

5. If theological and moral boundaries are indeed permeable, and if good and evil represent a continuum rather than dualistic opposites, what attitudes can you embrace or what actions can you take to ensure that good outweighs evil?

6. What message of hope do you find in chapters 12 through 14 of Revelation?

Chapter 7

Third Vision of Judgment: Seven Plagues (Revelation 15–16)

Summary: After Satan is thrown from heaven and goes stalking the earth, the imagery and symbolism of Revelation becomes even more terrifying, for the bowl plagues (Rev. 16) are twice as intense as the trumpets (Rev. 8–9). While we must deal with the element of violence and other problematic issues in Revelation, John's perspective does not promote violence and destruction but rather healing for the world. We understand this emphasis in terms of the biblical story of exodus and liberation. As in the exodus, salvation comes only through God's action and the blood of the Lamb. The plagues are meant for the conversion of the oppressors and for the liberation of God's people. Their intention is persuasive, not punitive. Like the plagues brought against Pharaoh, the plagues threatened against Rome are for the purpose of release and liberation rather than vengeance, cruelty, or war. Evil, however, does not escape, for it bears within it the seed of its own destruction. When evil gets out of hand, God will deal with it. The reference to Armageddon in 16:16, its only appearance in Revelation, provides assurance of the demise of evil, but should not be taken literally, since no actual battle is described.

Assignment: Read chapters 15 and 16 of Revelation

Key Passage: Revelation 15:3–4

Central Theme: Evil is temporary; ultimately it is God's love that changes the world.

150   PART III: God's Message of Judgment

Learning Objectives

Participants will examine:

1. The symbolic nature of Revelation's imagery of violence
2. How the message of the seven plagues correlates with the plagues in the book of Exodus
3. The relationship between the seven bowls and the seals and trumpets in Revelation's imagery of judgment
4. The meaning of Armageddon in 16:16
5. The meaning of "the great city" in 16:19

OUTLINE TO REVELATION 15:1—16:21

I. The Seven Last Plagues Introduced 15:1–8
   A. Preliminary Material 15:1–8
      1. Exodus Setting 15:1–4
      2. Heavenly Setting 15:5–8
II. The Natural Plagues 16:1–8
   A. The First Bowl 16:1–2
   B. The Second Bowl 16:3
   C. The Third Bowl 16:4–7
III. The Political Plagues 16:10–14, 16–21
   A. The Fourth Bowl 16:8–9
   B. The Fifth Bowl 16:10–11
   C. The Sixth Bowl 16:12–14, 16
      Interjection: Wake-up Call 16:15
   D. The Seventh Bowl 16:17–21

DÉJÀ VU ALL OVER AGAIN

Throughout Revelation John presents patterns of seven: seven seals, seven trumpets, seven signs, and now seven bowls. While the series appear formulaic, they are not mere reiterations, for John's artistry carefully lays out corresponding yet ever-progressing parallels to display from differing vantage points God's plan of judgment and redemption. While the accounts reinforce one another, they convey to the reader the certainty of God's rule over heavenly and earthly affairs. Within the imagery of seven angels pouring out the contents of seven golden bowls, John repeats his message, only this time with a marked stress on finality. These plagues are final; they announce proleptically that judgment is complete. The seven bowls of God's wrath are poured successively on the earth, the sea, the rivers and fountains, the sun, the throne of the beast, the great River Euphrates, and finally into the air (16:2–17). These are described as "seven plagues, which are the last, for with them the wrath of God is ended" (15:1). Here as elsewhere, when we hear of "God's wrath," we should think "God's justice," for God is not interested in destroying creation or humanity but in restoring justice. The seven plagues are the final cycle of visitations, bringing to a close God's warnings to the unrepentant and commencing the destruction of the forces of evil. John sets the stage with preliminary remarks, as he does in chapter 5 with the seals and in 8:1–5 with the trumpets.

ANALYSIS OF REVELATION 15:1—16:21: THE EXODUS REDUX

In our search to understand the violence of the seven trumpets and seven bowls, the exodus story provides great help. Imagine Revelation as a retelling of the exodus plot. In that story, when hearing the cry of the people suffering as slaves in Egypt, God threatens Egypt with ten plagues. These were designed to manifest God's power but also to persuade Pharaoh to let the Israelites go. Similarly, in Revelation God hears the people's cries and threatens to send new plagues against Rome. They too were designed to show God's power but also to liberate people from injustice. The book of Revelation is full of exodus imagery, linking the Christian journey to the Israelites' journey out of Egypt. God's people are not called to fight back or participate in violent activity; rather, as in the exodus, salvation comes through God's action and the blood of the Lamb.

The Seven Last Plagues Introduced (Chapter 15:1-8)

As Moses and his sister Miriam led the Israelites in a song of triumph after crossing the Red Sea (Exod. 15), in Revelation 15 God's people join together at the sea of glass, singing a new song praising God and the Lamb (Rev. 15:2–4). It is as if the song of the Lamb is another verse in the song of liberation and praise that Moses, Miriam, and the Israelites first sang at the sea. The "sea of glass" reminds us of the heavenly throne room in 4:6, only this sea is "mixed with fire," reminiscent of the suffering of the Israelite slaves in Egypt but also of the "martyrdom" of the bloody winepress of chapter 14—the trial by fire that Christ and his followers undergo on behalf of unrepentant humanity.

In Exodus 15:1–18 the words of the song of Moses after crossing the Red Sea are different from those of the song of the Lamb, though both celebrate deliverance from danger. The song of the Lamb (15:3–5) expresses confidence that all nations will be led to worship the one true God, because they will acknowledge God's justice and glory. One of the most striking features of this song of the triumphant believers is the absence of any mention of their own victory and their own achievement. The songs of believers through the ages celebrate the greatness of God's love and redemptive power.

The idea that the exodus is reenacted in Revelation is a valuable tool for comprehending the terrible plagues at the exodus as well as in Revelation 16. The plagues are warnings; their intent is to persuade. "They are meant for the conversion of the oppressors and for the liberation of God's people. Like the plagues brought against Pharaoh, the plagues threatened against Rome are the violence of release and liberation, not that of vengeance or cruelty."[1] In the exodus story there comes a time when the Pharaoh's heart is hardened, meaning he was no longer able to repent (Exod. 7:13). John leaves that reference out, suggesting that it is still not too late to repent. Earlier in Revelation we find an amazing moment of repentance, when the testimony of the two witnesses causes nine-tenths of the world's people to worship God (Rev. 11:13). The focus in Revelation is on the urgency of the present moment as a time of testimony and a call for change in the world. The threats of the seven bowls are like those of the exodus story. The goal of such horrific apocalyptic imagery is to bring about change, not to inflict cruelty, for God is not a cosmic destroyer.

In Revelation we learn that God grieves and laments over the world's pain. We hear this lament in Revelation 8:13 and 12:12. The word "woe" in these passages is not a foreboding of worse things to come but a cry of lament, like a mourner wailing "Oh, oh, oh!" at the death of a loved one. It is as if God is crying on behalf of a suffering world.[2] In the slain Lamb God hears our cries and comes to deliver. God will not curse the world, abandon his beloved creation, or leave anyone behind. At the end of Revelation God's

---

1. Rossing, "Journeys through Revelation," 57–58.
2. Ibid., 58.

Third Vision of Judgment: Seven Plagues (Revelation 15–16) 153

love for the world is consummated by coming to dwell in it. In Revelation 21:10 we read that "one of the seven angels who had the seven bowls full of the seven last plagues" (Rev. 21:10) reveals how everything turns out. When the holy city descends to earth, the earthly sea (representing all worldly evil, harm, and danger) is no more (21:1) and the heavenly glassy sea becomes part of the infrastructure of the New Jerusalem. John demonstrates this by incorporating the heavenly sea into his holy city: the city's wall, for example, is "clear as crystal" (21:11), the city itself is "clear as glass" (21:18), the street of the city is "transparent as glass" (21:21), and the river of the water of life is "bright as crystal" (22:1). Ideally married, the two become one, even as are heaven and earth.

Following the victors' song of praise, John sees that the "tent of witness in heaven was opened" (15:5), and out of this temple seven angels emerge with the seven plagues. Then one of the living creatures gives the angels golden bowls "full of the wrath of God" (15:7) and the presence of God is shrouded in smoke, making it impossible for ordinary comings and goings. The reason is clear: "we are honing in on the greatest showdown of them all . . . It is time, now, for the destroyers to be destroyed."[3]

We cannot overlook John's presentation of this final series of plagues within the context of worship. The language throughout chapter 15 is clearly that of worship and praise. The action denotes a liturgical setting, and the bowls are meaningful only to that setting. The bowls are holy vessels, used in the temple in Jerusalem (and previously, during the wilderness wanderings, in the tent of witness/ tabernacle) to carry ashes from the altar. John uses the same word in 5:8 as part of the equipment for the heavenly sanctuary. As the bowls are poured out on the earth to set the final plagues in motion, the earthly plagues emerge as the result of the heavenly worship, in which the prayers of earthly Christians play a part (cf. 5:8; 8:3–5). One can imagine Christians on earth praying "Thy kingdom come" and "Come, Lord Jesus!" (22:20; cf. 22:17 and Matt. 6:10; 1 Cor. 16:22). Yet before the final triumph, and as part of it, the eschatological woes are described once again, this time in their final intensity.[4]

The Seven Bowls (Chapter 16:1–21)

The final woes are not a chronological continuation of the preceding ones; they refer instead to the same period but present it from a different perspective. In them the preceding visions are intensified and finalized. Not merely

---

3. Wright, *Revelation*, 140.
4. Boring, *Revelation*, 174.

a fourth or a third but the entire world is struck by the blow against the sun and by the darkness, and everything in the sea dies. Not just the earth but the cosmos itself (heavens, sun, dry land, sea, rivers) is struck (16:1–8). Human rebellion against God has infected the cosmos, necessitating judgment as a means to its renewal. Like the plagues inflicted on Egypt during God's act of liberation, these terrors are viewed as manifestations of the righteous judgment of God. They are directed against those "who had the mark of the beast and who worship its image" (16:2).

The first four plagues bear a strong resemblance to the first four trumpets. They too are based on the plagues of Egypt and represent an attack on the same four elements of the physical world, and through them on humanity. But there is a difference: the trumpet plagues, like the Egyptian ones, are a call for repentance in the face of imminent doom. They symbolize, in a sense, the pre-exodus experience. The bowls, representing doom, correspond to the submersion of the Egyptians in the sea. In the series of seals and trumpets, John divided his sevens into groups of four, two, and one, interrupting the seals and the trumpets after the sixth vision by lengthy visions of the righteous witnesses, believing that faithful witness would succeed in bringing humans to repentance. Now, with the coming of the final plagues, the time for repentance has passed, and the series proceeds uninterrupted to its climax.

It is important to interpret individual plagues in light of the whole. The first four plagues are titled "the natural plagues" because they anticipate the judgment of Babylon and of those so deeply involved in Babylon's sins that they cannot be dissociated from her fall. The three final plagues are titled "the political plagues" because they represent the dethronement of the beast, the invasion of his empire by demonic hordes from beyond, and the destruction of his capital city, Babylon. If we maintain the integrity of the unit we see that the three final plagues no longer represent threats to nature or to individual humans for their contribution to the world's evil (this latter concern is addressed later, when the record books are opened in front of the great white throne, 20:11–12) but "the ending of persecution through the removal of the persecutor."[5]

When we read in 16:9 that those who bore the mark of the beast "cursed the name of God," this sets a distinctive interpretation upon the whole of this series. Outside of this chapter the apocalyptic part of the book attributes blasphemy only to the beast (13:1, 5, 6; 17:3). The threefold repetition of the statement that humans cursed God (16:9, 11, 21) can only mean that they have taken upon themselves the character of the false god they

---

5. Caird, *Revelation*, 201.

Third Vision of Judgment: Seven Plagues (Revelation 15–16) 155

serve. That foe must be defeated and annihilated (14:10–11; 20:15; 21:8; 22:15). The gospel message has been likened to a two-edged sword, and Christians must be faithful to both aspects of the message: God loves the world and longs for the repentance of his foes, but God will not allow evil to endure, for its days are numbered (cf. 12:12).

The disparaging statement by H. Richard Niebuhr, one of America's most famous twentieth-century theologians, is instructive at this point: "A God without wrath brought men without sin into a kingdom without judgment through the ministrations of a Christ without a cross."[6] Niebuhr's criticism of post-Enlightenment Christianity addresses not only John's concerns but those of our time as well. Evil must be named and addressed, its fruits judged and condemned, and its demise proclaimed and celebrated. That's what John does, and that's what we must do. The "wrath" of the creator God (16:1) may be viewed to consist of two things: (a) it allows human wickedness to work itself out, reaping its own destruction, and (b) it is something God addresses directly when evil gets out of hand. N. T. Wright notes how in the twentieth century three forms of evil—three marks of the Beast—reared their ugly heads and did untold damage to people and societies before they collapsed of their own weight and of the deception that sustained them: Communism, Fascism, and Apartheid.[7] The first four plagues represent a mixture of both types of "wrath."

When the first angel pours his bowl on the earth, painful and ugly sores appear. The irony is clear: the faithful witnesses of the Lamb in chapter 7 are sealed with God's protection, whereas the followers of the beast are marked with wounds that turn into festering sores and boils. This bowl is a reminder of the plagues of boils in Egypt (Exod. 9:10–11; cf. Deut. 28:35). When the second angel pours his bowl upon the sea, it turns to blood as its creatures die (cf. Exod. 7:17–21). Whereas during the sounding of the second trumpet a third of the creatures are destroyed, here everything dies. The third angel pours out his bowl into the rivers and springs of water, which also turn into blood (Exod. 7:17–18). The angel in charge—described as "the angel of the waters"—responds by acknowledging God's righteous judgment (16:5–6). While the designation for this angel has no known biblical parallel, there is nothing surprising about this expression. Because Jews thought of angels as responsible for specific areas of the universe, this angel is responsible for the waters. The angel's remark indicates that God's judgment is impartial, a case of the punishment fitting the crime. Unlike 1:4, where God is described as "who is and who was and who is to come," the third element is omitted

6. Niebuhr, *Kingdom of God*, 193.
7. Ibid., 142.

in 16:5, indicating that the consummation has arrived; the future is present in its finality. When the fourth angel pours his bowl on the sun, the sun burns people with fire (cf. Deut. 28:22). Those burned, we must note, are incorrigible, for they blaspheme even more. While this plague does not have a counterpart among the plagues of Egypt, it brings out an important characteristic of the series, the contrast between the fate of the idolaters and the reward of the redeemed.

Though the bowls of wrath are poured on the earth, sea, fresh water, and sun, their purpose is not to destroy nature but to enlist it in the service of divine retribution. The bowls end a time of repentance and begin the long progression that in chapter 20 culminates in a process by which God first rids the world of those who have assisted in its destruction and decay (chapter 16), then of the great imperial systems that have set up massive structures of injustice (chapters 17 and 18), and finally of the evil powers that lie behind those systems, ending with Death and Hades (chapters 19 and 20; cf. 1 Cor. 15:26–28). This powerful sequence affirms that God is loving and sovereign, and that his intervention is part of his love. As we noted with the various sequences of seven, the final scenes of judgment are not chronological accounts but different facets of the same ultimate reality. And in verse 15, where one least expects it and at a time when the hearer-reader might be considering Revelation as merely an entertaining story, John provides a "wake-up call": "Hey you," John seems to be saying, "stay awake. This message applies to everyone!"

The final three bowls—political in nature—are indirectly connected to the Egyptian plagues, but each is modified to denote impending doom. The darkness is not the three-day visitation of Exodus 10:21–29 but the total eclipse of the beast's imperial power. The frogs are no longer simply a minor nuisance from the Nile but are the frog-like demonic spirits of the false trinity, pervading the whole world with their deluding and seductive influences. The violent earthquake of the final bowl is unlike any before it in history. While appearing natural, like the first four plagues, these represent political disaster. They also parallel the three woes ushered in by the eagle (8:13) to denote the last three trumpets, for the first released from the abyss smoke that darkened the sun (9:1–3), the second released a demon army from beyond the Euphrates (9:14), and the third was accompanied by earthquake, thunder, and hail (11:19). Despite the similarities, the bowl triad is more obviously historical and political. The fifth plague refers specifically to the throne of the beast and its kingdom, Rome (16:10). The sixth bowl, like the sixth trumpet, reveals a demonic army released to cross the Euphrates and attack Roman civilization. As in the conquest of the Promised Land following the exodus, when God dried up the Jordan River to allow his people to attack the idolatrous Canaanites (Josh. 3:1—4:18), so God will dry up the Euphrates to allow the dreaded "kings from the east" to destroy the arrogant Roman civilization.

At this point the imagery shifts to the final battle on the Day of the Lord, commonly called Armageddon, though the place of the battle and the object of the battle are unclear. Neither is the battle described, though that will be the subject of 19:11–21. The armies amass at Armageddon, but instead of a battle, the scene shifts to the judgment of Babylon (16:19). The name Armageddon (Hebrew Harmagedon, lit. "Mountain of Magedon") is a composite image, comprising three different elements.

1. In the north of Palestine is a famous battlefield, beyond the city of Megiddo, a fortress town on the famous Via Maris, in antiquity the main highway connecting Egypt to Syria. This route was vital to commerce but also to armies in the region. Megiddo guards a pass close to mountains, beyond which lies the Plain of Esdraelon, where several major battles took place in ancient times (Judg. 5:19–21; 2 Kgs. 9:27; 23:29). Due to its strategic location, Megiddo was destroyed at least twenty-six times in antiquity and today lies in ruins, a remarkable archaeological site. According to prophetic symbolism, future battles might occur here once again. Of course it would be unusual for John suddenly to use a place name literally, particularly since there is no such place as the Mountain of Magedon.

2. Near Megiddo lies Mount Carmel, where Elijah defeated the pagan prophets of Baal, a Canaanite deity (1 Kgs. 18:20–46). This explanation would fit John's view that the prophetic Christian community stands in the tradition of Elijah in resisting Roman idolatry (cf. the allusion to Elijah and Mount Carmel in Rev. 11:5–6). John might have maintained such a connection, since he was originally from Palestine, but such a connection would have been missed by his readers.

3. Another possibility is that Magedon refers to the Hebrew word for "assembly," so Harmagedon would mean "Mount of Assembly." In this case it might refer to the expression in Isaiah 14:12–15, a text connected with the fallen angel Day Star, the beast's parody of the Lamb. As with much of John's imagery in Revelation, it is best to view Armageddon as a way to make concrete the expectation that the powers of evil would one day be brought together for their ultimate destruction. The term is symbolic and nothing more. John was not expecting a battle in northern Palestine, but at Rome.

Like the seventh seal and the seventh trumpet, the seventh bowl is the End. The splitting of the great city, the fall of the cities of the nations, and the punishment of Babylon are not three separate consequences of the earthquake but three aspects of the dissolution of imperial power. Although John describes the earthquake in physical terms, it is a political catastrophe he is depicting, not a natural one. Once again, as at the seventh seal (8:5) and the seventh trumpet (11:19), natural imagery indicates the doom of evil and the demise of the destroyers of the earth (11:18), which John addresses in chapters 17:1—21:8. The succession of plagues should be understood forensically, not emotionally or retributively. They do not represent divine rampage but rather divine justice against the destroyers of the earth. The repeated emphasis on lack of repentance (16:9 and 11) indicates the true allegiance of those who curse God. In these final plagues the focus narrows from the natural realm to the religious and political realms, leading to the climactic fall of "Babylon" in chapters 17 and 18.

Essay 7: Interpreting Revelation's Violent Imagery

One of the most serious criticisms of the book of Revelation is the charge that it promotes violence. Tragically, this portion of scripture has been used to endorse war, crusades, discrimination, and every kind of attack by Christians against perceived enemies, including people of other faiths. Such misuse of Revelation violates traditional Christian teaching of "just war," which forbids the use of violence except as a last resort. To be sure, there is violent imagery in this book, but the violence it depicts is the brute force of an oppressive, heartless empire. That, at least, is what we find in chapter 13, where John links the leaders of empire with the images of two beasts. Because they were its victims, the original readers of Revelation knew firsthand Rome's violent, conquering power over the whole world.

There are passages in Revelation, however, sometimes invoked with cries for vengeance, where violence is associated with God's judgment of evil, where the source of violence is God and the Lamb. The range of imagery poses a severe problem for interpreting Revelation as a Christian book, particularly when compared with the message of forgiveness in the Gospels. The picture of sinners being tormented forever in the presence of the Lamb (14:10) seems to present a different standard from that of Jesus praying for his tormentors and teaching his disciples to do the same (Luke 23:34; Matt. 5:43–44).

John's violent language can be properly interpreted by attending to four factors: (1) the fact of suffering, for John and his community, (2) John's appropriation of apocalyptic imagery, (3) John's metaphorical use of language, and (4) John's understanding of God's plan for the world, namely

Third Vision of Judgment: Seven Plagues (Revelation 15–16)

to eradicate evil and call people to repentance.[8] From John's theological and literary perspective, every event of apocalyptic violence in chapters 6 through 19 derives from chapters 4 and 5, meaning that the Lamb is the controlling image throughout; everything derives from the Lamb. In 19:13 the Messiah is clothed in the bloody garments of the eschatological victory, but the blood is his own (see 1:5). The scenes are scenes of "wrath," but it is the "wrath of the Lamb" (6:16). Death and Hades hold sway (6:7–8), but the Messiah holds the keys to Death and Hades (1:18) and will finally cast them—not their victims—into the lake of fire (20:14).

The concept of God's return in judgment, whether in a final sense or through periodic visitations, is prophetic and apocalyptic in nature. The seventh bowl, with its declaration of finality, "It is done!" (16:17), depicts the coming of God to make things right at the end of history. The same applies to the sixth seal, which mentions "the great day of their wrath" (6:17), apparently in reference to the final "Day of the Lord." Other warnings, including Old Testament admonitions such as "prepare to meet your God" in Amos 4:12 or "Alas for those who desire the day of the Lord" in 5:18–20, refer to events in history—in this case Israel's defeat at the hands of Assyria in 722 BC—and not to the end of history.

When Old Testament prophets spoke of God's coming to enact justice, they often used theophanic language, traditional poetic language associated with the coming or presence of God on earth (theophany). Literary theophanies in the Bible describe God's presence in language descriptive of earthquakes, thunderstorms, and other natural phenomena. The appearance of fire and smoke is characteristic of biblical epiphanies. At Mount Sinai, natural elements, cultic features, and mythological language combine to set forth the supreme theophany of the Old Testament. Yahweh speaks to the accompaniment of thunder, lightning, thick cloud, smoke, and the sound of a trumpet (Exod. 19:16–19), "while the whole mountain shook violently" (19:18; cf. Judg. 5:4–5; Deut. 33:2; Ps. 68:7–9). Natural features are also seen in Psalm 18:7–15; 29:3–9; 68:7–9; 77:16–20; 97:1–5; 114:3–8; 144:5–6. The author of the New Testament book of Hebrews (12:18–21, 25–29) has Old Testament theophanic references in mind when he refers to the new covenant mediated by Jesus as one that "cannot be shaken." In reality there are no true theophanies in the New Testament, for their place is taken by the manifestation of God in Christ (John 1:14; Col. 1:15; Heb. 1:1–3).

Theophanic language is used particularly to picture the day of wrath associated with God's final appearance. Examples of eschatological theophanies may be found in the prophetic literature of the Old Testament (Isa.

---

8. Boring, *Revelation*, 118.

30:27; 63:1–6; Zeph. 1:14–18; Hab. 3:3–16). Such theophanic descriptions are not uniquely Israelite. Sumerian and Akkadian hymns and Hittite and Ugaritic myths describe their storm god as a "divine warrior" who rides the storm and travels on cloudy chariots, and who hurls bolts of lightning as arrows. In response, the earth quakes, mountains stagger, and the ocean trembles.

The sixth seal (6:12–17) introduces the typical apocalyptic pattern for the end of history, much of it drawn from Old Testament symbolism. The language is highly colorful and need not, indeed cannot, be taken literally. The great earthquake that accompanies the opening of the sixth seal is not local or natural but cosmic and symbolic, a regular feature in the Jewish apocalyptic tradition. The use of cosmic convulsions to describe social and political upheaval is well established in biblical prophecy (compare the picture of chaos in Jeremiah 4:23–28, where the desolation caused by foreign invaders is intended). One can see an example of this pattern in the "little apocalypse" of Mark 13:5–36. Here, as elsewhere, the Gospels describe the second advent of Jesus Christ in the terminology of eschatological theophany (Matt. 24:29–31; Mark 13:24–27; Luke 21:25–28). The language is theophanic, used biblically to describe the Day of the Lord and judgment against evil. It reminds us that no one can hide from God. This scene would have been especially sobering to Christians who might have been tempted to seek security by assimilating into the dominant culture of their day. In Revelation John wants us to feel the threat of judgment—God's critique of evil—and not jump quickly to hope. These visions should not be viewed as predictions of actual events, but as warnings. Their goal is not destruction but repentance. John's aim is not to terrify Christians but to reassure them that God is in control and that God's purposes will be accomplished, even if the universe were to pass away.

In 6:12–17 John carefully builds up his picture out of Old Testament allusions, making particular use of five passages, each of which contributes something to the interpretation: (1) an early prophecy of Isaiah describes people hiding in caves from the terror of the Lord (Isa. 2:19); (2) a prediction of the utter destruction of Samaria in Hosea, which prompts the inhabitants to call to the mountains to cover their shame (Hos. 10:8); (3) a prediction by Isaiah that the sky would vanish "like a scroll rolling itself up" and all the stars would fall to the earth (Isa. 34:4; 24:21; in the ancient world heavenly bodies were commonly regarded as living beings with a divine authority, the principalities and powers that stood behind the authority of earthly kings); (4) a prediction in Joel of the turning of the sun to darkness and the moon to blood portends the judgment of the nations that have oppressed Jerusalem (Joel 2:30–31); (5) the question "who is able to stand?" is a quotation from

Malachi 3:2, from a prophecy of God's coming in judgment to purge Judah's sacred and secular life. In John's imagery the cosmic earthquake and the devastation of nature represent the overthrow of temporal orders organized in hostility to God.

This eschatological imagery found its way into the Roman Catholic Requiem Mass in a sequence known as the "Dies Irae" (Day of Wrath). The importance of this sequence in the Roman liturgy led to its use in musical settings such as those of Mozart and Verdi. It is also part of the traditional liturgy of All Souls Day (All Saints Day). The original musical setting for the "Dies Irae," a medieval Gregorian plainchant, has been used as a theme by many classical musicians, including Hector Berlioz, Charles Gounod, Gustav Holst, Gustav Mahler, and Camille Saint-Saëns. The finest representatives of this genre are Franz Liszt's *Totentanz* and Sergei Rachmaninoff's *Rhapsody on a Theme of Paganini*. A major inspiration for the Dies Irae came from the Latin Vulgate translation of Zephaniah 1:15–16 and from passages in the New Testament such as Luke 21:26, 1 Thessalonians 4:16, 2 Peter 3:7, and Revelation 20:11–15.

Questions to Ponder

1. What verse, passage, or theme stands out for you as the key to chapters 15 and 16 of Revelation? Support your answer.

2. What parallels do you see between John's first-century Christian churches and the people of Israel in the exodus? What are some differences? What parallels might we draw between the exodus and our own time?

3. How do you imagine God is concerned with the affairs of the world today, whether oppressive or compassionate and just? What aspects of violence in our world concern you most? How might God respond?

4. What is John's view on repentance? Are there times when you long to see people judged and punished instead of forgiven? Is it possible for Christians to live and witness faithfully without working for reconciliation between nations and races and creeds and genders and religions? Explain your answer.

5. What message of hope do you find in chapters 15 and 16 of Revelation?

Chapter 8

A Vision of the Harlot and Her Demise (Revelation 17–18)

Summary: Chapters 17 and 18 are a literary triumph of imaginative power. John is so certain that God will judge the persecutors of the church that he devotes two chapters to an account of the demise of the fabulous "grandeur that was Rome." Chapter 17 is a satire on Rome; it identifies Babylon (Rome) as a harlot and announces her fall; chapter 18 is a lament for the destroyed city. Earlier John introduced the four depictions of evil: the dragon, the two beasts, and the harlot. We come now to their defeat, in reverse order. The harlot is first to be destroyed, when the seven-headed beast turns against her (17:16).

Assignment: Read chapters 17 and 18 of Revelation

Key Passage: Revelation 18:4

Central Theme: Evil is bad business and will be judged; be careful the company you keep!

Learning Objectives

Participants will examine:
1. The power of symbols to communicate reality
2. Two forms of writing John uses in this section: satire and lament
3. The meaning of Babylon the whore

A Vision of the Harlot and Her Demise (Revelation 17–18)

4. The judgment pronounced against Babylon/Rome
5. The meaning of the political imagery in 17:9–14
6. The self-defeating nature of evil in 17:16–17
7. The triumph of good over evil, integrity over dishonesty, justice over injustice

OUTLINE TO REVELATION 17:1—18:24

I. The Fall of Babylon 17:1–18
   A. Description of the Harlot 17:1–6
   B. Significance of the Harlot and the Beast 17:7–14
   C. Punishment of the Harlot 17:15–18
II. The Lament over Babylon 18:1–24
   A. The Fall of Babylon 18:1–3
   B. A Call to Leave the City 18:4–5
   C. Judgment on the City 18:6–8
   D. Lament over the City's Fall 18:9–19
   E. Destruction of the City 18:20–24

A TALE OF TWO CITIES

The journey through Revelation culminates in a tale of two cities, Babylon and the New Jerusalem, with a call to choose between them. First comes the judgment of Babylon (Rev. 17–18), a metaphorical reference to Rome, the symbol of human community opposed to the things of God. John wants hearer-readers to be repulsed by its seductively violent ways, to be shocked at the collapse of its fabulous wealth and power. Even though Rome is still very powerful when John writes Revelation, he seeks to convince his audience that Rome is doomed. His urgent message is that believers must "come out" of the culture of Rome (18:4) before it is too late, so that they can participate as citizens in God's New Jerusalem, the city of blessing and promise. John paints a vivid portrait of Rome's elites lamenting the loss of their great wealth, while the victims of Roman injustice finally can rejoice. In painting this portrait, he personifies Rome in a shocking manner, describing the demise of all that Babylon represents. As elsewhere, the details of this angel's message are not meant literally. John's intent is not vindictive or violent in nature; his apocalypse is Christian and must be read in the light of Easter.

John's description of the angel introducing the vision as "one of the seven angels who had the seven bowls" (17:1) relates the fall of Babylon to the preceding seven last plagues, as the climax to which they were leading. When the angel introducing the vision of the New Jerusalem is later described in the same words (21:9), the fall of Babylon is represented as the parody of the Holy City. As the New Jerusalem is John's most extensive picture of salvation, so Babylon is his most extensive picture of judgment. As the New Jerusalem is a Bride (19:7), so Babylon is a Whore (17:5). Immorality, particularly political and economic immorality, is ultimately self-destructive (17:16).

Up to this point John has emphasized the sovereignty of God, repeatedly making the point that in the end evil will be eradicated. In the present, however, evil may be strong and believers helpless before it, but in reality evil's days are numbered; it can do no more than operate as God permits. John has deliberately structured his composition in order to place the detailed description of Babylon and its judgment prior to his description of the New Jerusalem, for the two cannot coexist.

ANALYSIS OF REVELATION 17:1—18:24

In the ancient world it was conventional to personify cities as feminine figures. The image of the gaudy "whore of Babylon" wearing gold jewelry and a scarlet dress and seducing nations with her cup of fornication (17:3–6) is one of the most unforgettable images of Revelation. That Babylon is a city (an empire) is made clear in 17:18: "The woman you saw is the great city that rules over the kings of the earth." Throughout Revelation Babylon is the nickname John gives to the hated Roman Empire. By doing so he triggers memories of the Hebrew scriptures. Just as the ancient Babylonian Empire destroyed Jerusalem in 587 BC, Rome violently destroyed Jerusalem in 70 AD, within the lifetime of John's initial audience. What makes Revelation so audacious is the way it overturns Rome's self-image as the goddess Roma with the image of a whore (17:4). While feminist scholars discuss the merits of the imagery of chapter 17, rejecting much as dangerous and demeaning of women (for example, Rev. 17:16 sounds like a horrific scene of gang rape), it is important to regard its intent as political and economic criticism. John's Harlot does not represent women or womanhood any more than Lady Liberty does.

A Vision of the Harlot and Her Demise (Revelation 17–18)

In addition to the imagery of the whore, John describes Rome in terms of drunkenness and fornication. The charge of "fornication" is cultural (with religious, political, and economic inferences) and has little to do with illicit sex (although that cannot be discounted altogether). Rome is an idolatrous city that seduces and oppresses nations and peoples with its fornication—its exploitation of everyone and everything around it. Here John is drawing on the cry of the Hebrew prophets against such enemies as Tyre, an ancient Phoenician maritime power north of Israel that terrorized its neighbors economically and seduced them religiously. The prophet Isaiah labeled Tyre's unjust trade as "prostitution" (Isa. 23:15–18). Nahum describes Nineveh, the ancient capital of Assyria, similarly (Nah. 3:4). Nations and rulers have become drunk on the "wine of the wrath of [Rome's] fornication" (18:3), John says. This image symbolizes Rome's wealth and power, which have become irresistibly enticing. In 18:23 John uses the imagery of "sorcery" to describe the spell cast by Rome's economic prowess. For a nation to fall prey to Rome's spell is to drink of her golden cup (17:4), which holds an intoxicating drug that poisons all who drink from it.

The Fall of Babylon (Chapter 17:1–18)

John's imagery often works in much the same way as modern political cartoons, which use well-known images to make sharp social critique. Like modern cartoonists, John also uses satire to expose the shortcomings of society. His portrayal of Babylon would make readers wonder why anyone would want to conform to Roman values, particularly its materialistic and militaristic qualities.

John's satire uses a template based on standard Roman imagery. A good example is a picture found on a Roman coin from the late first century. In the center of the coin is a graceful figure of the goddess Roma, the symbol of the city of Rome. John turns this picture into the image of a debauched prostitute. Instead of sitting calmly on the seven hills of Rome, John's version of Roma rides on a beast with seven heads. She no longer holds a sword gracefully in her hand but holds a goblet full of blood. John also changes the woman's name from Roma to Babylon in an effort to reveal something about her character. Giving her this name is a way of saying that Roman society has the same traits as Babylon, the capital of an empire remembered for its brutal conquests and its destruction of the temple at Jerusalem. This grotesque image of the harlot is designed to challenge the perceptions of Christians who thought that adopting the corrupt values of the imperial culture was perfectly acceptable. By creating this picture, John urges his readers to look beneath the surface to see the destructive currents at work in Roman society. The judgment of the kings who commit immoral acts with the harlot (17:2) serves as a warning to John's audience. Christians should be wary of rulers like Caligula and Nero and Domitian, who feign divinity while promising economic and social benefits, for such rulers are subject to the same temptations as are other humans.[1]

The mention of "the great whore" (17:1) represents the antithesis of the people of God, who are regularly seen in the Bible as God's bride. It is significant that in the present passage the word is "whore" (harlot) and not "adulteress." Here John is not speaking directly of Jews or Christians but of secular powers. The image, however, has a flip side, for in the Old Testament the prophets sometimes describe Israel's religious apostasy as harlotry: "How the faithful city has become a whore!" (Isa. 1:21; cf. Jer. 2:20; 3:1; Ezek. 16:15; Hos. 2:5; 3:3; 4:15). John is not identifying his audience with harlotry, but the message is clear: don't "sleep with the enemy"; don't compromise your faith or your values: "Come out of her, my people, so that you do not take part in her sins, and so that you do not share in her plagues" (18:4).

The fact that the whore sits on many waters may be an allusion to the mythological beast Leviathan, the chaos monster of the seas, but most likely it refers to seagoing commerce, a symbol of Rome's economic and military control over the Mediterranean (cf. 17:15). In the Old Testament, streams or rivers can refer to nations and peoples (Babylon is addressed as "You who live by mighty waters" in Jer. 51:13), and that is the meaning here (see Rev. 17:15). John has taken a conventional description of historic Babylon and reinterpreted it to give a picture of a world empire exercising dominion over subject nations.

Until now the angel has *spoken* about the whore. Now John is carried "in the spirit to a wilderness," where he *sees* her; this sight represents the start of John's third major vision (1:10 and 4:2 introduce the first and second visions). We have previously encountered the contrast between hearing and seeing. The city John sees is in the form of an alluring prostitute. There is no doubt that the harlot city is Rome, "the great city that rules over the kings of the earth" (17:18). The woman sits on her pimp, a scarlet beast with seven heads and ten horns, known for its blasphemy. This beast is no stranger to John's audience. It is the beast from the sea (13:1), one of the destroyers of the earth (11:18). Earlier John described this monster as having ten horns and seven heads, on which are blasphemous names (13:1; the same was said of the dragon in 12:3). The beast is imperial Rome, its heads representing

---

1. Koester, *Apocalypse*, lecture 10, "The Harlot and the Imperial Economy."

both the seven hills upon which Rome had been built and the "seven kings," the full line of its emperors (17:9–10).

The prostitute is ready for a night on the town (17:4–6); she is clothed in purple and scarlet, adorned with gold, jewels, and pearls, and holds a wine goblet full of impurities, designed to dupe her customers. She seems attractive, much as materialism and consumerism are attractive to us today, but her evil identity is clear: "Babylon the great, mother of whores and of earth's abominations" (17:5).

In verse 7 John indicates he will unveil the "mystery" of the woman and of the beast, that is, that he will make their reality clear. "Mystery" here, like the term "apocalypse," does not refer to a code or puzzle to be solved but rather to prophetic insight (cf. 1:20; 10:7). The harlot is clearly Rome, destroyer of Jerusalem, persecutor of Christians, and the mother of antichrists (17:6). The "mystery" is clarified in 17:7–18.

The harlot is insignificant apart from the beast. The beast's authority, indeed its very existence, is vacuous and devoid of substance. The beast is but a parody of God, who in Revelation 1:8 is called "the Alpha and the Omega . . . who is and who was and who is to come, the Almighty." In 17:8 the beast is described as one who "was, and is not, and is to come." The phrase can be understood in one of three ways. The fact that it once "was" indicates that imperial persecution of God's people occurred in the past. At the moment it "is not" means that there is currently no full-scale persecution of Christians by Rome. John believes this cessation may have lulled many Christians into a false sense of security and accommodation to Rome and what she represents. Scholars also find here a reference to the "Nero *redivivus* myth," the legend of Nero's return to life and the expectation of his return with Parthians to conquer Rome (see Dan. 8:8, a reference to Alexander the Great's premature death; cf. Rev. 13:3; contrast 5:6). A third possibility is that John (who was exiled for his faith) might have been thinking of Domitian as a second Nero, fearing he would unleash a second persecution of Christians. Whatever view we take, John saw the return of the beast as imminent (it "is to come") and was trying to prepare his congregations for the great persecution yet ahead. The Greek word for "is to come," *parestai*, is regularly used in the New Testament to indicate the advent of Christ. The beast here is clearly a parody of Christ, whose *parousia* ("coming") is from heaven, unlike the beast, whose sinister *parousia* is "from the bottomless pit" (the Abyss). The reference to the beast going "to destruction" means that from God's perspective the enemy is already defeated. Here John beseeches his followers not to accommodate to a lost cause. Yet this is exactly what many people do (called here "the inhabitants of the earth," an expression for unregenerate humanity, cf. 6:10). They are the ones "whose names have not been written in the book of life." The reference to "the foundation of the world" is a reminder of God's eternal purpose, something the unregenerate do not discern. The beast holds a fascination over some people, who simply can't resist its influence. For that reason they will be "amazed" at the reappearance of the beast after his disappearance.

John's pastoral function also underlies the rather complex symbolism of 17:9–12. The identity of the seven mountains (hills) has already been discussed, but the meaning of the seven kings, "of whom five have fallen, one is living, and the other has not yet come" (17:10) needs to be addressed. Their identity is much debated by scholars, particularly by those who view this as a reference to actual Roman emperors, to specific kingdoms in antiquity that persecuted Jews and Christians, or as an allusion to rulers at the end of history. A second approach interprets the imagery symbolically rather than allegorically. According to this interpretation, the seven emperors constitute a symbolic unit of seven but are not to be seen as actual emperors.

We can be spared much confusion if we follow this second approach and apply John's imagery consistently. Seven is a symbolic number in Revelation as well as in the rest of the New Testament. Seven represents totality and completeness, at least from God's point of view. For John, God is perfectly good and absolutely holy; conversely, Satan is completely evil and absolutely unholy. The beast and the whore are Satan's henchmen, representatives of imperialistic persecution and ethical degradation. Fitting Roman emperors or empires into the number seven actually detracts from John's intention and from the symbolism of Revelation. John is writing a pastoral letter, not a timeline or chronology of history. He is addressing the immediate problems of his audience, not presenting a puzzle for later readers to solve. If the number seven represents Roman imperialism in its totality, then five have passed away, which places John and his audience into the time of the sixth, which precedes the seventh (the climax), much as the sixth trumpet and the sixth bowl precede the finale. John locates himself at this point in time in order to let his readers know not only that they live at the height of the destruction perpetrated by imperial power, but also that God's judgment of this power is imminent. This interpretation also helps to explain why John indicates that the seven kings "have fallen" rather than "have died." Kings usually die or are slain; they don't fall. Amos 9:11 speaks of the "fallen" booth of David, a reference to David's kingdom having ended. John's figurative language in 17:10 is not about particular kings or groups of kings but about the end of evil imperialism, represented by Rome. To make enigmatic symbols correspond to something exact or precise is to desymbolize symbols, robbing them of their significance.

A Vision of the Harlot and Her Demise (Revelation 17–18)

Verse 11 returns to the image of the beast, "who was, and is not, and is to come." This beast is now identified with an eighth, and yet is also said to be of the seven. If we take the symbolic view that the eighth implies a parody of Christ, the beast is the false Christ ("antichrist") who claims to be special yet in reality is no more than one of the seven.[2] The seven do not reign alone or in their own might, for they have no "authority" apart from the beast (17:13). John tells us that their authority is derived from the beast, who persecutes Christ and his followers, but that his time is short (cf. 12:12), limited "to one hour," temporary at best. Evil's last hurrah will be its greatest defeat, because the beast and its minions are in a hopeless position.

Verses 15–18 describe the punishment of the whore. This passage shows the disunity of the forces of evil, their self-destructive power, and the certainty of God's triumph. In this passage Rome and all she represents (not culture in general but culture degraded) is defeated in a self-destructive battle, though it is clear that this defeat is God's doing (cf. 19:2, 11–21). After repeatedly depicting Rome as an embodiment of the beast, John now adds to the satire by providing a picture in which the beast and its allies, the ten kings, turn on the harlot and devour her. On a political level, empires and nations destroy one another; on a spiritual level, the biblical God uses the powers of evil as instruments of his judgment. God's power is the ultimate power, the "power-behind-the-power-behind-the-thrones. When evil turns on itself and the powers fall, it is the purpose of God announced in his words spoken by the prophets that is being fulfilled (17:17)."[3]

The message of chapter 17, embodied in verse 17, is one of hope. No matter what happens in this world, good and love will succeed, for God is love, and that love will defeat all evil, which ultimately is not sustainable. Eventually it will self-destruct. There will be times when suffering and persecution are great, but in the end the love of God will overcome anything detrimental.

The Lament over Babylon (Chapter 18:1–24)

In chapter 18 John provides a unique obituary for the harlot, describing the fall of Rome with pathos and realism. "The literature of the world contains few passages that compare in dramatic power with this dirge over the

---

2. In the Bible the number eight is often associated with Christ, with the resurrection "on the eighth day," and with new beginnings. If seven signifies completion, eight represents a new start, the new age, and the new covenant, said to be instituted by Jesus Christ.

3. Boring, *Revelation*, 185.

fallen city."[4] Like the tolling of a funeral bell, we hear the repeated lamentation, "Alas, alas, the great city" (18:10, 16, 19), and six times the refrain, "no more" (18:21–23). Despite her many sins and crimes, many mourn for Rome—kings of the earth, merchants, shipmasters, and sailors—because Rome's downfall is also their own. But from John's perspective, the fall of Rome is cause for rejoicing and praise to God (18:20; 19:1–3).

The language coincides with laments by Old Testament prophets, particularly in descriptions of the fall of Tyre (Ezek. 26–28) and of Babylon (Isa. 13; 14; 21; Jer. 50; 51). While there is similarity of language, John surpasses dirges from the past in realism and intensity, as if ancient poetry has lit a fire in the belly of his imagination, making this dirge a summation of all prophetic oracles against unrighteousness. The significance of John's lament is perhaps best captured in the poet Byron's memorable couplet: "When falls the Coliseum, Rome shall fall; And when Rome falls—the World." John has something like this in mind, for in announcing the fall of Rome, he is announcing the overthrow of all opposition to God.

The harlot's arrogance is seen in verse 7, where she deceives even herself with the thought, "I rule as a queen; I am no widow, and I will never see grief." Her motives are impure, and she is thoroughly self-deceived. She believes she can operate with impunity. She is greedy, materialistic, and violent, and her sins have found her out (Num. 32:23; this idea, of course, pertains to obstinate, arrogant, deceptive sin, characteristic of the harlot. Believers need not be anxious about such matters but rely instead on the testimony of such passages as Isaiah 1:18; Jeremiah 31:34; 1 Peter 4:8; and 1 John 1:9).

John's vision in chapter 18 depicts a world of unbridled materialism. He portrays the fall of Rome's vain and hackneyed world through the laments of those who profited from her wealth and commerce. As the merchants mourn, their lament reflects a worldview in which everything has been turned into a commodity. What really matters to them is not the city and its inhabitants but the money they have lost. The cargo list of verses 12 and 13 encompasses the span of Rome's extractions from the land and sea: gold, precious stones, pearls, exotic hardwoods and wooden products, ivory, metals, marble, luxury spices, food, armaments and war horses, and even "slaves—and human lives" (18:13). For John, the slave trade epitomizes life in Rome, a world in which humans have become a commodity. Those final two items in the cargo list furnish "the most explicit critique of slavery and slave trade in the New Testament."[5] In the nineteenth century, Christians

---

4. Metzger, *Breaking the Code*, 86.
5. Rossing, "Journeys Through Revelation," 66.

A Vision of the Harlot and Her Demise (Revelation 17–18) 171

in the abolitionist movement drew on John's eloquent expression of horror at the commercial sale of human beings to denounce slavery and the slave trade.

In Revelation 18 John puts an empire on trial; the final defeat of Rome/Babylon happens not on a battlefield but in a legal court scene. Instead of letting us see the ultimate destruction directly, the devastation of the evil city occurs "offstage," indirectly. The courtroom approach enables us to examine the guilt of Rome and the reasons for her judgment. This approach was utilized by the ancient Hebrew prophets in a literary format called "covenant lawsuit" (Heb. *rib*, often translated "indictment" or "a charge"; see Hos. 4:1; 12:2; Mic. 6:2). In Revelation the plaintiffs are the saints (all of God's servants, including apostles and prophets; see 18:20), representing Rome's victims who have suffered and died on earth; the charge is murder (18:24). The judge is God, who sentences Rome to receive "a double draught" in the cup she has mixed (18:6). The principle of double repetition in the Bible is emphatic, like the double "fallen" in 18:1 or the double "alas" in 18:10. Double does not mean that God's judgment is unfair. Rather it is a way of emphasizing that the judgment is fair, full, and complete. Babylon will get exactly what she deserves.

Joy breaks out in heaven and on earth when the sentence is announced, the post-trial celebration of plaintiffs extending to the celebration of God's angels in heaven (18:20). The message of the trial scene in the divine courtroom is that God desires justice. Verse 20b, therefore, is best translated: "God has exacted justice from her on the basis of your legal claims."[6] Those who oppress the world with unjust trade, oppression, and violence will be sentenced and punished accordingly. Their empires will come to an end. Jesus, the slain Lamb, represents in his resurrection the first fruits of God's new reign on earth. The harvest is being gathered; the new day is dawning. The scriptures make clear that we are not to fear God's wrath but hold fast to faith, participating in the joyous celebration of the victory of God's justice. As 19:1–5 makes clear, the church needs not postpone its celebration until the New Jerusalem. Amid the injustice of this world, Christians celebrate in their life and worship the victory of God's justice, in the sure hope that it will be realized ultimately throughout all creation. John allows readers the freedom to choose their response to the verdict. While the situation calls for celebration, the means of rejoicing is doxological and worshipful praise (19:1–8) rather than vindictive gloating. Hearer-readers may take the lamentation ironically or may actually join in mourning what was good in

---

6. Schüssler Fiorenza, *Revelation*, 99.

human culture but which has now been perverted and consequently subjected to the judgment of God.[7]

The vision culminates in 18:21–24 with a remarkable dramatization of Babylon's fall (cf. Jer. 51:63–64): an angel takes up a large millstone and throws it into the sea, proclaiming Babylon's destruction. When John wrote these immensely moving chapters about its fall, Rome was still very much alive, enjoying undisputed sovereignty and prestige. So great is John's faith in the sovereignty of God and so great is his confidence in the justice of God that he writes as though Rome had already fallen. As with many biblical judgments against evil empires, the fulfillment came eventually. For centuries Rome decayed and degenerated, but then, during a fateful week in August 410, Alaric, with his northern hordes of Goths, pillaged Rome; it was the beginning of the end for the Roman Empire.

In this climactic scene Revelation calls Christians to join God in his struggle for justice. With powerful exodus language God's servants are called to "come out" (18:4) of empire, to desist from participating in the sins of Babylon/Rome and to enter God's new reign. Revelation 18:4 is the key to this unit because it calls on God's people to be "a contrast community, witnessing to God's alternative way of life. The question for us today is to search out how the church can 'come out' of empire. How do we live according to a different story than the dominant stories of our contemporary culture and of empire? Revelation shows us the way—*God's people* become a sign of prophetic judgment against the exploitative empire by living differently."[8] One way to do so is to emphasize quality over quantity, to focus on our own character and to work to improve the character and priorities of all authorities, corporations, institutions, structures, and bureaucracies in our society and world, that they might reflect God's priorities and vision for his beloved world. Another way—a central way for those who wish to be Christ-like—is to embrace "Lamb power," the power of nonviolent love to change the world.[9]

A helpful analogy for understanding John's purpose in Revelation 18 is the story of Alfred Nobel, the inventor of dynamite. Nobel became wealthy by selling explosives to mining and construction companies. One day Alfred's brother was killed in an accident, and certain newspapers mixed up the names, believing that Nobel himself had died. So they wrote his obituary; the headline identified his legacy as one of wealth and violence: "The merchant of death is dead. Dr. Alfred Nobel, who became rich by finding

---

7. Boring, *Revelation*, 186.
8. Rossing, "Journeys Through Revelation," 67–68.
9. See the discussion on Revelation 5:6.

more ways to kill more people faster than ever before, died yesterday." When Nobel read his own obituary he became so depressed that he decided to do something that would leave a different legacy. He therefore created the Nobel prizes for contributions to science, medicine, literature, and peace as his legacy.[10] John's obituary in Revelation can produce a similar effect. It can startle readers into seeing the destructive legacy of their society and lead them to commit themselves to a different future, a future that John links to the Creator and the Lamb.

Essay 8: Interpreting Revelation's Symbolism

In addition to Babylon, her harlotry, and earlier images of the four living creatures and the four horsemen, many symbols in the book of Revelation are obviously drawn from the Old Testament, where their content helps to define them. Twelve such symbols include (1) *the tree of life* (2:7; 22:2, 14, 19), a reference to Genesis 3:22, where the tree is an emblem of eternal life; (2) *the hidden manna* (2:17), a reference to the food that sustained the Israelites during their wilderness sojourn (Exod. 16:32–34) and possibly an allusion to the Jewish idea that at the temple's destruction the prophet Jeremiah hid the pot containing the manna from the Ark of the Covenant, which would reappear when the Messiah came; (3) *the rod of iron* (2:27), an echo of Psalm 2:9, which indicates that those who overcome will share in Christ's decisive victory over his enemies; (4) *the morning star* (2:28; 22:16), which is Christ himself (cf. 2 Pet. 1:19), a reference to the prophecy of Balaam in a passage commonly taken to refer to the Messiah (Num. 24:17); (5) *the key of David* (3:7), a reference to Isaiah 22:22, where the key represents control over the royal household and authority to grant or refuse access to the king's presence; (6) *the mighty angel* (10:1–7; cf. 5:2; 18:21), whose description owes much to Daniel 10:4–6; cf. Dan. 12:5–9; 8:26); (7) *the beast out of the sea* (13:1–10), a composite of the four beasts of Daniel's vision (Dan. 7:3–8), which John combines into the picture of the Roman world order; (8) *the two witnesses* (11:3–12), which are not named but may be explained on the basis of their connection with the lampstands and the olive trees of Zechariah 4:11–14, though the description of them accords better with Elijah and Moses, who "have authority to shut the sky, so that no rain may fall during the days of their prophesying, and they have authority over the waters to turn them into blood, and to strike the earth with every kind of plague" (Rev. 11:6); (9) *fire and sulfur/brimstone* (14:10; 19:20; 20:10), which

---

10. Koester utilizes this analogy in his analysis of Revelation 18 in *Apocalypse*, lecture 10, "The Harlot and the Imperial Economy."

seem to be modeled on the burning of Sodom and the cities of the plain described in Genesis 19:24; (10) *the book of life* (3:5; 17:8; 20:12, 15), a feature found in Luke 10:20 and Hebrews 12:23 and a reference to Psalm 69:28; (11) *lightning, thunder, earthquake* (8:5; 11:19; 16:18), a feature appearing at the conclusion of the seals, trumpets, and bowls and a reference to the Sinaitic theophany in Exodus 19:16; (12) *the wine of God's wrath* or *the wine of the wrath of her fornication* (14:8, 10; 16:19; 17:2; 18:3), the former a reference to God's judgment upon evil and the latter to the process of evil that God tolerates throughout history. These related concepts are based respectively on Isaiah 51:17 and Jeremiah 51:7.

Taken as a whole, the symbols of Revelation are not fanciful or imaginary but are related to ideas that would be readily recognized by the original audience. The Old Testament, apocalyptic writings, and the common phenomena of everyday life provided the background for John's figures. They are partially obscure to the modern reader because they belong to a bygone era, but when explained biblically, they take on new meaning. Of course it is presumptuous to claim that their meaning is perfectly explained by relating them to their original setting. There will always remain an aura of mystery around them because one is never quite certain what concepts, events, or trends they denote. The interplay of disturbing and inspiring images is a key to how Revelation works. The images move in cycles, with the author taking us through scenes that threaten us and into a vision of something hopeful and life-giving. It is helpful to keep in mind that John's images are not final; they are not designed to dispense bits of data for readers to absorb. Instead, like great works of art, they are open-ended, engaging our imagination and stimulating our thoughts. The closer one looks at the imagery, the more possibilities one sees.

Questions to Ponder

1. What verse, passage, or theme stands out for you as the key to chapters 17 and 18 of Revelation? Support your answer.

2. How would you describe the seductive effects of "empire" on current political and economic practices and policies? What might be the hidden dangers in a booming economy or a favorable political climate?

3. What might it mean for you and your church (or social group) to "come out" of empire? How might communities of faith embody a different way of life?

A Vision of the Harlot and Her Demise (Revelation 17–18) 175

4. How do you respond to the courtroom scene in 18:20, particularly the rejoicing of the winners? Does it foster discomfort, confidence, or some other feeling?

5. What message of hope do you find in chapters 17 and 18 of Revelation?

PART IV

God's Message of Hope
Making All Things New

Chapter 9

A Vision of Final Judgment and the Demise of Evil (Revelation 19–20)

Summary: When we read Revelation as a literary work, we find that the second half of the book is dominated by the struggle against the agents of evil. The introduction of the four depictions of evil—the dragon, the two beasts, and Babylon the harlot—began systematically in chapter 12. Chapters 17-20 provide an account of their defeat, in reverse order. The harlot is first to be judged and destroyed (chapters 17–18), then the two beasts are defeated, when Christ overpowers them with the sword (the word) that comes from his mouth (19:11–21). That leaves only Satan, who is temporarily banished from earth to the abyss below, only to emerge for one final stand against the saints and "the beloved city" (20:7–10). By way of contrast to the harlot and immediately after her fall, John introduces the church, the resplendent bride of Christ dressed in fine white linen (19:7–9). The voices in the heavenly sanctuary announce the festive celebration of "the marriage supper of the Lamb" (19:9; in chapters 21 and 22 the bride is transformed into the magnificent Holy City, the New Jerusalem). This section also introduces the much-debated concept of the millennium, also called the "first resurrection," a time when Satan is bound (20:2–3) and faithful Christians reign with Christ for "a thousand years" (20:4–6). Because God's justice finally prevails, John includes a scene of the final judgment (20:11–15), where the dead gather before the throne to be judged according to the records found in two books, the Book of Merit and the Book of Mercy. In the end cosmic evil is annihilated; Satan is hurled into the lake of fire, together with Death and Hades (20:11–15) and those who refuse God's love (21:8).

180 PART IV: God's Message of Hope

Assignment: Read chapters 19 and 20 of Revelation

Key Passage: Revelation 19:13

Central Theme: In the end God will annihilate evil and judge the world with equity and love.

Learning Objectives

Participants will examine:

1. The power of symbols to communicate reality
2. The judgment announced against Satan, the beast, and the false prophet
3. The meaning of the church as the Bride of Christ in 19:7–9
4. The nature of Christ's *parousia* (return) in 19:11–16
5. The nature of Christ's defeat of evil in 19:21
6. The meaning of the "double eschatology"—Satan's twofold punishment—in chapter 20
7. The meaning of the millennium in 20:4–6
8. The meaning of the "lake of fire" (second death) in 19:20 and 20:14
9. The meaning of the great white throne judgment in 20:11–13
10. The triumph of God's justice and love

OUTLINE TO REVELATION 19:1—20:15

I. Visions of Final Judgment and Eternal Reward 19:1—20:15
   A. Celebrating the Fall of Babylon 19:1–5
   B. The Marriage of the Lamb 19:6–10
   C. The *Parousia*: The Coming of Christ 19:11–16
   D. Armageddon: Overthrow of the Beast and the False Prophet 19:17–21
   E. The Binding of Satan 20:1–3
   F. The First Resurrection: The Millennium 20:4–6
   G. Satan's Last Stand: Gog and Magog 20:7–10
   H. The Last Judgment 20:11–15

A Vision of Final Judgment and the Demise of Evil (Revelation 19-20)

ANTICIPATING THE NEW JERUSALEM: OVERVIEW

Following the model established by the author of the book of Daniel, John's visions collapse ultimately into a pattern of four, each given a unique geographical setting: an island (1:9—3:22), heaven (4:1—16:21), a wilderness (17:1—21:8), and a high mountain (21:9—22:5). Chapters 19:1—21:8 form the second half of John's third vision, which chronicles the systematic defeat of the four depictions of evil.

Eugene Boring presents a different compositional scheme, one that divides Revelation into a threefold apocalyptic pattern that (a) begins with the present troubles, (b) portrays them as intensifying before the End, and (c) then pictures the ultimate victory of God in the End itself. This means that things get worse before they get better, an intensification immediately followed by the demise of evil. Some interpreters understand this to be the meaning of John's enigmatic expression "time, times, and half a time" (12:14), also borrowed from Daniel (7:25; 12:7). If one follows Boring's pattern, each of his three major divisions of Revelation begins with a transcendent scene of the glory of God and/or Christ, from which proceeds a sevenfold vision. In part one the inaugural vision of Christ (Rev. 1:9-20) results in the seven messages to the churches (2:1—3:21). Part two is introduced by the vision of the throne room of God and the Lamb (4:1—5:14), which opens into the sevenfold visions of the last plagues, culminating in the fall of Babylon (6:1—18:24). Part three is preceded by a vision of the heavenly glory of God (19:1-10), which results in the final septet of visions portraying the *parousia*, last battle, binding of Satan, millennium, defeat of Gog and Magog, last judgment, and the New Jerusalem (19:11—22:21). Boring's model is attractive in its simplicity and offers a compelling explanation for 19:1-5. Whether a continuation of the theme of the judgment of Babylon begun in 18:1 or the start of a new group of visions, that passage plays a transitional role and clearly has a unique identity.

ANALYSIS OF REVELATION 19:1—20:15: ONE DOWN, THREE TO GO

The Messianic Banquet: Weal and Woe (Chapter 19:1-21)

Worship is the dominant note at the start of this passage. The jubilation over the judgment of Babylon is not gloating but celebration of the enactment of justice by the true judge of the cosmos. Worship is characterized by praise, summarized in the word "Hallelujah," a word unique to John. It occurs only here in the New Testament, where it appears four times (19:1, 3, 4, and 6). Hallelujah, meaning "praise the Lord" or "salvation to our God," is found frequently in the Psalms, expressing God's victory. When we hear "Hallelujah" many of us think of Handel's "Hallelujah Chorus," where the composer used the word in repetitions of fives, adding his own (fifth) praise to John's fourfold usage. In Revelation 19:1–6 God is praised for (a) his salvation (victory), yet to be unveiled, for (b) the justice of his judgments, and for (c) his destruction of evil. The antiphonal response, Amen (verse 4), is a way of saying "it is true," or "you bet!" In verse 5 "Hallelujah" is translated for the first time: "Praise our God." Verse 6 celebrates the omnipotence of God, the Almighty. The unfolding eschatological events disclose what had always been known and declared, that God alone is the true sovereign of the world.

John introduces this segment on the judgment of evil with the language of worship, not with the language of conflict. While the passage speaks of the harlot and of her demise ("the smoke goes up from her forever and ever," verse 4), the scene is described as taking place in heaven, where hallelujah choruses are sung by multitudes praising God for his judgments, which "are true and just" (verse 2). The harlot is gone and evil's doom is sure: one down, three to go!

After celebrating the destruction of decadent Babylon, the wedding feast is the next element in God's redemptive plan. Mention of the wedding feast signals that the climax of the drama is close at hand. The image of the relationship between God and his people as a marriage comes from the Old Testament, where Israel is called God's bride (Isa. 54:18; Ezek. 16:7; Hos. 2:16–20). The Song of Solomon, included in the Jewish scriptures because it was seen as an allegory of the love between God and his people but read often at Jewish weddings as a poem of erotic love, points to God's great banquet feast (Song 2:4; cf. Isa. 25:6–10). In the New Testament the church is represented as the bride of Christ, beloved of Christ to the point that he gave himself up on her behalf (Eph. 5:25). The concept is captured in the words of a familiar hymn: "With his own blood he bought her, and for her life he died."

The majestic chorus of praise records the fourth of the seven beatitudes found in Revelation: "Blessed are those who are invited to the marriage supper of the Lamb" (19:9). The way that John sees things is that God/Jesus is the bridegroom, Israel/church is the bride, and the redeemed are the attendants. The wedding guests are also the citizens of the Holy City, and the unresponsive guests are those who reject Jesus and his invitation to the feast. The wedding feast also corresponds to the coming of the kingdom and the bride to the New Jerusalem (21:2).

A Vision of Final Judgment and the Demise of Evil (Revelation 19-20)

In verse 10 John is said to fall down in front of the angel to worship him, to the angel's chagrin. In biblical times people often worshipped angels, but this practice was criticized in the New Testament (see Col. 2:8), for to worship anything other than God is idolatry. The angel calls himself a "fellow servant" and bids John worship God alone. The last part of the verse, "For the testimony of Jesus is the spirit of prophecy" reminds us of the beginning of Revelation, where the central thing about prophetic inspiration was the testimony that Jesus bore upon the cross—faithfulness to death—and which the church now bears to Jesus.[1]

Heaven opens in 19:11 and the tempo of the action increases in a succession of seven visions, preparatory to the end; each vision begins with the words "I saw." This is the point at which the perspective of heaven prevails on earth, finally dispelling all the lies of the beast. Out of the opened heaven there comes into view a white horse, symbolic of victory (19:11). Its rider is called "Faithful and True." His eyes are piercing, like a flame of fire (cf. 1:14) and on his head are many crowns, indicative of his rule over many nations and peoples. The "white horse" reminds us of the first horseman of 6:2, but this rider is not to be identified with the earlier one. Here there can be no doubt that the figure is Jesus, "clothed in a robe dipped in blood" (19:13). In Isaiah 63:1-3 the conqueror's garments were stained with the blood of his enemies, but here with his own blood (see 5:6 and 9). Whereas the seven-message series in the beginning of Revelation (2:1—3:22) had depicted Christ as the judge of the Christian community, 19:11-21 presents him as the judge of the nations. The title "Faithful and True" indicates that like the Lord God Almighty, he judges with justice (19:11; cf. 16:5-7; 19:2). This title stresses that the justice meted out by Christ is just and refers simultaneously to 3:14, which calls Christ "the faithful and true witness."

Among the various titles and names of Jesus in this section is the enigmatic reference to "a name inscribed that no one knows but himself" (19:12). In ancient Judaism, to know someone's name was to know that person's character or essence (hence Moses's desire to know God's name in Exod. 3:13, to which only a circumlocution is given in response, Exod. 3:14). This interpretation points to something mysterious about Christ, which must be guarded. The reference is also reminiscent of the biblical prohibition against magical use of divine names, a prohibition implied in the third commandment (Exod. 20:7). The statement probably correlates with the comment in Matthew 11:27 that "no one knows the Son except the Father," meaning that some aspects of Jesus, including intimacy with the Father, are reserved for God only.

---

1. Wright, *Revelation*, 170-71.

The rider is called "The Word of God" (19:13), a title reminiscent of John's Gospel (1:1, 14) and of Wisdom 18:15–16: "your all-powerful word leaped from heaven, from the royal throne, into the midst of the land that was doomed, a stern warrior carrying the sharp sword of your authentic command . . ." The title is not Christ's name but a reference to his office; it is through him that God has spoken fully and finally to humanity (see Heb. 1:1–2).

In 19:14 Jesus is accompanied by his armies, dressed in fine white linen and riding on white horses (19:14). What a strange army, and what odd armor! John adds one final detail, the most important and most intriguing of all. As in the initial vision of the heavenly Christ (1:16), so here "from his mouth comes a sharp sword with which to strike down the nations" (19:15). That sword is his word, his only weapon, the Word of God, which he is (19:13). By that word "he convicts, convinces, and exonerates."[2] This is not the slaughtered Lamb turned slaughterer, but it is the witness turned judge. The "faithful and true witness" (3:14) is now called "Faithful and True," but not witness. His faithfulness to the truth now makes him the judge of those who persist in lies. In consequence of this victory over deceit on earth, the devil himself, the source of all lies, is bound so that he may not deceive the nations (20:1–3).

On the Last Day, the Word serves as judge. With this understanding of the witness of Jesus to the truth of God, intended to liberate people from error, but which must in the end judge those who reject it (19:20), it is useful to compare John 12:46–48: "I have come as light into the world, so that everyone who believes in me should not remain in the darkness. I do not judge anyone who hears my words and does not keep them, for I came not to judge the world, but to save the world. The one who rejects me and does not receive my word has a judge; on the last day the word that I have spoken will serve as judge . . ." This passage, conveying the same thought in an idiom rather different from Revelation's, helps to explain how Christians understand Jesus as both Savior now and Judge at the end, without feeling any incongruity in that combination.

In a figure without parallel in the New Testament, John portrays the return of Christ (the *parousia*) as the Messiah who will rule the nations with a rod of iron (see Ps. 2:9). His many crowns denote his rightful sovereignty over the world and he properly bears the title claimed by the emperors of Rome: "King of kings and Lord of lords" (19:16). While this militaristic imagery seems alien to Jesus of Nazareth, the Prince of Peace (Isa. 9:6; cf. Matt. 21:1–9), John has not forgotten the definitive picture of the nature of

---

2. Metzger, *Breaking the Code*, 91.

Christ's conquest—a Lamb standing as if it had been slaughtered—given in 5:6. John uses traditional messianic imagery, but he consistently asks his audience to interpret the Lion as the Lamb, even in the bloody scene to follow (19:17–21), probably the same final battle narrated already in 16:13–16, known as Armageddon. The blood is not that of his enemies "but his own martyr blood in union with the martyr blood of his followers who, like him, have suffered/testified at the hands of Rome."[3] This is the meaning of the fact that he treads (not "will tread" as in the NRSV) "the wine press of the fury of the wrath of God" (19:15; see the discussion on 14:17–20). John's theology as a whole calls for this unexpected interpretation (see 7:14). He uses ancient imagery but fills it with new content. Before the final battle (Armageddon) ever begins, Christ's garments are already bloody with his own blood. This important change from Isaiah 63 reflects the fact that for Revelation, the crucifixion is the key battle, not some future battle of "Armageddon." The battle of Armageddon is over as soon as it begins because the victory has already been won by Jesus on the cross.

Moreover, there is no reason to think that Christian believers take part in chapter 19's war, certainly not as traditional warriors. The fact that the armies are said to be clothed in white linen means that they have been washed in the blood of the Lamb (7:14), unlike the garments of Jesus, which are red with his self-sacrifice. The "armies of heaven" may be simply the angelic host that was expected in apocalyptic tradition (see Matt. 25:31; Mark 13:27; 2 Thess. 1:7–8), but the image may also suggest the church triumphant in heaven (7:9–17; 14:4; 17:14), for this army wears the same white garments as the faithful church (19:14; cf. 6:11; 7:14; 19:8; 22:14). Unlike certain Jewish eschatological battles (such as depicted in the War Scroll of the Dead Sea Scrolls, where thousands of warriors take the field at the end of the age, arrayed in sophisticated military weaponry), the saints do not actually participate in the final battle, for the victory belongs to God/Christ alone, and was already achieved in the life and death of Jesus.

The message of the book of Revelation thus reframes the whole concept of victory, away from the militaristic meaning given it by Rome. Nowhere in Revelation do God's people wage war. When they "conquer" or "become victors," this is accomplished through the blood of the Lamb and through courageous witness. For all its holy war imagery, Revelation does not promote war. God's wrath, ultimately, is the wrath of the Lamb (6:16), not that of a Lion.

Surprisingly, the final coming of Christ does not figure prominently in John's account. It is one of several pictures about the End, described briefly

---

3. Boring, *Revelation*, 196.

by comparison with the detailed description of the New Jerusalem; but it does bear significance. John's first response to the perennial question, "What will the End be like?" is to provide a picture of the return of Christ. For John, the End is a person; not something but someone. And that someone is not a stranger but a bridegroom. For John, the second coming of Christ is not to be rationalized or made into a chronological timetable; that is not its purpose. Rather it is one aspect of a set of symbolic pictures that convey a variety of confessional possibilities:[4]

1. Christ came as the revelation of God and *never left*. Christ remains in the world, present not only to and with his church but also to unbelievers. The indications of the Holy Spirit's presence in the church and the world, identified as the continuing presence of Christ, belong to this way of thinking. John affirms this view in Revelation 1:13, 20, and 2:1;

2. Christ came as the revelation of God and departed, though he makes himself present from time to time; he *comes again in judgment and in grace*, within the events of history and the experience of the church and individuals. Christ comes in judgment if the church or individuals do not repent and in grace to make himself known in the church's worship. John affirms this view in Revelation 2:5, 16, and 3:3, 20;

3. Christ came as the revelation of God and departed, but he *will return unconditionally at the end of history* to bring this age to fulfillment and establish God's new order. John affirms this view in Revelation 19:11–21.

John's picture of the *parousia* merges with that of the last battle to form a bizarre aftermath of Armageddon called "the great supper of God" (19:17). The imagery, taken from the mythical pictures of ancient Near East religion, depicts the primeval battle between the deity and the chaos monster. Though the monster is provisionally defeated by the act of creation, the struggle goes on. Israel's adaptation pictures a warrior leading the people of God against the monster and his minions (including Israel's historical enemies), thus bringing the reign of evil to an end. In apocalyptic literature, God's salvation of Israel from traditional enemies, the longing for the return to an idealized past, and the joyous celebration of the final defeat of evil were all projected onto a cosmic screen, where God defeats the ultimate enemy in a final battle (Ezek. 38—39). John's Christianized version of this apocalyptic scenario is presented in 19:17–21.

The losers in the battle are the seven-headed beast and the beast from the land (the false prophet). The first personifies tyranny and the second

---

4. For an extended discussion see Boring, *Revelation*, 198–99.

A Vision of Final Judgment and the Demise of Evil (Revelation 19-20)

promotes religious compromise by turning political leaders into gods. Both entities are destroyed, but in different ways. No battle is described, because the decisive battle has been won long ago. Without a struggle, in a manner reminiscent of the messianic king of Isaiah 11:1–5, the transcendent powers of evil are taken and cast into the ultimate place of destruction, the lake of fire (19:20). The victory, without bloodshed, is a victory only Christ can accomplish, for it is "a victory over violence itself."[5]

The rest—the historically rebellious human community—are killed with the "sword" and receive the judgment reserved for those who have rebelled against God. It is important to note that their punishment is different from that of the satanic trio, which is tormented in the lake of fire. Human devotees of the destructive political and imperial cult of Babylon/Rome are killed instantly (19:17). The image of the messianic banquet ("the marriage supper of the Lamb," 19:9), is resumed, this time in an ironic reversal, for the banquet has become the slaughter-meal of the vanquished. In a reversal of Zephaniah 1:7–9, those who supposed themselves to be guests turn out to be the menu (Rev. 19:21). The imagery of birds of prey is taken from Ezekiel 39:4 and 17–20. This is not the last time we see in Revelation the vanquished, who reappear in 20:3, 8; 21:24–26; and 22:2. The conjunction of terror and celebration fitted into one conceptual picture "makes clear that both God's judgment and God's grace are more than we can imagine."[6]

All this is symbolism at its highest. No one imagines that such statements are literal. While the descriptions are not of real events, they are symbols of real occurrences. The message that John conveys through his symbolism is that evil will surely be banished. Christ, the King of kings and the Lord of lords, will be victorious, both in protecting his followers and in defeating his foes. To those who refuse his love, he stands knocking at the door (3:20). (For further discussion see essay 10, "Interpreting Revelation's Inclusive Language.")

Judgment Day (Chapter 20:1–15)

Having related the destruction of the beast and of the false prophet, John turns to the ultimate foe, identified in Revelation by four sinister titles: the dragon, the ancient serpent, the devil, or Satan. His punishment is described in two stages, called John's "double eschatology." In the first stage (20:1–3), an angel descends from heaven carrying in his hand a chain and the key to the bottomless pit (20:1). The image of the key to the Abyss appeared

---

5. Wright, *Revelation*, 173.
6. Boring, *Revelation*, 200.

earlier (see 9:1), where it opened the shaft of the pit, releasing a horde of demonic locusts upon the earth. This time the pit is locked and sealed, suggesting defeat and finality. The final battle is over: Armageddon culminates when Satan is captured, chained, and banished below the earth, where he is bound for a thousand years. In the second stage (20:7–10), the dragon, released from his prison in the underworld, gathers a ghost army and marches against the camp of the saints. However, as in 19:19–21, no battle ensues. Instead, fire from heaven devours the army of Gog and Magog, and the devil suffers the same fate as the two beasts. Their punishment signals the final and everlasting destruction of all evil and demonic power.

Revelation 20:1–10 is one of the most difficult passages in the entire book, the source of great contention and endless disputes, particularly among Protestant evangelicals (the various millennial positions are introduced and discussed in essay 9). Revelation 20 introduces John's "double eschatology," one of the most mystifying scenarios in Revelation. After Satan's banishment he "must be let out for a little while" (20:3). To this point John has taken ideas from Jewish and Christian eschatology—the great banquet, the last battle, and the last judgment—and applied them to his own vision and understanding, indicating how he saw these expectations fulfilled. But then follows the millennium, and after the millennium an entirely new set of fulfillments of the same expectations: Gog and Magog are defeated in battle, the dead are judged, and the New Jerusalem descends from heaven like a bride adorned for her husband. Why would evil be defeated and banished, only to emerge again? One way to solve this dilemma is to downplay the concept of the millennium itself, regarding it as an item of traditional eschatology that John felt bound to include, although it played no integral part in his own thinking—it occurs only in this one passage in Revelation and nowhere else in the New Testament. But the concept does have validity for John, as we shall see. Dual fulfillment, including the intervening millennium, is vital to his theology.[7]

Revelation 20:4–10 bristles with questions. Why, for example, must Satan be loosed after having been securely sealed in the Abyss, and why the millennium? Why should the martyr church wait a thousand years for the bliss of the New Jerusalem? Who or what are Gog and Magog, and what part do they play in eschatology? And what is the first resurrection, and how does it relate to the second death? These questions will be answered in due course, but first we must provide perspective, gained from two sources: the

---

7. This interpretation of the millennium and its place in John's theology is adapted from Caird, *Revelation*, 235–36 and 249–58.

A Vision of Final Judgment and the Demise of Evil (Revelation 19–20)

Jewish apocalyptic tradition, particularly that found in Ezekiel 37–39, and John's own theology of history.

For modern readers to comprehend this imagery, they need to understand that the millennial period at the end of history was not an original concept with John, but was a part of the tradition he inherited. John's distinctive elements will become apparent once we compare and contrast his picture with that tradition. The idea of a millennial period resulted from the combination of two different kinds of eschatology: (a) prophetic eschatology and (b) apocalyptic eschatology. *Prophetic eschatology* was essentially optimistic, tending to picture a this-worldly fulfillment of God's purpose at the end of history, when the world's evil would be overcome and when salvation (eschatological bliss), championed by an earthly Messiah, would emerge in continuity with history. In contrast, *apocalyptic eschatology* saw this world as too burdened with evil for redemption to occur from within. The present world must pass away to make way for eschatological fulfillment in the setting of new heavens and a new earth (Isa. 65:17; 66:22; 2 Pet. 3:12–13). In this conception the Messiah is no earthly figure but a transcendent one that brings redemption from the other world. In apocalyptic eschatology, the final kingdom of God does not emerge out of this world but breaks into it from the beyond. "By John's time these two views had already been combined into a scheme in which a this-worldly messiah brought this-worldly salvation during a transitional kingdom, which was then superseded by eternal apocalyptic salvation in the new world."[8] The "two ages" were bridged by an intermediate period of messianic rule, a period varying from forty years to one thousand years.

According to the Epistle of Barnabas (a second century AD Christian writing), Jewish belief in a millennium had its origin in a combination of Genesis 2:2 and Psalm 90:4, whereby each of the seven days of creation becomes a thousand years of history, ending with the messianic Sabbath and succeeded by the timeless new world of the eighth day (this view is found in 2 Enoch 32:2—33:2, though without reference to the Messiah). The Apocalypse of Weeks (1 Enoch 91:12–17; 93) presents a similar perspective but divides world history into ten weeks of indeterminate length and singles out the seventh week as the period of apostasy. In 2 Esdras 7:28–30, the Messiah is expected to reign for four hundred years before dying along with the rest of his generation. In the Apocalypse of Elijah (AD 261), many ways resembling Revelation, the age of the Messiah is to last only forty years. In other Jewish writings, such as the Similitudes of Enoch (1 Enoch 37–71), there is no earthly kingdom intervening before the transformation of heaven and earth.

---

8. Boring, *Revelation*, 206–7.

John adopts this picture partly because he stands in this tradition but also because he is influenced here as elsewhere by the storyline of Ezekiel. The "first resurrection" and millennial period (20:4-6) corresponds to Ezekiel 37, the defeat of God and Magog (20:7-10) to Ezekiel 38-39, and the coming of the Holy City (21:1—22:5) to Ezekiel 40-48. In addition, John inherits from his Jewish background the tradition that only the just are raised (Isa. 26:19) and the tradition that all the dead, good and bad alike, are raised (Ezek. 37; Dan. 12:2-3). By adopting the scheme of an intermediate eschatological period, he discovers a conceptual means of affirming both traditions. It was the Jewish tradition that provided the elements for John's conception but his own vision that provided the additional features.

The uniquely Johannine features of the millennium can be determined from the clues John provides. The first is that Satan is confined so that he cannot continue deluding the nations (20:3). This implies that throughout the millennium there would be a considerable world population, otherwise susceptible to the influence of Satan, and therefore a population in addition to the faithful church, which has resisted this corrupting influence. If we admit this line of thought, we cannot then treat the "battle" of the previous chapter as the end of world history. The battle is the end of something, but not the End per se, for the nations as a whole survive.

The second clue is that John saw thrones, whose occupants "were given the authority to judge" (20:4a). Despite the eccentric syntax that follows, added in the English translation but not found in the original Greek ("I also saw"), we can assume that those who sat on the thrones were none other than the Christian martyrs of 20:4b. The combination of thrones and judgment suggests that John had in mind the judgment scene in Daniel 7:22, which he has interpreted in his own way. According to Daniel, the Ancient of Days sat in judgment and rendered a favorable verdict on behalf of Israel (the holy ones/saints). But since Daniel speaks of thrones (9:9) and of the saints gaining possession of God's kingdom (9:18, 27), the Christian tradition assumed that the thrones would be occupied by a plurality of judges (cf. Matt. 19:28; Luke 22:29-30; 1 Cor. 6:2-3). More significant, however, is that in Daniel the judgment is not the last judgment but one that happens in the course of history. In an earlier chapter of Daniel we learn that God is sovereign over the kingdoms of the world and that he gives that sovereignty to "whom he will" (4:17, 25, 32) and "sets over it the lowliest of human beings" (4:17). In Revelation 20, the judgment committed to the martyrs is not the right to determine the ultimate destinies of mortals—that final judgment is God's—but the right to assume the empire of the defeated monsters.

The third clue is that "they came to life and reigned with Christ a thousand years" (Rev. 20:4). To understand John's intent here we must return to

A Vision of Final Judgment and the Demise of Evil (Revelation 19-20)

the book of Daniel and to the fact that throughout the formative period of Old Testament eschatology (from Amos to Daniel) the Jewish people had no expectation of an afterlife. It never occurred to them that the wrongs of this present world might be redressed in a different one, for the only other world they believed in was Sheol, a shadowy netherworld of death, not of life. When they began to entertain hopes of life after death—and the author of Daniel was the first to clearly enunciate the doctrine that the saints of the past would be restored to life in order to participate in the glories of the age to come (12:2-3)—they naturally envisioned it as a return to the only life they knew, the life of this present world. Once this belief in resurrection took hold, it was only a matter of time before they imagined a place more solid and lasting than earth.

John seems to want the best of both worlds. He believes that the ultimate destiny of the redeemed is in the heavenly Jerusalem, but he also retains the earthly paradise, the millennium. He therefore requires not one but two resurrections. The first resurrection (Rev. 20:6) restores the martyrs to life for their millennial reign; the second brings all the dead before the great white throne. Whatever John meant by "resurrection," it seems clear that he did not expect the martyrs to return to their fleshly bodies and resume a physical existence, for they had already put off their mortal garment of flesh and received the white robe of immortality (6:11). The breath of life from God having already come into them (11:11-12), they went up to heaven in a cloud. It is unlikely that John should have used the word resurrection in two completely different senses, since the resurrection of remaining humanity is clearly not to earthly, bodily life.

The decisive point, however, is the parallel between the resurrection of the martyrs and that of Christ. Since it is said that they "reigned with Christ a thousand years" (20:4), he and they must share a common mode of existence. It is safe to assume that the rule of the martyrs, like that of Christ, has a double reference for John: it refers to both a heavenly rule (cf. 3:21), past and present (cf. 6:11 and 11:12), and its millennial sequel on earth. The first resurrection is therefore not a postponement of heavenly bliss, for already the martyrs are "blessed and holy" (20:6); already they walk with Christ in white (6:11); already they are before the throne of God and serve him day and night in his temple (3:5; 6:9; 7:15). For them the great white throne holds no terror, for they have passed the most exacting test—faithfulness unto death—and the second death (the annihilation that awaits those who fail the final test) has no claim on them (cf. 2:11).

During their millennial reign, in addition to ruling with Christ, the martyrs will serve as priests (20:6); this is John's fourth clue. In Old Testament times priests had a sacramental role, meaning that they mediated to

God the prayers and hopes of the people and to the people the blessings and promises of God. John foresees the continuation of this mediatorial role during the heavenly/earthly millennium (cf. 1:6; 5:10). The martyrs will have a role in bringing the nations to God and in making them fit to be presented to God. Whatever else may have stopped, the work of the gospel must continue during this period. John envisions generations coming and going at this time, for Death and Hades have not yet been destroyed; their end follows the last judgment (20:14).

John's enigmatic reference to the release of Satan at the end of the millennium and the ensuing invasion of Gog and Magog in 20:7–10, events beyond the scope of time and space, make better sense when connected to the visions of Ezekiel. For John, the prophecy of Gog and Magog, recorded in Ezekiel 38–39, must have its fulfillment. Once again, however, John modifies his sources. Earlier he had introduced the prophecy of the banquet of the birds (Ezek. 39:17) and its fulfillment (Rev. 19:17–18), and now he turns Ezekiel's "Gog, of the land of Magog" (38:2) into a pair of nations (Jewish sources follow suit; in the Talmud, for example, Gog and Magog are said to be the rebellious nations of Psalm 2:2, 9). That John introduces Gog and Magog during the millennium is not really a mystery. Three times in Ezekiel 38 it is said that Gog will come upon Israel only when she is living in security (38:8, 11, 14), a prophecy enabling us to understand the meaning of John's symbolism. The myth of Gog relates a profound spiritual truth: the resilience of evil. "However far human society progresses, it can never, while this world lasts, reach the point where it is invulnerable to such attacks. Progress there must be . . . [b]ut even when progress issues in the millennium, men must remember that they still have no security except in God."[9] Victory, however, is guaranteed, when the devil who had deceived the nations (Gog and Magog, 20:8) is cast into the lake of fire, where the beast and the false prophet were annihilated. The concept of a "lake of fire" cannot, of course, be taken literally, it being a contradiction in terms, like a "bottomless pit." It symbolizes the profound spiritual truth that though evil is real, its presence is provisional, for its doom is guaranteed.

The reference to "the camp of the saints and the beloved city" in 20:9 seems confusing, since John has not yet seen the holy city descend from heaven. Once again we need to focus on the spiritual truth: the descent of the city is not a single far-off event but a permanent reality. Just as the beast is a rising-from-the-abyss sort of monster, so the beloved city is a

---

9. Caird, *Revelation*, 257.

A Vision of Final Judgment and the Demise of Evil (Revelation 19–20)

descending-from-heaven sort of city. Wherever and whenever God's people are gathered, there is the City of God (3:12; cf. 11:2).[10]

John's next vision is awesome and sobering in nature; it is the scene of the Last Judgment (20:11-15). He sees a great white throne, great because it is God's throne and white because of God's eternal purity. What follows is astounding imagery, theophanic in nature: "the earth and the heaven fled from [God's] presence" (20:11). We are reminded that in John's cosmology earth and heaven are one unit, spiritual rather than spatial in significance. This scene represents the end of the old and sets the stage for "a new heaven and a new earth" (21:1), based on the premise that God is "making all things new" (21:5). In the new age two elements disappear: whatever is transitory and whatever hinders God's purpose.

The judgment itself is described starkly. Two books are opened, the Book of Merit (Works) and the Book of Life (Mercy). The first volume contains a record of the deeds of those who stand before the throne; it suggests that our earthly lives are important and meaningful, for we are to be judged by our works. The Book of Life, based on the work of Christ, shows that our destiny is determined by God's amazing goodness, for we are saved solely by grace. According to John, Christ's death is universal in scope, for it represents God's desire to ransom and save "every creature in heaven and on earth and under the earth and in the sea" (5:13), effected in the "mighty multitude that no one could count, from every nation, from all tribes and peoples and languages" (7:9).

The idea that books would be consulted in the final judgment is found in many ancient texts and traditions, including the Old Testament (Exod. 32:32-33; Ps. 69:28; Mal. 3:16), particularly the book of Daniel, which profoundly influenced John's eschatology at this point (see Dan. 7:10; 12:1, 4). While the idea of heavenly registries need not be taken literally, the concept carries significant meaning. John obviously found the image of the book of life to be suggestive, for he refers to it six times in Revelation (3:5; 13:8; 17:8; 20:12, 15; and 21:27).

John's concept of two books is useful. The Book of Works reflects what people have done, and there is no basis for judgment other than that (see 1 Cor. 3:11-15), whereas the Book of Mercy indicates the profundity of God's love for his creation, a love spurned by the destroyers of the earth (11:18), the unholy trinity, and those deceived by Babylon's counterfeit gospel. Having rejected God's mercy and love, their punishment is described starkly in 14:10, where they are said to "drink the wine of God's wrath, poured unmixed into the cup of his anger, and they will be tormented with fire

---

10. Ibid.

and sulfur" (14:10). In 20:14 John summarizes their judgment even more succinctly as "the second death," meaning that evildoers are cast into the lake of fire, together with Death and Hades, where they will be banished forever (see 21:8). The righteous, described elsewhere as those who "die in the Lord," will be blessed forever; "they will rest from their labors, for their [righteous] deeds follow them" (14:13). The deeds of God's saints, the consequences of loyalty and faithful witness, are vital and blessed, but Christ's vicarious work is indispensable because it determines their identity in God's sight. Those who love God/others (1 John 4:7–12, 20–21) need not fear the Day of Judgment, for "perfect love casts out fear" (1 John 4:18). The biblical message is clear: when God sees his children, he sees Christ.

In 20:11–15 John presents a spiritual perspective better than reasoned argument could ever do. The entire scene prepares the way for the establishment of the new heaven and the new earth, from which imperfection and death are banished.

Essay 9: Eschatological Approaches to Revelation

The book of Revelation is one of the most amazing depictions of Christian faith and life ever written; it is also divisive, having become the source of endless disputes and sectarian conflict. For generations, Revelation has tapped into some of people's deepest hopes but also their darkest fears. Sometimes the results have been spectacular and sometimes they have been tragic. A point we need to keep in mind has relevance to the assumptions we make about this book and to the questions we ask. If we assume that Revelation provides a literal outline of events leading up to the end of history, then we tend to view events described in the book as actual and as chronologically connected. From this perspective, material that appears early in the book precedes material found later in the book. Events described in chapter 20, for instance, would still be in the future, and would occur at the very end of time, probably on earth, and immediately before the eschatological bliss. If we assume that the symbolic imagery in Revelation is spiritual in nature, then we focus on its meaning for John's original audience and for spiritual life in the present. In that case the timing of things—their interrelationship chronologically—diminishes into near irrelevance.

This essay examines the concept of the millennium under four categories: (1) historic premillennialism, (2) dispensational premillennialism, (3) postmillennialism, and (4) amillennialism. (To these a fifth can be added—panmillennialism—which affirms that everything will "pan out" in

A Vision of Final Judgment and the Demise of Evil (Revelation 19–20)

the end.) These views may be said to correspond indirectly with the four methods of interpreting Revelation described in the Introduction (preterist, idealist, historicist, and futurist). Each of these interpretations involves difficulties, but the central truth of all four is the affirmation that Christ will return to destroy the forces of evil and establish God's eternal kingdom.[11]

1. *Historic premillennialism*: this view, a moderate form of premillennialism, maintains that Christ will return to earth before the millennium. Despite attempts to Christianize society, conditions will become worse as history unfolds, and in the final days the antichrist will gain control of human affairs. At Christ's return, the Christian dead will be raised and believers will reign with Christ during the millennium, the golden age of one thousand years of peace on earth. Then Satan will be released for a short period, after which all other dead will be raised. This explanation accounts for the two resurrections in Revelation 20:4–6. Finally there comes the judgment before the great white throne.

2. *Dispensational premillennialism*: this view, an extreme form of premillennialism, maintains that the purposes of God in scripture can be understood through a series of time periods called dispensations. The basic premise of dispensationalism is the distinction between Israel and the church. Dispensationalists argue that the purposes of God are expressed in the formation of two groups, Jews and Christians, whose distinction continues throughout eternity. Exponents of this view follow a literal system of biblical interpretation, adhering to a timetable that considers everything after Revelation 4:1 as future. Since dispensationalists expect Old Testament promises to be fulfilled literally, the Jews must establish a theocratic kingdom in the land of Palestine, which they will possess forever. These predictions will be fulfilled in the millennium, a literal thousand-year period on earth.

Dispensationalists maintain that the coming of Christ before the millennium consists of two stages: the first, a secret rapture that removes living Christians from earth to meet Christ in the air (1 Thess. 4:17), whence they will proceed to heaven to be spared the devastation of the Great Tribulation, a time of earthly persecution championed by the antichrist. The second stage involves Christ's coming with his saints (a select group of followers, including resurrected believers) to establish the kingdom on earth. This millennial reign, rather than being established through the conversion of individuals over a long period of time, will come about suddenly. The Jews will be converted during the millennium and will have a central role during this time. Evil will be held in check (for Satan is bound) and nature will

---

11. For a discussion of the pros and cons of each of the main views of the millennium see Clouse, *Meaning of the Millennium*, and Grenz, *Millennial Maze*.

flourish during this golden age, to the point where even ferocious beasts are tame (cf. Isa. 65:25). At the end of the millennium Satan will be released and precipitate a rebellion. Following the millennium the non-Christian dead are raised and the eternal states of heaven and hell are established.

3. *Postmillennialism*: adherents of this view believe that Christ will come after the millennium has taken place. The kingdom of God is present on earth during the church age and is now being extended in the world through the preaching of the gospel and the saving work of the Holy Spirit. This activity is causing the world to be Christianized and will result in a lengthy period of peace and prosperity called the millennium. Christ is presently reigning through his faithful church and will bring to the world a thousand years of peace and righteousness prior to his return at the conclusion of history. According to this scenario, evil is not eliminated from history but is being minimized as the moral and spiritual influence of Christians deepens in society. As the church develops through history, it will assume such great importance that many social, economic, and political problems will be solved. This period closes with the Second Coming of Christ, the resurrection of the dead, and the final judgment.

4. *Amillennialism*: proponents of this view regard the thousand years, like other numerals in Revelation, to be symbolic. Instead of being a literal period of exactly one thousand years, the expression refers to a long time, extending from the first to the Second Coming of Christ. During the entire period Satan is "bound," meaning that evil's power is limited by the preaching of the gospel (Luke 10:18). The "last days" correspond to the church age, a period beginning with Jesus and with the outpouring of the Holy Spirit on the day of Pentecost and ending when the "last day" arrives. Instead of the optimism of postmillennialism or the pessimism of premillennialism, amillennialists take seriously the teaching of Jesus that good and evil will develop side by side until the end of the world (Matt. 13:24–30, 36–43). Amillennialists look forward to a glorious and perfect kingdom on the new earth in the life to come. Some amillennialists interpret the millennium mentioned in Revelation 20:4–6 as describing the present reign of the souls of deceased believers with Christ in heaven.

Although these interpretations are represented throughout the history of the church, in certain ages a particular outlook has dominated. During the first three centuries of the Christian era, premillennialism appears to have been the dominant eschatological interpretation. Among its adherents were Papias, Irenaeus, Justin Martyr, Tertullian, Hippolytus, Methodius, Commodianus, and Lactantius. During the fourth century, when the Christian church was given a favored status, the amillennial position was accepted. The famous church father Augustine articulated this position,

A Vision of Final Judgment and the Demise of Evil (Revelation 19–20)

which became the dominant interpretation in medieval times. His teaching was so fully accepted that at the Council of Ephesus in 421, belief in a literal millennium was condemned as superstitious. The Protestant Reformers stayed with Augustinian amillennialism, particularly in opposition to the premillennial views of Radical Reformers (Anabaptists) such as Jan Matthys, who called for the establishment of a millennial kingdom in the city of Münster, considered to be the New Jerusalem. As premillennialism waned, postmillennialism became the prevailing eschatological interpretation, receiving its most impressive formulation through the work of Daniel Whitby (1638–1726). During the nineteenth century premillennialism again attracted widespread attention, fostered in part by the violent social and political upheaval during that period. There was also a renewed interest in the conversion and status of the Jews. The writings of J. N. Darby (1800–1882), popularized in the United States by D. L. Moody and C. I. Scofield, contributed greatly to the emergence and propagation of dispensational premillennialism. During the second half of the twentieth and the start of the twenty-first centuries, books by Hal Lindsey (particularly the bestseller titled *Late Great Planet Earth*, 1970) and the *Left Behind* series (sixteen novels written by Tim LaHaye and Jerry B. Jenkins between 1995 and 2007) greatly enhanced the popularity of dispensational premillennialism, particularly among conservative Christian audiences.

If John believed that the world he knew would continue for the long but indeterminate period represented by a symbolic thousand years, it follows that only the events that happen after that period can strictly be called eschatological. Yet there is no question that eschatological events prior to the millennium have occurred regularly throughout Revelation. We must conclude that John deliberately used eschatological language and imagery to depict events that possess only a qualified finality, historical events that address ultimate issues of life. When John spoke in Revelation 1:1 of matters that "must soon take place," he certainly was not thinking of the End, since it was at least a millennium away. He expected a momentous event, so important that it could properly be described in eschatological terms, an event in which the End was so embodied that through their involvement in it people would be committed to taking sides in the great battle between good and evil and be judged before the throne of God. That event was the forthcoming persecution. Incidentally, during the third and early fourth centuries Christians survived empire-wide persecution so severe that the future of Christianity was at stake, and the bravery and tenacity of persecuted and martyred Christians set the stage for a spectacular reversal of fortune under Emperor Constantine and his successors, leading to the globalization of Christianity and its eventual spread to northern Europe and the Americas.

If this is the nature of John's eschatology, it raises the further question whether the same is not true of all eschatology. Could it be that ancient writers used eschatological imagery primarily as a way to express confidence that God's providential purpose was working itself out in the events of contemporary history? If eschatological language is more concerned with the present—the critical moment we call Today (cf. Heb. 3:13)—than with the remote future, then literalistic approaches to Revelation really do miss the point of John's theological language.

Questions to Ponder

1. What verse, passage, or theme stands out for you as the key to chapters 19 and 20 of Revelation? Support your answer.

2. What is your understanding of the biblical portrayal of the end of evil? Do you see John's depictions of the final defeat of evil as primarily symbolic, literal, or as a combination of both?

3. Christians hold various positions on the return (second coming) of Christ, called "the blessed hope" in Titus 2:13. Do you find attractive one of the three positions mentioned above or do you prefer some other understanding of this event? If so, describe your view in a few sentences or short paragraph.

4. Despite its minimal role in the Bible, the concept of Christ's millennial reign on earth (see Rev. 20:4–6 and 2 Pet. 3:8; cf. Ps. 90:4) is viewed as significant by many traditional Christians. Which view do you find most attractive? Explain your answer.

5. What message of hope do you find in chapters 19 and 20 of Revelation?

Chapter 10

A Vision of the Church Perfected (Revelation 21–22)

Summary: Revelation 21 and 22 complete John's hopeful vision for God's people by presenting a joyous picture of New Jerusalem, the opposite of the earthly Babylon. Readers are invited to see each detail of the new city and experience the landscape of God's renewed world. The blessed city is described in exotic language, with golden streets and a pearly gate, where death is no more and where God wipes away all tears. This wondrous scenario of renewal and joy for the universe fulfills the promises made to those who conquer in the opening letters to the seven churches. This vision invites us to see ourselves already as citizens of this wondrous city and to live our lives in terms of this powerful vision of hope, which transforms the way we live our lives each day.

Assignment: Read chapters 21 and 22 of Revelation

Key Passage: Revelation 21:5

Central Theme: Because God is always coming to dwell with humanity, Revelation calls people to live as citizens of God's New Jerusalem in the present.

Learning Objectives

Participants will examine:
    1. The meaning of "a new heaven and a new earth" in 21:1

200   PART IV: God's Message of Hope

2. John's vision of the New Jerusalem
3. What it means to live as citizens of God's New Jerusalem
4. The meaning of "its gates will never be shut" in 21:25
5. The meaning of John's inclusive language in Revelation
6. How Revelation provides a fitting conclusion to the biblical storyline and its underlying message
7. The hope that Revelation offers humanity

OUTLINE TO REVELATION 21:1—22:21

I. The New Jerusalem 21:1—22:5
  A. The New Heaven and the New Earth 21:1-8
    1. All Things New 21:1-4
    2. Separation between Good and Evil 21:5-8
  B. The Holy City 21:9—22:5
    1. Overall Description 21:9-14
    2. The City's Gates and Walls 21:15-21
    3. No Night There 21:22—22:5
      a. The City's Glory 21:22-27
      b. The Water of Life and the Tree of Life 22:1-3
      c. God's Presence in the City 22:4-5
II. Coda 22:6-21

HERE COMES THE BRIDE

We all want answers to impossible questions such as how everything is going to end and whether good triumphs over evil at last. If we only knew how all things were going to turn out, human history might become intelligible and even credible. Revelation 21 and 22 provide a vision that makes comprehensive sense. In some ways this passage is the most important part of John's vision, anticipated all throughout Revelation: the promises to those who conquer, the white-robed multitude, the triumph song of Moses and the Lamb, and the wedding feast of the Lamb and his bride. Now at long last John examines the New Jerusalem, the city of God, descending from heaven in splendor. Here is the source of John's prophetic certainty, for only in comparison with the New Jerusalem can the lures of Babylon be recognized as the enticements of a haggard whore. When we see the bride we recognize true splendor; all other attractions pale by comparison.

The bride of Christ is first introduced immediately after the fall of Babylon (Rev. 19:7-9) as a woman dressed in white linen. The invitation to the marriage of the Lamb comes as beatitude: "Blessed are those who are invited to the marriage supper of the Lamb" (19:9). The expected wedding scene shifts, however, when the bride becomes a magnificent city in Revelation 21 and 22. This vision presents the bride, the wife of the Lamb, as a wondrous, radiant city, a place of welcome and renewal for the whole world.

Revelation 21 and 22 provide an exceptional look at the New Jerusalem, a description of something ultimately indescribable. The radiant city comes like a bride adorned with golden streets and gates of pearl, where suffering and tears—even death—are gone forever; this splendid vision has shaped the dreams of God's people throughout the ages. But John's talk of streets paved with gold and gates made of single pearls cannot be reduced to material value. It is simply his way of highlighting the inestimable value of what God has in store for his people. John is certainly concerned with physical realities, but even more so with spiritual realities.

As we examine John's vision of the new creation in more detail, the following analytical categories are useful: (1) cosmic dimensions of New Jerusalem; (2) social dimensions of New Jerusalem; (3) political dimensions of New Jerusalem; and (4) sacred dimensions of New Jerusalem. In exploring the glorious city and its implications, keep these categories in mind.

ANALYSIS OF REVELATION 21:1—22:21

The New Heaven and the New Earth (Chapter 21:1-8)

Revelation 20 presents a picture of a zone with the caption "Under Construction," meaning that earth and heaven are under renovation. The first verse of chapter 21 indicates that the renovation is complete. The final scene of Revelation provides John's vision of a new heaven and a new earth. The word "new" doesn't mean simply another, but a new kind of heaven and earth. Heaven and earth are part of God's creation; God is not about to destroy it all just to start over, but rather will bring about radical alteration. As in Isaiah's earlier vision (65:17): "For I am about to create new heavens and a new earth," "new heavens" suggests "new spirituality" and "new earth" suggests "new physicality." In this case newness need not be equated with discontinuity or dissimilarity, for embedded in the biblical concept of newness is the notion of continuity as well as discontinuity with what precedes. When Paul states that the whole creation is longing for redemption (Rom. 8:19–22), he has in mind the double connotation of the Greek word for "new," which means either "renewed" or "new." Newness—like resurrection—is an image of renewal, similar to Paul's description of "new creation" in Galatians 6:15 and 2 Corinthians 5:17. T. S. Eliot's classic statement about life's journey, "and the end of all our exploring will be to arrive where we started and know the place for the first time," can be read in this way, as a statement about renewal. This is the sense in which there will be a new creation in Revelation. There will be continuity in that the earth is renewed but also discontinuity in the distinction between God's vision of what the world can be and the imperial visions that came before (21:1–2).

In the *Chronicles of Narnia*, C. S. Lewis describes the place he calls "New Narnia" in terms of both continuity and transformation. In *The Last Battle*, the New Narnia where the children find themselves at the end of their journey is not an escape from old Narnia but rather an entry more deeply into the very same place. New Narnia has the same hills and the same houses as their hometown, but everything is more radiant. New Narnia is a "deeper country; every rock and flower and blade of grass looked like it meant more." New Narnia is "world within world," where "no good thing is destroyed." This kind of vision provides a wonderful picture of how all of creation will be renewed.[1] The fact that John refers twice (21:2 and 10; cf. 3:12) to the holy city "coming down" does not mean that he saw the city come down from heaven on two separate occasions. John is identifying a permanent characteristic of the city; its nature is defined by its having come down.

Belief in a heavenly city of Jerusalem, often personified as a feminine figure or "mother," was widespread in biblical times (see Gal. 4:26). According to Isaiah 54, the renewed Jerusalem would be made of precious stones and would be "married" to God in covenantal love. Following the destruction of Jerusalem in AD 70, people's longings for a renewed Jerusalem intensified. John would have been well aware of such a longing and likely experienced it himself. What is unique to Revelation is that the heavenly city does not stay in heaven. It comes down from heaven to earth, offering a welcoming home to all humanity. A fundamental example of apocalyptic hope is the message we find at the end of Revelation: God is coming to make a home among us. "See, the home of God is among mortals," this vision

---

1. Rossing, "Journeys Through Revelation," 72.

A Vision of the Church Perfected (Revelation 21-22)

declares (21:3). Contrary to ideas about the "rapture" of the church from earth, there is no "rapture" in Revelation. Instead it is God who is "raptured" to earth to live with us. As we come forth out of Babylon, God comes to us. At the end of Revelation, humans are not in heaven; there is no longer need for dualistic thinking, because God dwells on earth; and where God is, there is heaven.

This vision fulfills the people's deepest longings for residing with God. The promise of God's dwelling on earth recalls God's "tabernacling" with Israel in the wilderness, after the exodus. The theme also echoes Ezekiel 37:27, "My dwelling place shall be with them; and I will be their God, and they shall be my people." This idea is also found in John 1:14, where the verbal form of the word translated "dwell" (Greek *skene*) refers to the residence of God in Jesus and Jesus with us, and then again here in Revelation 21:3, where God's presence with mortals is made permanent. Matthew's usage of Isaiah's promise of the birth of a child named Emmanuel (Matt. 1:23), which means "God is with us" (Isa. 7:14), reminds us that God's intention has always been to dwell with humanity. In Revelation that promise is fully consummated. There will be no temple in God's new city, for the presence of God and the Lamb will be the temple.

Two strands of language and symbolism run through John's account of the New Jerusalem, a combination of particularism and universalism. In the first place, the history of both Israel and the church comes to fulfillment in this vision, the fulfillment of God's promises to the covenant people, whose destiny is portrayed as being "a kingdom and priests" serving God (5:10; cf. 1:6 and 22:3b-5). It is, after all, the New *Jerusalem*. On the other hand, references to the nations as sharing in the promised blessings are equally prominent. The nations will walk by the city's light, the glory and honor of the nations are brought into it (21:26), and the kings of the earth bring their glory into it (21:24). The significance of 21:3, which states the overall meaning of 21:1—22:5 at the outset, is to reiterate evidence found throughout Revelation to the effect that the witness of the church is intended to bring about the conversion of the nations. The implication of 21:3—that all nations are to become covenant peoples—is stunning. John's intention in this passage seems clear: the history of God's covenant people (both Israel and the church) will culminate in "the full inclusion of all the nations in its own covenant privileges and promises."[2]

To the earth God makes a commitment in Revelation, earth being the location of salvation. Such is the meaning of "a new heaven and a new earth," a phrase coterminous with God's bridal city. But the "new heaven"

---

2. Bauckham, *Theology of Revelation*, 139.

will be on earth, and God will dwell in the midst of that renewed city. There can be no more sea in that city, neither the heavenly sea before the throne nor the earthly sea, symbolic of the chaos monster and all the Leviathans of violence, injustice, and despair in the old order of things. And there can be no more tears, sorrow, and mourning in this new world of joy and life eternal. Positioned at the end of the Bible, the vision of the New Jerusalem brings to fulfillment all biblical promises of restoration and renewal. It fulfills Isaiah's promise of newness (Isa. 43:19; 65:17) as well as the promises made to the seven churches in the opening letters of Revelation, when those who "conquer" receive their inheritance (21:7). As we might expect, John dismisses seven elements of the old order in the holy city: sea, death, grief, crying, pain, all that is under God's curse, and night (21:1, 4; 22:3, 5).

Even in the midst of such hopeful scenes the warnings and threats continue, however, for one of John's ultimate goals is repentance. The purpose of threats like those in 21:8 and 21:27 is not to predict who will be saved and who will be lost, for Revelation does not predestine anyone to damnation. John's goal is to persuade the faithful to greater faithfulness and the rebellious to repentance; he desires that everyone's name be written in God's book of life, so that all can enter as citizens into God's holy city. We must recall that Revelation is a letter, from beginning to end, and here, as in Paul's letters (see Rom. 12:1), John is making his appeal, urging unbelievers to join the winning team and believers to step up to the plate and not simply to sit on the bench as "pew warmers." When John indicates that this new world will not include "the cowardly, the faithless, the polluted, the murderers, the fornicators, the sorcerers, the idolaters, and all liars" (21:8), he is depicting qualities associated with the dragon and with the absence of God. He is not saying that all people who have committed one or more of these acts will be cast into the lake of fire, but rather that such deeds are forgivable (see Eph. 2:1–10; Col. 2:13–15; 3:5–11). When the new earth and new heaven appear, such acts cannot occur, and for a very obvious reason: God's presence prevents all evil and wrongdoing.

Earlier in Revelation God was kept at a distance from humans, behind the veil of the sea and his own glory of smoke, but God is fully present in the New Jerusalem, residing with mortals. God's presence is depicted as an everlasting light (21:23–24; cf. Isa. 60:19), not necessarily a physical light, but a revelatory light. Prior to the New Jerusalem, faith required belief in God's existence and providential care. Now faith is confirmed. Also, since God now dwells with humans, there is no need for a temple (21:22), a place where people go to worship and communicate with God, for God is wholly present on earth. Furthermore, there is no temple in the city because the whole city is the new temple.

The Holy City (Chapter 21:9—22:5)

In 21:9—22:5 John becomes a tour guide, leading us through this amazing city. Like the visions of chapter 20, the New Jerusalem vision derives from Ezekiel 37-48, coupled with features from a wide range of apocalyptic traditions about the New Jerusalem. John, however, molds features taken from traditional materials and sources in such a way that they express his own vision of future bliss. The same angel that showed John the judgment of the hated Babylon becomes the agent of revelation. He takes John—and us—to a high mountain to see the glorious city and its twelve gates always open.

The "great high mountain" (21:10), to which the holy city descends, derives from Ezekiel 40:2, though it has a long mythological ancestry. It is the cosmic mountain where heaven and earth meet, where the gods dwelt, where sacred cities were built with temples at their center.[3] According to Ezekiel 28:14, paradise was on "the holy mountain of God." Mount Zion, on which Jerusalem and the temple stood, was not in reality so very high, but was mythologically a very high mountain (Ps. 48:2). In the last days it was to be elevated above all other mountains, becoming actually the cosmic mountain, and the temple on its summit would draw all the nations to it (Isa. 2:2-4). Moreover, it was to be the site of paradise restored (Isa. 11:9; 65:25). Thus the very site of the New Jerusalem in Revelation suggests paradise, the natural world in its ideal state.

The city and the wall around it are clearly distinguished. Whereas the city seems to function as the universal cosmic representation of redemption, the wall appears to represent the eschatological community. The inscriptions over its gates bear the names not of emperors or local deities but of the tribes of Israel. The names on the city's foundations are of the apostles of the Lamb. These foundation stones resemble those precious stones that adorned the breastplate of the Jewish high priest (Exod. 28:17-20; cf. Isa. 54:11-12). They also represent the precious stones and metals of paradise (cf. Ezek. 28:13). When the whole city is said to have "the glory of God and a radiance like a very rare jewel, like jasper, clear as crystal" (21:11), we recall that the glory of God is "like jasper and carnelian" (4:3) and that the sea of glass before his throne in heaven is translucent like crystal, to reflect God's glory (4:6). John probably means that the city in its entirety shines with the reflected glory of God (cf. 21:23).

3 Ibid., 132-33.

The dimensions of the city are mind-boggling, measuring 1,500 miles on each side and 1,500 miles high. The city is a perfect cube, shaped like the Holy of Holies, the location in the temple where God dwells (cf. 21:3). John seems to model his depiction of the New Jerusalem after the historical city of Babylon, known to us from the Greek historiographer Herodotus, insofar as John says that the city stands "foursquare" and gives its size in furlongs (12,000 stadia), measurements that are found in Herodotus's text. It is therefore possible that John's audience may have recognized in this visionary description of the New Jerusalem an allusion to the historic Babylon and thereby an "anti-image of Babylon."[4]

This city has an unshakeable heritage. New Jerusalem is a welcoming place for all, including foreigners, who are invited to participate in its eternal newness (21:24, 26). The city is walled, offering protection and security to its inhabitants but also possessing distinct identity, its citizens guided by standards of faith, hope, and love (see 1 Cor. 13:13). In antiquity, the image of a city was a key source of individual identity and belonging. Like cities, John is offering readers not a private heaven but a community in which they can participate.

The story of alternative authority is reflected in part in the city's name. John's early readers would have identified Jerusalem with the history of Israel and with the earthly time of Jesus. But by AD 70 much of historic Jerusalem had been destroyed in the Jewish revolt against Rome, leaving the future of the city uncertain. The vision of New Jerusalem reiterates the idea that God's purpose cannot be equated with any earthly city, even Jerusalem itself. It is clear from the vision of New Jerusalem that God's designs go beyond a simple restoration of the old order of things. The city descends from heaven rather than arising from earth, and its splendor goes beyond even the most fantastic hopes of the Hebrew prophets.

Revelation fulfills global hopes for the "golden age," imagining God's new heaven and new world as a place in which nature and culture are integrated. The New Jerusalem is a paradise of open spaces and rivers. The vision of verdant space and God's river of life draws on the prophet Ezekiel's vision of a wondrous, tree-lined river flowing out from the temple (Ezek. 47:1–12). Everyone is free to drink from the river. Water flows "as a gift"— that is, without payment or price, even for those who have no money (Rev. 21:6; 22:17; cf. Isa. 55:1). What a wonderful promise for those too poor to buy the essentials of life!

On the other side of the river grows the tree of life. When God's voice speaks from the throne to declare that all things are being made "new"

---

4. Schüssler Fiorenza, *Revelation*, 111.

(21:5), such reality revolves around that tree, symbolic of the paradisiacal Garden of Eden, where its fruit was prohibited to humans. The tree reappears in the New Jerusalem, its medicinal leaves available to everyone and its fruit always in season (22:2). This healing is for "the nations," not ethnic groups, religious bodies, or nationalities, but for those who walk by the city's light and bring their glory into the city (21:24–26). Like the multicultural multitude in Revelation 7:9–12, John's New Jerusalem is inclusive; not only the Christian community but now all the nations will be the people of God (21:3; cf. 5:13 and 15:4). How different this vision and invitation to the nations are from Roman life, which was filled with privilege, violence, and famine.

With the final scene around the throne of God and the Lamb (22:1–3) we are brought back to the central symbol of Revelation: the divine throne, with its combination of cultic and political images, which first appeared in chapters 4 and 5. The contrast is obvious. The throne of God, located in heaven in Revelation 4, is now on earth, at the center of the beloved city. Whereas in chapters 4 and 5 the living creatures form an inner circle of priests in the immediate presence of God and the twenty-four elders form an inner circle of thrones sharing God's rule, in chapter 22 all who may enter the New Jerusalem have immediate access to God's throne. Nothing expresses this sense of immediacy more evocatively than the words: "they will see his face" (22:4). This is the face of God that no mortal could see and survive (Exod. 33:20–23), a joy to be realized only beyond this mortal life (1 Cor. 13:12). The throne—the symbol of God's power and authority—becomes now the source of eternal life and happiness. Unlike the Roman Empire, oppressive and dehumanizing, where minorities were citizens and the rest common laborers and slaves, the eschatological vision of God's universal empire promises new life, health, and happiness. Although Revelation 2:26–27 had promised that those who are victorious would share in Christ's rule over the nations, the New Jerusalem pictures no subjects of this reign. Not oppressive rule or subordination but only life-giving and life-sustaining power characterizes God's eschatological reign. The point is that God's rule in the New Jerusalem is participatory, for all citizens will share in that rule.

The vision of God's life-giving creation is a vision not just for the future but for the present. Revelation calls people to live now as citizens of God's New Jerusalem, even in the heart of Babylon. The holy city coming out of heaven can provide incentive for us to examine the world's cities and communities today. The message of Revelation is that God wants to heal human wounds and the wounds of all creation. In the face of climate change and other urgent crises that threaten so many people in our world, the world-healing vision of Revelation can help us live in terms of a different future, before it is too late. While New Jerusalem holds implications for the future, it also holds promise and hope for this world, including cities in the Middle East and the global South that are ravaged by violence, war, disease, famine, and overpopulation.

The heart of the message of Revelation is not that God plans to destroy the world but that God's desire is to heal. That healing comes as a gift of God from creation, through the waters of a river and the leaves of a tree. The image of a life-giving tree is common to many of the world's religious traditions. Each of us, in our own way, receives wisdom to see the river flowing from the heart of God and the Lamb, even now. It flows through the midst of our cities, a life-giving river by which each of us is renewed. We need New Jerusalem; we need the tree of life, with leaves for the healing of the nations. We need eyes to see the gifted resources already available, within, above, below, and around us.[5]

SUMMARY OF REVELATION 21:1—22:5

The final scene of Revelation is an explosion of light and color. We can focus on the details, such as the pearly gates or the streets paved with gold, or we can ponder the larger cosmic, social, political, and sacred dimensions of the scene. If with John we find ourselves transported to the great, high mountain (21:10), we take from this vision four grand conceptions.[6]

1. *Cosmic perspective*: this final scene of Revelation does not focus on where individuals go when they die, but rather provides a picture of a new creation, which integrates the future of the individual with the future of the world. The promise that God makes "all things new" (21:5) tells readers that the scale of God's action is cosmic and his goal transformative. The challenge for the reader is to ponder the practical implications of that hope for life in the present.

2. *Social perspective*: the final chapters of Revelation portray the New Jerusalem as a bride. For John's readers, bridal imagery would have conveyed values that centered on faithfulness and commitment. Here John reaches back to the tradition of the Hebrew prophets, who pictured Israel's covenant with God as a marriage. According to the prophets, the sense of commitment went both ways: God would be faithful to Israel and Israel was to be faithful to God. Early Christians extended this imagery by referring to Jesus as the bridegroom and the church as the bride. Just as Jesus is the faithful

---

5. Ibid., 75.

6. This perspective is taken from Koester, *Apocalypse*, lecture 12, "New Creation and New Jerusalem."

witness, so the bride is called to the same path of fidelity and commitment. Revelation uses the image of the bride to define a way of life different from the self-absorbed ways of the harlot and her clients. The bride of the future is called to follow those ways in the present.

3. *Political perspective*: the cities lived in by the first readers of Revelation were monuments to human achievement, with structures that expressed the greatness of ancient rulers and loyalty to pagan deities. The New Jerusalem reflects a different kind of power structure, one that is egalitarian, inclusive, and salutary. The imagery John uses is designed to show that the city of God can never be equated with any earthly city. Its splendor exceeds human imagination.

4. *Sacred perspective*: John's description of New Jerusalem includes an intriguing detail. He says that he sees no temple in the city, its temple being the Lord and the Lamb (21:22). For ancient readers, a temple was essential to life in the city. For Jewish people, only one temple was needed because there was only one God and the temple symbolized God's presence on earth, indirect and veiled, nevertheless present. In New Jerusalem there is no longer a barrier between God and human beings, for New Jerusalem is the relationship of God and humanity made intimate and permanent.

Alpha and Omega, the Beginning and the End (Chapter 22:6-21)

The closing section is no epilogue, there being little in this section that is new except the prohibition formula about not adding or taking away words from John's prophecy (22:18-19), an attempt often found at the conclusion of ancient documents to prevent "copyright" infringement (cf. Deut. 4:2). In a scene reminiscent of 19:10, John again warns his parishioners against a false fascination with spiritual phenomena (22:8-9). The list of vices found in 21:8 is repeated almost verbatim in 22:15, and a prophetic oracle of impenitence and righteousness is pronounced in 22:10-11. At the same time, John emphasizes that Christ, who comes imminently, will reward everyone according to their life-work (22:12; cf. 20:13; Rom. 2:6; 1 Pet. 1:17).

It is no surprise that a book theocentric throughout concludes with the command to worship only God. The God who is worshiped is the one who came in Jesus and is forever present in the Spirit. This God is the one who always comes soon, for God is the *eschaton*, the one who is the beginning and the end, the one in whom "we live and move and have our being" (Acts 17:28). Unlike the book of Daniel and apocalyptic literature in general, the book of Revelation is not to be sealed, as though its message were for future generations, but is to remain open, since it was written specifically for John's generation (22:10). In Jewish-Christian fashion, John concludes his beatitudes with a call for his audience's faithful response (22:14), since his revelation has throughout been a call to action. He includes a severe reminder of the call to decision by picturing again the two groups into which humanity is divided by its choice of whom to worship/obey (22:14–15). As in 21:8 and 27, there are outsiders, and there are consequences for deeds, choices, and allegiance—but the gates remain forever open (21:24).

God— Father, Son and Holy Spirit—has the final word in Revelation. At times it is difficult to distinguish among them. In 1:8 God had said that he is the Alpha and the Omega and again in 21:6, where he adds, "the beginning and the end." Now the identical expression is found in 22:13, with the insertion "the first and the last." All three expressions mean much the same. If they apply to Christ, as surely they must in this case, then they set Christ apart from all created beings, since none other than God could share in these titles. Like God, Christ is the beginning and the end (cf. 1:17; 2:8). As a way of stating unambiguously that Jesus Christ belongs to the eternal being of God, the statement in 22:13 surpasses anything in the New Testament.[7]

It must be noted that the third and final appearance of the Alpha and the Omega title in 22:13 identifies the speaker as one who is "coming soon . . . to repay according to everyone's work" (22:12), precisely the office already claimed for Jesus in 2:23. Revelation 22:12 follows common early Christian practice in quoting an Old Testament prophecy of God's coming to judgment (Isa. 40:10; 62:11) with reference to the *parousia* of Christ, and expands it with the well-known principle of divine judgment ("to repay according to everyone's work"), drawn here from Proverbs 24:12. But if Christ's judgment at his coming is the divine judgment, the same must be said of his sacrificial death, which, as we have seen, is also central to the theology of Revelation. When the slaughtered Lamb is seen "at the center of the throne" (7:17; cf. 5:6) in the heavenly throne room, "the meaning is that Christ's sacrificial death belongs to the way God rules the world."[8] If God is not present in the world as the one "seated on the throne" (4:2), he *is* present as the Lamb who conquers by suffering. Christ's suffering witness is, as previously noted, the key event in God's conquest of evil and establishment of his rule on earth. Moreover, Christ's presence (walking among the lampstands, 2:1; cf. 1:13) with his people who continue his witness and sacrifice is also God's presence.

---

7. Bauckham, *Theology of Revelation*, 57.
8. Ibid., 64.

A Vision of the Church Perfected (Revelation 21–22)

At this point, a linguistic clarification is in order. When John speaks of the hope or warning of Christ's imminent coming, he never uses the word *parousia*, which is common elsewhere in the New Testament, though he regularly uses the verb "to come." Seven times in Revelation, Christ announces that he is coming (*erchomai*, 2:5, 16; 3:11; 16:15; 22:7, 12, 20). In these cases, John employs the same verb he uses elsewhere to designate God as eternal in three tenses: the One "who is and who was and who is to come" (1:4, 8; cf. 4:8). But this "coming" of God to the world to execute his purposes for his creation—his eschatological coming to the world in salvation and judgment—is the coming of Christ.

The book of Revelation is the revelation of Jesus (22:16), since this has been his revelation all along (1:1). The concluding verses reiterate four times (22:6, 7, 12, 20)—a theme found only three times in the rest of the book (1:1; 2:16; 3:11)—that Christ will come soon. Since Christ is the fulfillment of that hope, then it is to Christ that the titles in verse 13 apply. These expressions of imminent expectation focus not on the Day of Judgment but on the eschatological coming of Christ, who in verse 16 is imaged in Davidic messianic terms (cf. 5:5; Num. 24:17). Christ also is compared with the "morning star," the star of Venus heralding a new day, sorely needed by John's audience and by those of all ages who are marginalized, victimized, and hard-pressed.

The Spirit speaks in 22:17; the Spirit has been a mysterious presence throughout Revelation: sometimes sevenfold (1:4) and sometimes "the spirit of prophecy" (1:10; 4:2; 17:3; 21:10). The focus seems to have been on God and the Lamb, but that is not quite correct. It is this Spirit that enables the bride to be the bride; it is the Spirit that enables the martyrs to bear true witness; it is the Spirit that inspires the shouts and songs of praise. The Spirit goes out from God's throne and returns in praise to the Father and the Lamb. Revelation is Trinitarian, and the bride is caught up with that Spirit so that when we hear "Come"—the invitation to worship, intimacy, and expectation—we can't tell whether the Spirit or the Bride is speaking, because the answer is both.[9] The apocalyptic journey of Revelation concludes with a liturgical dialogue. The antiphonal "Come" (22:17) is a liturgy in which the Spirit and the bridal New Jerusalem call the community to participate. The invitation for everyone who thirsts to "take the water of life" (22:17) draws the New Jerusalem vision to a sacramental close, representing a summons to the Eucharist.

The letter—always a letter, as well as a prophecy and a revelation—ends with a closing greeting: "The grace of the Lord Jesus be with all the

---

9. Wright, *Revelation*, 206.

saints. Amen" (22:21). The concluding note is one of comfort, love, and encouragement. The closing, while conventional, is also a benediction given in the name of Jesus. This book has been a revelation of Jesus, a testimony to Jesus, and an act of homage to Jesus. John closes his book with visions of hope, promising that at the last we shall enjoy the vision of God because of the grace of the Lord Jesus. It is this Jesus who has come, is coming, and will come again. In that sense, every generation both awaits and experiences his coming, for his time is always near.

Essay 10: Interpreting Revelation's Inclusive Language[10]

When Christians speak of "salvation" they often refer to the afterlife and to the blessedness of eternal life in God's presence. Such an interpretation, however, is peripheral to the Bible and foreign to the book of Revelation. John never uses the verb "save" or the noun "savior," and only uses the word "salvation" three times, never as the destiny of human beings but only as an ascription of praise to God (7:10; 12:10, 19:1). John deals in pictures, not theological concepts, and offers overlapping or inconsistent pictures concerning human destiny. Many texts portray or imply universal salvation (meaning that all humans will be redeemed/restored to a state of grace) while others portray or imply limited salvation (meaning that only those who prior to their death are converted to the worship of Christ will experience eternal life with God). Some texts in Revelation that portray or imply universal salvation are 1:7; 4:3; 5:13; 15:4; 21:5; 21:22—22:3. Texts in Revelation that portray or imply limited salvation include 14:9–10 and 20:11–15. Passages from other books of the Bible support each position as well; passages such as John 3:36, 2 Corinthians 5:10, and 2 Thessalonians 1:6–10 portray ultimate salvation as limited, while passages such as Matthew 20:1–16, John 3:17, Romans 11:32, and 1 Corinthians 15:22 portray salvation as inclusive or universal.

How shall we understand these data from Revelation? Three options address the inconsistency: (1) that John's real view is universal salvation, meaning that texts seeming to imply limited salvation must be understood in the light of the universalistic texts; (2) that John's real view is limited salvation, meaning that texts seeming to imply universal salvation must be understood figuratively; (3) that John has no one consistent viewpoint, meaning that John presents opposing views deliberately. The solution—if

---

10. This segment is adapted from Boring, *Revelation*, 226–31.

A Vision of the Church Perfected (Revelation 21–22)   213

there is a solution—is not to arrive at solutions prematurely but to live within the tension, admitting that our knowledge of ultimate truth is limited. That, after all, is why John chose the apocalyptic medium, in which pictures may be worth a thousand words, but their meaning not reducible to words. John's intention is to call people to repentance and faithfulness, not to arrive at solutions to abstract questions. Central is faith's confession of the meaning of the act of God in Christ, not determining who makes it into the "club."

Those who adhere to universal salvation need to consider the following precautions: (1) the doctrine of universal salvation should not relativize the ultimate event of Jesus Christ, as if Christ is only one of many paths to God. John does not do this. For John, humans are not saved through conversion to a particular religion. It is God who saves humanity, the God who acted definitively in Jesus. (2) The doctrine of universal salvation should not permit the relaxation of human responsibility. John's dialectic avoids this; he includes pictures that make humans responsible for their own destiny. (3) The doctrine of universal salvation should not be held in such a way that it minimizes God's judgment on human sin. Alongside pictures of universal salvation, John offers pictures of the terror of God's judgment. (4) The doctrine of universal salvation should not be held in such a way that it minimizes the importance of faith, commitment, and obedience. The corollary of the doctrine of universal salvation is not that evangelism is unnecessary. The New Jerusalem would be "pie in the sky" for everyone if there were no consequences for one's actions and choices. This is not John's view.

There is a corresponding list of dangers in affirming a doctrine of limited salvation: (1) such a doctrine, with its depiction of judgment and damnation, should not be affirmed in a way that depicts God as vindictive or frustrated. God's wrath is part of his justice but should never be associated with lust for revenge or torture of enemies. This is not the God revealed in Jesus Christ. Likewise, John avoids pictures of a frustrated God who wishes to save the cosmos but was able to salvage only a small fraction. This is not the God praised in Revelation 19:6. (2) Such a doctrine should not explain judgment or damnation by reducing them to purely remedial terms. Biblical pictures of hell should not be reduced to purgatorial references (cf. 1 Cor. 3:10–15), as though they were only a purifying, redemptive stage on the way to universal salvation. (3) Such a doctrine should not be affirmed in a way that it places the acts of Christian preaching, evangelism, and belief on the same plane with God's act in Christ. John's dialectical affirmation of both sets of pictures avoids this arrogance. It also avoids the petty, insecure understanding of salvation that derives meaning and value from the reassurance that most will be damned and that only a select few will receive an invitation to the celestial party.

There is also a danger in resolving John's dialectical method through paradox. "Paradox is not a cure-all for every difficult theological problem. Paradox affirms what must be affirmed in order to communicate the truth of the gospel, whether it can all be made logically consistent or not, but it is not an excuse for fuzzy thinking, a cop-out on rigorous theologizing. In John's method, one begins with faith in God's saving act in the Israel-Christ event and thinks to the paradoxical pictures in which it must be expressed, rather than using paradox or picture-language as an excuse for not thinking."[11]

A good way to end this discussion is with insights from Revelation 20–22. John's emphasis on the martyr church becoming priests during the millennium (20:6) is in keeping with previous statements in Revelation where faithful Christians are told they would be kings and priests on earth (5:10; cf. 1:6), having authority over the nations "to rule them with an iron rod" (2:26–27; cf. 12:5). The nations in mind are those mentioned in the second psalm, who rise in their wrath against God and Christ (11:18). They are the peoples among whom Christians were living, from whom they had been ransomed (5:9; 7:9), and by whom they were to be persecuted (11:2). They were the people made drunk and seduced by the great whore (14:8; 17:15; 18:3, 23). But they were also the people to whom John was to speak his prophetic message (10:11) and to whom the angel of the eternal gospel was sent (14:6). They are the ones whose conversion the martyr church had confidently celebrated (15:4) and who are now given the assurance of future freedom from Satan's deceptions. The "striking down of the nations" and the rule of them "with a rod of iron" (19:15) cannot mean their disappearance from the earth but rather the demolition of the political power that had organized them in resistance to the sovereignty of God.

In his vision of New Jerusalem, John does not have in mind a small remnant or a faithful few citizens. It is a vast city he envisions. Against everything we might have expected from prophetic passages in the Old Testament or from Jewish apocalyptic literature, John has modified his tradition in order to portray a radically inclusive city. In 21:3 John quotes Ezekiel 37:27, "My dwelling place shall be with them; and I will be their God, and they shall be my people," but the final word is modified to read "peoples" (the plural is read by the best Greek manuscripts). The New Jerusalem is not populated by the "chosen people" only but by the peoples of the earth, including the very nations and even their kings (21:24) that had opposed God's rule and oppressed the church. Ezekiel pictures the restored Jerusalem as having trees whose leaves will be used for healing. John modifies this from individualistic terms to geopolitical terms: the tree of life in the New

---

11. Ibid., 231.

Jerusalem will be for the healing *of the nations* (22:2). The nations of the earth are said to walk in the light of the glorious city, bringing into it their glory and honor (21:24–26). Ezekiel's city had twelve gates, which served as exits for its citizens (Ezek. 48:30–34); the New Jerusalem's gates are open to only one-way traffic—outside to inside (21:24, 26, 27). The temple in the old Jerusalem had a wall separating men from women and Jews from Gentiles; the New Jerusalem has no such temple. The most significant of all references is 21:5, where God is said to make "*all* things new"; the "all" is added by John to his Old Testament source (Isa. 43:19).[12]

Does John then teach universalism? I believe it would be wrong to argue dogmatically that he teaches that all human beings will be with God eternally. But as it would be wrong to assert universalism, it would be equally wrong to assert that he teaches that some people can never be saved; he doesn't say that either. What we can say with confidence is that if "the kings of the earth" can find their way to redemption, then it is a possibility for anyone. If we dare not be dogmatic as to what God will do, we dare not suggest what God can do. What we can say is that John leaves open the universalistic possibility. The remainder of the New Testament has the net effect of doing the same, although not quite in the way John does. It does, however, fail to give unanimous support to any other alternative.[13]

Questions to Ponder

1. What verse, passage, or theme stands out for you as the key to chapters 21 and 22 of Revelation? Support your answer.
2. Describe your understanding of John's vision of "a new heaven and a new earth." In what ways does this concept represent continuity with the present and in what ways does it represent discontinuity?
3. Does New Jerusalem represent a reality at the end of history or something else entirely? Does John's depiction of the New Jerusalem as coming down out of heaven imply that heaven and earth are ultimately different perspectives of the same reality, or do you view heaven and earth as eternally separate realities?
4. What parallels can you find between the New Jerusalem and the Garden of Eden in Genesis? What new ideas does John's vision add to that of Genesis?

---

12. Ibid., 221–22.
13. Eller, *Revealing Book*, 204.

5. In your view, how inclusive is God's kingdom? What are the standards for citizenship in the New Jerusalem?

6. What message of hope do you find in chapters 21 and 22 of Revelation?

Epilogue

WILL HOPE HAVE CHILDREN?

Three features are said to progress, increase, and become climactic in Revelation (and by implication throughout history): (a) the severity of evil, (b) the severity of judgment, and (c) the perfecting of the faithful church. Today's headlines speak of amplified tension among nations, ideologies, socio-economic groups, and religious groups, with individuals and nations resorting to ever-increasing draconian scenarios for resolution of differences. Recent examples include nuclear threats against the United States by Kim Jong Un, the world's youngest head of state; faith-driven detonations of weapons of mass destruction by Chechen brothers at the Boston marathon; and civil war in Syria, resulting in the loss of thousands of lives and the displacement of hundreds of thousands more of its citizens. Natural calamities are also on the rise, including the devastating effects of global warming; the desolation of Chinese earthquakes; the ravages of a tsunami on Japan; and the increasing severity and destructive power of hurricanes and storms such as Katrina and Sandy. And that's just the start of a list of tragedies, natural and manmade, that humans confront at the start of the twenty-first century. Potentially greater devastation lies ahead.

These conditions, apparently, are not new; today's headlines read like lines from the Gospels, particularly their apocalyptic passages: "When you hear of wars and rumors of wars, do not be alarmed; this must take place, but the end is still to come. For nation will rise against nation, and kingdom against kingdom; there will be earthquakes in various places; there will be famines. This is but the beginning of the birth pangs" (Mark 13:7-8; cf. Matt. 24:6-14; Luke 21:10-11). As we look ahead, will our cup be half full or half empty? Will we live with hope or succumb to fear?

As did John of Patmos, we live in a culture of violence, in which it is becoming increasingly common to retaliate when others threaten. In the name of security and protection, many families are stockpiling weapons against the day when procurement of such weapons may become more difficult. Children who do not strike back are labeled sissies, just as adults who emphasize forgiveness are said to be soft on crime. Yet many who are belligerent and terroristic—in America and abroad—adhere to some form of the motto, "In God we trust."

Under similar circumstances, John of Patmos turned to the Hebrew scriptures for hopeful imagination. Like John, I turn to scripture as well, in this case to biblical scholar Walter Brueggemann, who speaks profoundly of hope in history. In his book *Hope within History* Brueggemann raises the question, "will our faith have children?" pondering whether Christians will succumb to pessimism or remain resilient in the face of global anxiety, open enough to conceive a surprising future from God. In the context of Revelation, Brueggemann's question can be modified to read, "Will hope have children?" Can we, like John, be hopeful of the future?

Brueggemann notes that the juxtaposition of "hope" and "history" articulates both a central claim and a central problem of biblical faith. It also presents a central problem for belief and nonbelief. While there is no doubt that the Bible narrates a genuine history of humanity with the reality of pain and death, it also narrates the hope-filled purposes of God that seem to operate in history. Joseph's words at the end of Genesis powerfully address the inscrutability of God's hope within history: "Even though you intended to do harm to me, God intended it for good, in order to preserve a numerous people, as he is doing today" (Gen. 50:20). On a later occasion, God's hope within history is proclaimed confidently by the prophet Isaiah, in the face of overwhelming foreign power threatening to undo the fabric of Judah's social order: "The Lord of hosts has sworn: As I have designed, so shall it be; and as I have planned, so shall it come to pass . . . For the Lord of hosts has planned, and who will annul it? His hand is stretched out, and who will turn it back?" (Isa. 14:24, 27).

Having in this study referred frequently to hope without any attempt at definition, since it is the purpose of Revelation to envision the concept, it is time we clarify its meaning. Biblical hope is the "resilient conviction that the processes of historical interaction are to be understood in relation to some overriding purpose that prevails in odd but uncompromising ways."[1] Such a conviction of prevailing purpose is expressed in the biblical text as God's "plan": "For surely I know the plans I have for you, says the Lord,

---

1. Brueggemann, *Hope within History*, 2–3.

plans for your welfare and not for harm, to give you a future with hope" (Jer. 29:11). The temptation is to split hope and history. As a result, we hold to a religious hope that is detached from the historical process, or we participate in a history that ends in futility and despair because the process itself delivers no enduring victory for participants. Such a split between "a historyless hope and a hopeless history is a betrayal of biblical faith. It is precisely the wonder and burden of the biblical texts that hope is relentlessly historical and history is cunningly hope-filled."[2]

What then is the function of hope? What happens when people hope? They keep the future open and make the present provisional. Hope is realistic in that it reminds us that the present is precarious and in jeopardy; hence we should refrain from absolutizing it. This means that the current power structures and norms should not be treated too honorably or taken too seriously, because they will not last. Biblical hope is suspicious of secular systems and ideologies. It permits a critique of the status-quo while encouraging alternative realities. In Isaiah 65:17-25 the promissory vision of new heaven and new earth is an act of hope. It comes from a disenfranchised community that was oppressed by the dominant ecclesiastical system, a priesthood that controlled and preempted everything in terms of power, influence, and privilege. Isaiah 65 is the poetry of a minority asserting an alternative mode of historical existence. Elsewhere, another minority—three companions in Daniel 3:16-18—protest against the totalitarian demands of the Babylonian king Nebuchadnezzar. There too hope produces courage not to submit to present realities. In these passages Israel's perspective is shown to be noncompliant with current norms and endlessly suspicious of existing power arrangements. Such discontent can be labeled "sacred" in that it comes of God; such discontent is rooted in hope.

In the Bible, the promise of children is rooted in hope. That, of course, is the main theme of the Abraham-Sarah narrative. Although Sarah was barren, she and Abraham were promised descendants like the stars in the heavens (Gen. 15:5). The metaphor of a future child is most poignant in Isaiah 54:1-3, which begins memorably: "Sing, O barren one, who did not bear; burst into song and shout, you who have not been in labor! For the children of the desolate woman will be more than the children of her that is married, says the Lord." This passage is addressed to believers in exile. They were without resources, cut off from Jerusalem and the temple, doubtful of God's power, and enmeshed in a Babylonian culture that shaped everything in ways alien to them. They had no prospect of a way out, no hope for the next generation. Isaiah uses many poetic devices to announce fresh

2. Ibid.

possibilities for the future, none more astonishing than this metaphor of the barren one having children. The barren are Sarah, Rebekah, Rachel, and Hannah. Ours too is a community of barren women and unproductive men (cf. Heb. 11:12), with no possibility of creating a future of our own. "The barren one in Isaiah 54 is exiled Israel as well as the church whenever it reaches the end of its resources, which is often and soon and surely now."[3]

Trust in newness, however, must not be shallow. Faith in God is not escape to a naïve, never-never land. Will hope have children? It has already had them—and lost them. During the exodus Pharaoh forbids the birth of boy babies (Exod. 1:16); Second Isaiah (Isaiah of the exile) cannot announce the new birth until there had been two generations after Jeremiah to grieve the loss (see Jer. 31:15); in the New Testament Matthew writes of the brutality of Herod, who tries to eliminate the gospel by killing the male children (Matt. 2:17-18); in verse 19 Matthew cites Jeremiah: "A voice was heard in Ramah, wailing and loud lamentation, Rachel weeping for her children; she refused to be consoled, because they are no more" (Jer. 31:15). Herod wants to make sure that hope has no children, because the only sure way to preserve the old order is to be sure this hope yields no children.

Will hope have children? Yes, says the entire biblical narrative, but only when we read these texts from the dialectic of Good Friday and Easter. Paul knows from Isaiah and Jeremiah that it is precisely suffering—embraced, practiced, and articulated—that produces hope: "suffering produces endurance, and endurance produces character, and character produces hope, and hope does not disappoint us, because God's love has been poured into our hearts through the Holy Spirit that has been given to us" (Rom. 5:3-5). Like nothing else, suffering produces hope, but it must be suffering in faithful ways: non-violent, non-vindictive, non-harmful suffering.

Will hope have children? Not if we simply hold on to the old ways or glibly rush to newness. Hope will not have children if we imagine we can merely move from strength to strength, from children to children, and simply keep things going. Needed are the honesty to relinquish and the courage to receive. Hope is rooted in the sort of newness in which Jesus excels: newness that comes only through dying and being raised. And that good news, our newness, cannot be ours alone. Hope must include hope for all nations, peoples, and creatures on the globe. That is God's vision, God's dream, God's hope: "and in you all the families of the earth shall be blessed" (Gen. 12:3; cf. Rev. 5:13; 7:9; 21:24-26). The news of future children inexplicably given by the mercy of God is indeed the gospel. The future is given to us by the God

---

3. Ibid., 94.

known fully in Jesus Christ, crucified and risen. Of that one Rachel weeps on Friday and Sarah sings on Sunday.[4]

Throughout its twenty-two chapters, Revelation invites us to drink deeply from its metaphors of promise and warning, vision and blessing. This is not a book of judgment but of justice, of radical hope for the world's future. God is with us through every beginning and every ending, our Alpha and Omega. If Revelation is a journey, then the final scene of the New Jerusalem is the homecoming. Listening to Revelation being read aloud in the worship service, early Christians traveled with John on a life-changing apocalyptic journey. They traveled to heaven to see the throne of God and the Lamb, to taste and see the gifts of God. They witnessed conflict and victory, and they endured. Their journey of worship now comes to a close. As worshippers return from behind the apocalyptic veil, as they gather around the Eucharistic table, they see their own world more clearly, their own lives glimpsed in a new and deeper way.

That kind of transformational vision is the goal Revelation has for each one of us. Like Dorothy in *The Wizard of Oz* waking up in Kansas, everything is different for us now because of our apocalyptic journey. The message is clear: stay on course, keep the faith—follow the yellow-brick road. Faithful companions and a vision of the New Jerusalem can help us resist the temptations of Babylon and lead us to celebrate boldly: "Ding dong! The witch is dead; the wicked witch is dead!" With new eyes, ears, voices, limbs, and hearts we can see the Lamb standing in the middle of the street, reminding us that love never fails (1 Cor. 13:8). Together we find ourselves transported beyond our invisible mountains into thin places, glimpses of New Jerusalem beyond belief. We see rivers of life flowing from the heart of God; we catch a glimpse of God's tree of life and taste its medicinal healing leaves.

Visions of the new creation are essential; we cannot live without them, for they bring healing to our lives and to our troubled world. The message of Revelation is clear: the One who dwells in our midst is making all things new. That is the promise of Revelation: God's people gather around the throne of the Lamb, beside the river, beneath the healing tree of life, singing "Amen. Come, Lord Jesus!" Faith indicates that if Christ is our companion and the Spirit is within, then God's dwelling is with us. If that perspective holds true, then heaven is here, evil is defeated, the world is renewed, and all creatures are beloved, for reality is undergoing cosmic transformation. This vision of promise and faith keeps "making all things new."

4. Ibid., 108.

In the Bible, when all is said and done, we are left not with a new heaven only but with a new heaven and a new earth—joined together completely and forever (cf. Eph. 1:10). The new city is not just a dream, a comforting fantasy. Those who follow the Lamb already belong in that city and already have the right to walk its streets, for that city is the Bride. The new creation is God's kingdom; its citizens are dressed in white—the garment of the bride—and all have childlike faith, for it is "to such as these that the kingdom of heaven belongs" (Matt. 19:14). Surely here is hope revealed!

Appendix

The Essentials: Key Ideas from Revelation

Students in my classes on the book of Revelation are often asked to keep a journal, noting insights and questions from readings and class discussion. They are asked to list and prioritize ten key ideas learned during the term. These are my essential ideas:

1. Evil is temporary; in the end God wins and justice prevails.
2. God's wrath (justice) is part of God's love; like a loving parent or a skilled surgeon, God disciplines those he loves and wounds in order to heal.
3. God is creator and not destroyer of life. Humans, made in God's image, are to live peaceably and nonviolently on God's earth, caring for its resources, the environment, and every living creature.
4. Jesus is a Lion that is a Lamb. His only weapon is his word of truth.
5. Worship (liturgy) is both responsive and constitutive; it not only addresses the God of love but constructs the theological world in which humans viably, joyously, and obediently live.
6. While all language about God is metaphorical, it is essential to preserve personal and traditional language for God.
7. "Heaven" for John, is not about cosmic geography but about cosmic perspective; heaven represents the deeper dimension of what happens on earth.

8. Biblical prophecy is essentially present-oriented, focusing on its target audience.
9. Truth, like John's imagery, is polyvalent.
10. The message of Revelation is helpful, not vindictive, and hopeful, not pessimistic.

Properly interpreted, the book of Revelation provides a reliable overview of Christian doctrine and suitably concludes the biblical narrative.

Bibliography

Aune, David E. *Revelation.* 3 vols. Word Biblical Commentary 52. Dallas: Word: 1997–98.
Barclay, William. *The Revelation of John.* 2 vols. 2nd ed. Philadelphia: Westminster, 1960.
Bauckham, Richard. *The Climax of Prophecy: Studies on the Book of Revelation.* Edinburgh: T&T Clark, 1993.
———. *The Theology of the Book of Revelation.* Cambridge: Cambridge University Press, 1993.
Beale, Gregory K. *The Book of Revelation: A Commentary on the Greek Text.* New International Greek Testament Commentary. Grand Rapids, MI: Eerdmans, 1999.
Blount, Brian K. *Revelation: A Commentary.* Louisville: Westminster John Knox, 2009.
Boring, M. Eugene. *Revelation.* Interpretation: A Bible Commentary for Teaching and Preaching. Louisville: John Knox, 1989.
Bowman, John W. "Revelation, Book of." In *The Interpreter's Dictionary of the Bible* 4:58–71. Nashville: Abingdon, 1962.
Brueggemann, Walter. *Hope within History.* Atlanta: John Knox Press, 1987.
———. *Israel's Praise: Doxology against Idolatry and Ideology.* Philadelphia: Fortress, 1988.
———. *The Prophetic Imagination.* Philadelphia: Fortress, 1978.
Caird, George B. *Revelation of St. John the Divine.* Harper's New Testament Commentary. New York: Harper & Row, 1966.
Clouse, Robert H. *The Meaning of the Millennium.* Downers Grove, IL: InterVarsity, 1977.
Collins, Adela Yarbro. *The Apocalypse.* New Testament Message 22. Wilmington, DE: Michael Glazier, 1979.
Collins, John J. *The Apocalyptic Imagination: An Introduction to Jewish Apocalyptic Literature.* 2nd ed. Grand Rapids, MI: Eerdmans, 1998.
———. *The Encyclopedia of Apocalypticism: The Origins of Apocalypticism in Judaism and Christianity*, Vol. 1. New York: Continuum, 1998.
Drane, John. *Introducing the New Testament.* Rev. ed. Minneapolis: Fortress, 2001.
Ehrman, Bart D. *A Brief Introduction to the New Testament.* 3rd ed. New York: Oxford University Press, 2013.
Eller, Vernard. *The Most Revealing Book of the Bible: Making Sense out of Revelation.* Grand Rapids, MI: Eerdmans, 1974.
Ellul, Jacques. *Apocalypse.* New York: Seabury, 1977.

Bibliography

Ewing, Ward. *The Power of the Lamb*. Eugene, OR: Wipf & Stock, 2006.
Foster, Richard J. *Celebration of Discipline*. New York: Harper & Row, 1978.
Grenz, Stanley J. *The Millennial Maze*: Sorting out Evangelical Options. Downers Grove, IL: InterVarsity, 1992.
Hahn, Scott. *The Lamb's Supper*. New York: Doubleday, 1999.
Hays, Richard B. and Stefan Alkier. *Revelation and the Politics of Apocalyptic Interpretation*. Waco, TX: Baylor University Press, 2012.
Hendriksen, William. *More Than Conquerors*. Grand Rapids, MI: Baker, 1939.
Jewett, Robert. *Jesus Against the Rapture: Seven Unexpected Prophecies*. Philadelphia: Westminster, 1979.
Koester, Craig. R. *The Apocalypse: Controversies and Meaning in Western History*. Transcript of 24 lectures. Chantilly, VA: The Great Courses, 2011.
———. *Revelation and the End of All Things*. Grand Rapids, MI: Eerdmans, 2001.
Ladd, George Eldon. *A Commentary on the Revelation of John*. Grand Rapids, MI: Eerdmans, 1972.
Metzger, Bruce M. *Breaking the Code: Understanding the Book of Revelation*. Nashville: Abingdon, 1993.
Moltmann, Jürgen. *Theology of Hope*. Minneapolis: Fortress, 1993.
Morris, Leon. *Revelation*. Tyndale New Testament Commentary Series. Rev. ed. Grand Rapids, MI: Eerdmans, 1994.
Mounce, Robert H. *The Book of Revelation*. The New International Commentary on the New Testament. Grand Rapids, MI: Eerdmans. 1977.
Niebuhr, H. Richard. *The Kingdom of God in America*. New York: Harper & Row, 1957.
Pagels, Elaine. *Revelations: Visions, Prophecy, & Politics in the Book of Revelation*. New York: Penguin, 2012.
Rossing, Barbara R. "Journeys Through Revelation." *Horizons* 23:3 (2010), 1–76.
———. *The Rapture Exposed: The Message of Hope in the Book of Revelation*. Boulder, CO: Westview, 2004.
Schüssler Fiorenza, Elisabeth. *Revelation: Vision of a Just World*. Rev. ed. Minneapolis: Fortress, 1998.
Swete, H. B. *The Apocalypse of St. John*. London: Macmillan, 1911.
Tenney, Merrill C. *Interpreting Revelation*. Grand Rapids, MI: Eerdmans, 1957.
Thompson, Leonard L. *The Book of Revelation: Apocalypse and Empire*. New York: Oxford University Press, 1990.
Wainwright, Arthur. *Mysterious Apocalypse: Interpreting the Book of Revelation*. Atlanta: Abingdon, 1993.
Walvoord, John F. *The Revelation of Jesus Christ*. Chicago: Moody, 1966.
Ware, Kallistos. "Eastern Christendom." In *The Oxford History of Christianity*, edited by John McManners, 131–66. New York: Oxford University Press, 1993.
Weber, Eugen. *Apocalypses: Prophecies, Cults, and Millennial Beliefs through the Ages*. Cambridge, MA: Harvard University Press, 1999.
Wright, N. T. *Revelation for Everyone*. Louisville: Westminster John Knox, 2011.

Subject/Name Index

Abaddon, 105, 146
Abyss, the, 103, 104, 110, 121, 127, 128, 132, 133, 146, 167–68, 187–88, 192
afterlife, 191
Alexander the Great, 167
All Saints Day, 161
Alpha and Omega, 35, 92, 210, 221
altar, 84, 91, 100
amillennialism, 195, 196–97
angel(s), 31–32, 34–35, 91, 106
  fallen, 103, 105, 122, 127
  message of, 138
  of the waters, 155
  twenty-four elders as, 65
  worship of, 183
antichrist, xii, 69, 90, 131, 132, 135, 136, 169, 195
  See also beast from the sea
anti-Semitism, 46
apartheid, 155
apocalypse, 24–25, 30, 59, 79, 127, 167
Apocalypse of Baruch, 8
Apocalypse of Elijah, 189
Apocalypse of Zephaniah, 8
apocalyptic hope, 94, 202, 221
apocalyptic eschatology, 8–10, 61, 189, 197–98
apocalyptic literature, xi, xiv, 2, 6–10, 24–25, 30, 68, 69, 127, 160, 186, 209
  and time, 61, 114, 146
Apollo (god), 105, 119, 125–26
apostles and prophets, 56–57
  as conflicting traditions, 53–57

Armageddon, xii, 149, 157, 185, 186, 188
Ascension of Isaiah, 8
Asclepius (god), 48–49
Augustine (bishop), xi, 196

Babylon, 122, 139, 143, 166, 167
  and New Jerusalem, 164–65, 206
  as harlot, 3, 121, 126, 129, 163, 164–67, 169, 179, 182
  as symbol of Roman Empire, 17, 68, 121, 162, 163, 164, 171
  fall of, 138, 139–40, 154, 157, 158, 165–69, 170–72
  king of, 102
  lament over, 162–73
Balaam, 43, 49, 53, 55, 134
baptism, 87
Battle Hymn of the Republic, 74, 142n23
Bauckham, Richard, xvi
Bauer, Ferdinand Christian, 52n5
beast from the land, 3, 119, 121, 129, 131–32, 134, 169, 186–87
beast from the sea, 3, 119, 121, 131–34, 135–36, 166–68, 173, 186–87
Berlioz, Hector, 161
Bible, inspiration of, x–xi
bishop(s), 56–57
Blount, Brian, 25
book of life, 51, 133, 168, 174, 193, 204
Book of Mercy, 179, 193
Book of Merit, 179, 193
Boring, M. Eugene, xvi, 16, 124, 141
  outline of book of Revelation, 181

Subject/Name Index

bottomless pit. *See* Abyss
bride of Christ, 137, 138, 166, 179, 182, 201, 208–9, 211, 222
Brueggemann, Walter, 1, 2, 218
Bultmann, Rudolph, xi
Byron, George, 171

Caird, G. B. xv, xvi, 64
Caligula (emperor), 166
Calvin, John, xi
Christ. *See* Jesus Christ
Christian(s), 131
   assimilation to culture, 41, 49, 50
   complacency of, 41, 50–51
   faithful witness of, 3, 14, 32, 107, 109–12, 114, 119, 124, 128, 130, 136, 138, 140, 145, 172
   internal conflict among, 52–57
   origin of the term, 54, 56
   persecution of, 3, 5, 40–41
Christology, 26, 32–38, 70, 71, 110
   shared, 37–38, 45
   See also Revelation, book of: Christology of
cloud(s), 93, 106
code language. *See* Revelation, book of: code language in
Commodianus, 196
communism, 155
conquer, conquest, 5, 38, 44, 45, 56, 68, 70, 81, 82, 111, 128–30, 185, 204
   in Paul, 44
Constantine (emperor), 197
cosmology, biblical. *See* Revelation, book of: cosmology of
covenant lawsuit, 171
cross, 125, 127
   theology of, 5, 44, 85, 86, 90, 93, 119, 128, 129–30, 139, 144

Daniel, book of, 25, 92, 93, 106
   afterlife in, 191
   Alexander the Great in, 167
   Ancient of Days in, 31, 36, 190
   as apocalyptic literature, 8
   as secret message, 25, 68, 106, 108, 209–10
   divine council, 65
   hope, 219
   judgment, 190, 193
   Michael the archangel, 128
   Son of Man, 31, 142
   symbols of time, 108–9, 181
   tribulation, 108–9
   vision of four beasts, 122, 132–33
Darby, John Nelson, 12, 197
Day of Judgment, 187–94, 211
Day of the Lord, 8, 10, 157, 159, 160
Day Star, 103
Dead Sea Scrolls, 8, 185
Death, 32, 82, 86, 121, 140, 159, 192, 194
Dies Irae. *See* wrath, *Dies Irae*
dispensationalism, 12, 87–88, 90, 194, 195
Domitian (emperor), 29, 30, 33, 67, 105, 126, 166, 167
double eschatology, 187, 188
doxology, 35
dragon. *See* Satan as dragon
Dürer, Albrecht, 81

Egypt, 107, 122, 125, 140
   plagues. *See* plagues in Egypt
elders. *See* twenty-four elders
Eliot, T. S., 202
Eller, Vernard, 69
Ellul, Jacques, 86
Emmanuel, 203
Enoch, book of, 8, 66, 89
   Apocalypse of Weeks, 189
   Similitudes of Enoch, 189
Ephesus, church of, 43–44, 52, 55
Epistle of Barnabas, 189
eschatological approaches. *See* Revelation, book of: eschatological approaches
eschatological language, 198
eschatology. *See* apocalyptic eschatology; double eschatology; prophetic eschatology
eternal life, 9, 89
   in Gospel of John, 9
eternal torment, 140
Eucharist, 143, 211, 221
European Common Market, 132

evil, 4, 7–9, 10, 14, 56, 81, 84–85, 104, 111–12, 121, 133, 134, 135, 145, 154, 155, 192, 196, 223
  agents of, 121, 131, 179
  and good, 8, 122, 146, 147, 196
  cosmic, 8, 154, 179
  defeat of, 5, 61, 85, 91, 105, 111–12, 119, 121, 128, 129–30, 134, 140, 141–42, 144–45, 149, 151, 155, 156, 159, 160–61, 164, 169, 179, 181, 186, 187–90, 194, 195, 196, 204, 210
  government as, 136–37
Ewing, Ward, 70
exodus, the, 27, 64, 87, 98, 102, 119, 122, 124, 131, 149, 151–52, 154, 157, 172, 203, 220
  theology of the, 1
  See also plagues in Egypt
Ezekiel, book of, 92, 186, 203
  apocalyptic passages in, 8
  birds of prey, 187
  Gog and Magog, 190, 192
  millennial period, 190
  new temple imagery, 108, 190
  prophecy of the New Jerusalem, 144, 188–89, 190, 205, 206, 214–15
  scroll imagery, 68, 107
  vision of four creatures, 7, 65–66
  vision of heavenly throne, 63–66, 92
  visions of hope in, 7
Ezra, Fourth book of (2 Esdras), 8, 189

false prophet. *See* beast from the land
fascism, 155
first resurrection, 179, 188, 190, 191
forty-two months. *See* numerical symbols
Foster, Richard, 72
four horsemen, 80–83
four living creatures, 60, 62, 63, 65–66, 70, 81, 91, 138, 207
Fourth Ezra (2 Esdras). *See* Ezra, Fourth book of

Gandhi, Mahatma, 130
gematria, 135

glassy sea. *See* sea, crystal
gnosticism, 53
God, 62–63
  Ancient of Days, 31, 36, 190
  and Satan, 146–47
  as Creator, 66–67, 80, 121
  faith in, 2
  holiness of, 62, 66, 71, 168
  humans as image of, 1, 223
  judgment of, 14, 62–63, 81, 84, 85, 91, 94, 100–101, 110–12, 114, 138–40, 141–45, 152, 155–57, 158–61, 168–69, 171, 179, 186–87, 210
  kingdom of. *See* kingdom of God
  love of, 9, 72, 85, 144, 152–53, 156, 170, 193
  mystery of, 7, 106–7
  Old Testament imagery of, 92–93
  See also Day of Judgment; God, wrath of
Gog and Magog, 188, 190, 192
Gounod, Charles, 161
great white throne, 37, 154, 191, 193, 195

Hades, 32, 82, 86, 140, 159, 192, 194
Hahn, Scott, 123–24
Handel, George Frederick, 70, 74, 182
harlot. *See* Babylon as harlot
harvest, the, 138, 142
  of grain, 142–43
  of grapes, 142–43
heaven, 84, 85, 111, 145
  and New Jerusalem, 201–3, 205–8
  as permeable boundary, 145–47
  as place of perspective, 60, 61, 62, 83, 127, 146–47, 183, 223
  cosmic war in, 127–28
  millennial reign in, 196
  on earth, 19, 202–3
  vision of, 59–60, 62–67, 83–85, 182–83
  See also cosmology, biblical
heavenly altar. *See* altar
Hebrews, letter to the, 4, 35, 73, 159–60
Herodotus (historian), 206
Hippolytus, 196

Hitler, Adolf, 135
Holst, Gustav, 161
Holy City, the. *See* New Jerusalem
Holy Spirit, 33, 36, 64, 72, 132, 134, 186, 196, 211
  "in the Spirit," 14
hope, 4, 6, 7, 8, 18, 25, 27, 51, 52, 80, 94, 114, 128, 131, 133, 137, 138, 169, 211, 212, 218–22
  prophetic, 7
  within history, 218–22

idolatry, 105, 135, 183
Ignatius, 54, 57
inspiration. *See* Bible, inspiration of
interludes. *See* Revelation, book of: interludes in
Irenaeus, xi, 196
Isaiah, book of, 219–20
  Alpha and Omega, 92
  apocalyptic passages in, 8
  eagle imagery, 103
  fall of Babylon, 139
  fall of Lucifer, 102, 103–4, 127
  messianic king, 32, 187
  mountain imagery, 102, 205
  opus alienum, 144
  Servant of the Lord, 32, 69, 144
  theophanic language, 159–60
  vision of Emmanuel, 203
  vision of heaven, 7
  vision of new heaven and new earth, 189, 196, 201, 204, 219
  visions of hope, 7
  winepress imagery, 144, 183

Jacob's ladder, 83
Jeremiah, book of, 102, 107, 220
  "call" passage, 2
  fall of Babylon, 139
Jerusalem, 56, 107, 108, 109, 140, 143, 164, 167, 206
  See also New Jerusalem
Jesus Christ, 5
  as faithful witness, 35, 138, 155, 183, 184, 208–9
  as God, 36, 37, 45, 63
  as Lamb, 34, 36, 37, 63, 67, 68–70, 87, 88, 89, 90, 91, 93, 119, 128, 130, 136, 137, 152–53, 159, 185, 210, 223
  as Lion, 68, 70, 88, 93, 185, 223
  as Lord, 32–34
  as mediator of revelation, 34–35
  as redeemer, 37, 44, 82–83, 90, 182, 183, 193
  as Son of Man, 31, 37, 142
  as Word of God, 32, 81, 184
  John's vision of, 30–32
  King of kings, 92–93, 184–85, 187
  messianic office of, 36, 68, 86, 93, 189
  resurrection of, 9, 10, 18, 26, 35, 125
  return of, 185–86
  See also parousia
Jezebel, 43, 50, 53, 55, 134
Johannine school, 29, 43, 136
John (apostle), 28, 29
John, Gospel of, 28, 29
  and glory of Christ, 125
  and Revelation, 28–29
  apocalyptic perspective, 9–10
  discipleship, 138–39
  eternal life, 9
  heaven, 83
  Jesus as Word of God, 184
  judgment of the world, 139
  love of God, 9, 120
John of Patmos, xv, 2, 3, 4, 5, 7, 26, 27–30, 52n5, 89, 218
  and Paul, 52–57
Judgment Day. *See* Day of Judgment; God, judgment of
judgment language, 4, 113–14, 144–45, 158–61, 187, 221, 224
Justin Martyr, 196

King Jr., Martin Luther, 130
kingdom of God, 9, 13, 18, 37, 73, 111, 112, 130, 135, 142, 147, 182, 189, 196, 222
Koester, Craig R., xvi

Lactantius, 196
LaHaye, Tim, 197

lake of fire, xiii, 47, 86, 121, 129, 140, 159, 187, 192, 194, 204
Lamb power, 58, 70, 110, 111, 172
  See also Jesus as Lamb; song of the Lamb
lament, 162, 170
lampstands, 31, 32, 34
Laodicea, church in, 30, 41, 43, 44–45, 50
Lawrence, D. H., xii
Left Behind series, 197
Leviathan, 104, 131, 133, 166, 204
Lewis, C. S., 202
Lindsay, Hal, 197
Liszt, Franz, 161
little scroll, 105–7
living creatures. *See* four living creatures
locusts, 104–5
love, 5, 9–10, 43–44, 45, 68, 82–83, 128, 169
Lucifer. *See* Day Star
lukewarm, 44–45
Luther, Martin, xi, 33, 135

Mahler, Gustav, 161
Mandela, Nelson, 130
Maranatha, 33
mark of the beast, 134, 135, 154
marriage supper of the Lamb. *See* wedding feast
martyr(s), martyrdom, 84–85, 87, 100, 107, 109, 114, 129, 130, 138–39, 140, 141, 143, 152, 190, 191, 192, 198, 211, 214
Mass, Roman Catholic, 123
  Requiem, 161
materialism, 170
Matthys, Jan, 197
Messiah. *See* Jesus Christ, messianic office of
Methodius, 196
Metzger, Bruce, xv, xvi
Michael (archangel), 128, 131
millennial views, 195–98
millennium, 85, 179, 181, 187–92, 194–97, 214
  See also first resurrection

Milton, John, 127
Minear, Paul, xi
Moody, D. L., 197
Mozart, Wolfgang Amadeus, 161
mystery, 106–7, 167

Napoleon Bonaparte, 135
nations, 107, 214
  redemption/healing of, 71, 141, 203–4, 208, 210, 214–15
Nero (emperor), 29, 30, 133, 135, 166, 167
  redidivus myth, 133, 167
new heaven, new earth, 90, 189, 193, 194, 201–5, 219, 222
New Jerusalem, 7, 19, 51, 108, 129, 137, 138, 143–44, 153, 163, 164, 186, 188, 197, 199, 200–209, 214–15, 221–22
  descent of, 192–93, 202–3, 206
Newton, Isaac, xii
Nicolaitans, 43, 51, 53, 134
Niebuhr, H. Richard, 155
Nobel, Alfred, 172–73
nonresistance, 134
nonviolence, 141–42, 172
  See also Lamb power
numerical symbols,
  42 months (1260 days), 108, 109, 128, 133
  666, 135–36
  144,000, 56, 87–89, 113, 133, 137–38, 143

opus alienum, 144
Owens, Jimmy, 74

Pagels, Elaine, 54
Papius, 196
parousia, 167, 184, 185–86, 195, 196, 210, 211
Parthians, 105, 133, 167
Paul (apostle), 2, 5, 10, 16, 26, 31, 43, 53, 54, 56–57, 70, 84, 88, 204
  and death, 10
  and government, 137
  and John of Patmos, 52–57
  Christology, 33

Paul (apostle) *(continued)*
  church as bride of Christ, 138
  food laws, 50, 55
  hope, 10, 220
  new age, 10
  new creation, 202
Pax Romana, 41, 82
Pentecostalism, 72
Pergamum, church in, 32, 37, 43, 48–49, 51, 125
persecution. *See* tribulation
Philadelphia, church in, 45, 47–48, 52, 54, 56
Picasso, Pablo, 6
Pius X (pope), 123
plagues in Egypt, 102, 104, 105, 145, 149, 151–52, 155–57
Polycarp, 30
postmillennialism, 194, 196
praise, 65–66, 70, 71–73, 89–90, 112, 152
prayer, 91, 110
predestination, 133, 204
premillennialism, 12, 87, 194–96
progressive parallelism, 13–15, 78–80
prophetic eschatology, 189
Protestant Reformation, 53

Rachmaninoff, Sergei, 161
rainbow, 63–64, 106
rapture, 61, 85, 87, 111, 195, 203
Rauschenbush, Walter, xi
Renan, Ernst, 52n5
repentance, 100, 105, 111, 160, 204
resurrection, 191
  See also first resurrection; Jesus, resurrection of; second resurrection
Revelation, book of
  acceptance into biblical canon, xi, xiii
  and Gospel of John, 28–29
  as apocalypse, 10, 24–25, 79, 85–86, 100, 127, 154, 158–59, 160
  as biblical capstone, xi, 5, 18
  as letter, 26–27, 168, 204, 211
  as prophecy, 25–26, 211, 224
  Christology of, xi, 33–38, 110
  code language in, 15, 79
  cosmology of, 59–60, 83, 127, 128, 145–46, 193
  date of, 29–30
  eschatological approaches, 194–98
  hyperbole in, 16–17
  interludes in, 86, 105, 112, 113–15, 138
  Jews and Christians in, 54–57
  methods (schools) of interpretation, 11–12
  Old Testament background, 91–94, 106, 138, 159–61, 173–74
  original audience of, 27–28
  outline of, 14, 181
  principles for the study of, 15–19
  purpose of, 5–6
  violent imagery in, 141, 149, 151–52, 158–61
  worship in, 27, 65, 66, 71–74, 112
Roma (goddess), 126, 164, 165
Roman Empire (Roman imperialism), 28, 40, 44, 56, 69, 93–94, 110, 133, 136, 158, 166–67, 168–69
  defeat of, 61, 156–57, 158, 170–72
  economic exploitation, 3, 4, 81–83, 136, 137, 167, 170–72
  imperial cult, 3, 134
  political power, 3–4, 110–11, 119, 136, 137
  rule, 80, 81–82, 122
  symbols of, 3, 132
  See also beast from the land; beast from the sea; Babylon
Romero, Oscar, 130
Rossing, Barbara, xvi

Sabbath, 71, 91, 136, 189
Saint-Saëns, Camille, 161
salvation, 87, 89, 90, 133, 151, 182, 203, 212–15
  images of, 139, 143
  limited, 212, 213, 215
  universal, 212, 213, 214–15
Sardis, church in, 47, 48, 50–51
Satan, 103, 104, 121, 127–28, 130, 131, 136, 168
  and God, 146–47

Subject/Name Index   233

as dragon, 121, 122, 125, 127, 128, 131–32
defeat of, 119, 121, 127, 128, 130, 179, 187–88, 190, 195
release of, 192, 196
See also Lucifer; Day Star; throne(s) of Satan
satire, 137, 162, 165, 169
Scofield, Charles Ingersoll, 12, 197
scroll, 67–68
See also little scroll
sea, crystal, 63, 64, 151–52, 153, 205
as symbol of evil, 64
Second Coming of Christ. *See parousia*
second death, 47, 129, 140, 188, 192, 194
second resurrection, 191
Septuagint, 36, 92, 104, 133, 142
seven bowls, 78, 79, 91, 113, 130, 149–58
seven elements of the old order, 204
seven heads, 122
seven kings, 169–70
seven letters, 39–52, 54, 56, 204
seven seals, 78, 80–86, 91, 100
seven signs, 79, 113, 119–45
seven stars, 31–32, 104
seven thunders, 101, 106
seven trumpets, 78, 79, 91, 96–105, 130, 154
seventh bowl, 79, 135, 157–58
seventh seal, 79, 90–91, 135, 157, 158
seventh sign, 141–45
seventh trumpet, 79, 112, 115, 120, 122, 135, 157, 158
Sheol, 32, 103, 127, 191
Sibylline Oracles, 8
silence, 90–91
Sinai, Mount, 64, 159, 174
Sinclair, Jerry, 74
slavery, 170–71
Smyrna, church in, 30, 45, 46–47, 51, 54
Sodom, 107, 122, 140
song of the Lamb, 152
Spirit, Holy. *See* Holy Spirit
Stalin, Joseph, 135
symbolic language, 15–16

steno symbol, 15
tensive symbol, 15–16
synagogue of Satan, 46, 55–56

Temple, William, 71
Tertullian, 196
theophanic language, 94, 159–61, 193
throne(s), 18, 37, 45, 60, 62, 63, 64, 65, 67, 89, 91, 100, 103, 108, 125, 127, 169, 184, 190, 191, 204, 205, 206, 207, 210, 211, 221
great white, 154, 179, 191, 193, 195, 197
of Satan, 49
of the beast, 151, 156
throne room, heavenly, 62–64, 73, 84, 89, 100, 210
Thyatira, church in, 43, 49–50, 51
Tiberius (emperor), 46, 47
Tillich, Paul, 15
time, times, 108
Tolstoy, Leo, 135
tree of life, 19, 173, 206, 208, 214, 221
tribulation, 5, 40–41, 61, 84, 85, 87, 90, 109, 110, 111, 133, 136, 154, 167, 195, 197
Trinity, Trinitarian, 34, 36, 64, 66, 126, 131, 211
counterfeit, 126, 131, 134, 156, 193
twenty-four elders, 60, 65, 66, 70, 71, 91, 138, 207
two resurrections, 191
See also first resurrection; second resurrection
two witnesses, 109–11, 112, 132, 152, 173–74

van Gogh, Vincent, 6
Verdi, Giuseppe, 161
victory, 128, 185, 187, 192
vindication, vengeance, 85, 140, 141, 158, 172
violent imagery. *See* Revelation, book of: violent imagery; theophanic language; wrath
Virgin Mary, 123, 124
virgins, 56, 89, 138

wedding feast, 179, 182, 187, 200, 201
Wesley, Charles, 74
Wheelwright, Philip, 15
Whitby, Daniel, 197
whore. *See* Babylon as harlot
winepress, 141, 143–45, 152, 185
Wizard of Oz, 221
woe, 102, 103, 111, 152, 156
Word of God. *See* Christ, as Word of God
Wormwood, 99, 102
worship, 27, 49, 71–74, 91, 132, 134, 136, 152, 153, 172, 181, 182, 204, 223
  definition of, 71–72
  See also Revelation, book of: worship in
wrath, 155, 159
  Dies Irae, 161
  grapes of, 142
  of God, 66, 91, 93, 138, 142, 143, 144, 151, 153, 155, 171, 173, 185, 193, 213, 223
  of the Lamb, 85, 144, 159, 185
Wright, N. T., xvi, 64, 74, 155
Wyrtzen, Don, 74

Yousufzai, Malala, 130

Zechariah, book of, 93
  apocalyptic passages in, 8
  depiction of Satan, 127
  mountains/gates of heaven, 83
  vision of four horses/winds, 81, 86
  vision of lampstands, 31, 107, 173
Zeus (god), 48, 49, 125, 126
Zwingli, Ulrich, 33

www.ingramcontent.com/pod-product-compliance
Lightning Source LLC
Chambersburg PA
CBHW051635230426
43669CB00013B/2313